THE GREAT DINOSAUR HUNTERS and Their Discoveries

THE GREAT DINOSAUR HUNTERS and Their Discoveries

by Edwin H. Colbert

Dover Publications, Inc.
New York

This Dover edition, first published in 1984, is an unabridged republication of the work first published in 1968 by E. P. Dutton & Co., Inc., New York, under the title *Men and Dinosaurs: The Search in Field and Laboratory*. It contains a new preface by the author.
Grateful acknowledgment is made to the following for copyright material quoted in this book:
Encyclopedia Britannica, for excerpt from Roy Chapman Andrews' article, "Mongolia—Explorations" (1929).
Holt, Rinehart and Winston, for excerpt from *The Life of a Fossil Hunter* by Charles H. Sternberg (1909).
The Lawrence Daily World-Journal, for excerpt from *Hunting Dinosaurs on Red Deer River, Alberta, Canada*, by Charles H. Sternberg (1917).
The National Geographic Magazine for material by Barnum Brown from its May, 1919, issue.
H.F. and G. Witherby Ltd., for excerpts from *The Dinosaur in East Africa* by John Parkinson (1930).
Yale University Press for excerpts from *Marsh's Dinosaurs* by John Ostrom and John S. McIntosh (1966) and from *O. C. Marsh, Pioneer in Paleontology* by Charles Schuchert and Clara Mae LeVene.

Manufactured in the United States of America
Dover Publications, Inc., 31 East 2nd Street, Mineola, N.Y. 11501

Library of Congress Cataloging in Publication Data

Colbert, Edwin Harris, 1905-
The great dinosaur hunters and their discoveries.

Rev. ed. of: Men and dinosaurs. 1st ed. 1968.
Bibliography: p.
Includes index.
1. Dinosaurs. 2. Paleontologists. I. Colbert.
Edwin Harris, 1905-   Men and dinosaurs. II. Title.
QE862.D5C6785 1984   567.9'1'0922   84-4204
ISBN 0-486-24701-5

PREFACE TO THE DOVER EDITION

The Great Dinosaur Hunters and Their Discoveries was originally published by E. P. Dutton & Company in 1968 under the title *Men and Dinosaurs*. This republication presents the story of the men who hunted and studied dinosaurs as it was seen almost two decades ago, and because it is a reprint, it is not possible to bring the story up to date within the body of the text.

Yet many things have happened and many things have been done since the appearance of the original edition. Important new discoveries have been made, and these would have been noted and discussed if a thoroughly new and revised edition were being presented. Instead, certain new facts, especially as they relate to the reprinted text, will be set forth below. Some of the people mentioned in the text as contemporaries are no longer with us, and they will be listed. This is a sad task for the author, because almost all of them were personal friends.

With these few corrections and additions in hand, it is hoped that the reader will find this book a useful account of the worldwide hunt for dinosaurs in field and laboratory as it has now been going on for something more than a century and a half.

First of all is a listing of those students and hunters of dinosaurs mentioned in the text, but deceased since 1968:

M. N. Bien (Chapter 5).
R. T. Bird (Chapter 6).
I. A. Efremov (Preface, Chapter 8, Plate 89).
R. F. Ewer (Plate 93).
Anatol Heintz (Chapter 10).
F. von Huene (Chapters 4 and 9, Plates 31 and 32).
Werner Janensch (Preface, Chapter 9, Plates 96 and 98).
W. S. B. Leakey (Chapter 9).
L. I. Price (Chapter 9, Plate 105).
Charles M. Sternberg (Preface, Chapter 7, Plates 65, 68 and 115).
George Sternberg (Chapter 7).
Levi Sternberg (Chapter 7, Plate 67).
G. E. Untermann (Chapter 6).
T. E. White (Preface, Chapter 6).
C. C. Young (Chapter 5).

A few people have changed institutional affiliations:

Marlyn Mangus (Preface) is no longer at The American Museum of Natural History in New York.
Elwyn Simons (Preface) is now at Duke University.
A. W. Crompton (Chapter 5) is now at Harvard University.

Here a few remarks will be made concerning information in the text that has been revised or updated since 1968.

With regard to the chart on pages 6 and 7, some recent calculations would establish the duration of the Cretaceous Period as 70 million years, of the Jurassic as 55 million years, and of the Triassic as 35 million years. Certain changes also have been made concerning the duration of the Paleozoic periods.

In recent years there has been intensive discussion and debate about the origin of the birds, mentioned on pages 37, 104, and 107. Some authorities still consider the birds to have been descended from thecodont reptiles; others regard the birds as directly descended from primitive theropod dinosaurs. The latter view would require a slight revision of the chart shown on page 107.

In the pictures of dinosaurian pelves on page 101, some authorities would prefer to label the parts of the pubic bone in the ornithischian pelvis as prepubis and pubis, rather than pubis and postpubis.

Discoveries made during the past decade have revealed primitive ornithischian dinosaurs in sediments of late Triassic age. Thus in the phylogenetic chart on page 110, the line below the word *Ornithischians* should be solid, not dotted. This fact is noted on page 144.

The large taxonomic category *Euryapsida*, as shown in the chart on page 113, has been questioned by some students as being an artificial assemblage of reptiles. However, the term is still widely used.

In 1969, the bridge mentioned on page 135 was demolished, and two large sandstone blocks selected by Dr. John Ostrom and his associates were found to contain the additional bones of *Ammosaurus major*.

The excavation of *Coelophysis* at Ghost Ranch, New Mexico, described on pages 141–142, was supplemented by extensive cooperative work carried on in 1981 by the Carnegie Museum of Pittsburgh, the New Mexico Museum of Natural History in Albuquerque, the Museum of Northern Arizona in Flagstaff, and Yale University, and by the Carnegie Museum in 1982.

The proper designation for the National Museum in Washington is now Smithsonian Institution, National Museum of Natural History.

Since the discussion of continental relationships that appears on page 254 was written, extensive geophysical, geological, and paleontological field work and laboratory research have established beyond much doubt that there was a direct connection between Africa and South America in Mesozoic times. In other words, there was a supercontinent known as Pangaea at the beginning of the age of dinosaurs, made up of a northern-hemisphere part known as Laurasia, and a southern-hemisphere part known as Gondwanaland. During Mesozoic times this great land mass began to break up, with the result that the continental blocks as we know them became defined. Eventually these blocks drifted to their present positions, but during the Mesozoic Era sufficient connections between them remained so that there were broad avenues of communication whereby the dinosaurs could move from one part to another of the ancient supercontinent. This view of past continental relationships, as based upon the modern concept of Plate Tectonics (and continental drift), is one of the great milestones in the study of earth history.

EDWIN H. COLBERT

The Museum of Northern Arizona
Flagstaff
1984

PREFACE TO THE FIRST EDITION

It is all too easy to think of science as something large and impersonal, as something outside the understanding of most of us, as something rather distant, and removed from the affairs of the average person. Even in this day, when the lives of all of us are touched every hour, and almost every minute, by the products of technology, the handmaiden of science, we are still inclined to accept the impersonal view of science. Science is so manifestly complex, so compartmentalized by specialization, and to all but those who are initiated into the priesthoods of these specializations, so largely incomprehensible, that we can hardly think of it in other than impersonal terms.

Yet science is the work of scientists, who, in spite of stories and plays and pictures, are very real people, with very real feelings. This is true of scientists today, when science is large and complex, and it was very true of scientists yesterday, when science was small and simple. So in order to understand science it is helpful to understand scientists. If one can look at the men who are practicing science, one will get some very revealing glimpses of just what goes into the subject. The view of the men at work, of their triumphs and failures, of their hopes and disappointments, of their likes and dislikes, of their responses to one another and to other people around them, helps to bring science out of its impersonal aspect and to show it for what it is—one great and interesting phase of human thought and activity.

To get down to details, one of the many compartments of modern science is paleontology, the study of past life on the earth. And one of the most interesting aspects of paleontology, at least to those people who are not paleontologists, has to do with the study of dinosaurs. Dinosaurs today have a tremendous fascination for people of all ages in all lands. Perhaps this is because so many of the dinosaurs are of gigantic size, and to our eyes of strange aspect. Certainly the dinosaur skeletons in museum halls attract visitors in great numbers, some of whom come to view these ancient relics of long-extinct life with understanding and knowledge, some just to look at them in wonder.

There is much work back of those skeletons: the work of finding them, of digging them out of the ground, of patiently chipping them out of their rock matrices in the laboratory, of studying and interpreting them, of publishing the results of these studies, and finally of setting up the skeletons in museum halls so that they can be seen by students, by interested visitors, and by those who are merely curious. Who does this work? Who has done it in the past? These are important questions, because the story of the dinosaurs is inextricably entwined with the story of the men who have hunted and studied the dinosaurs. And although the story of the dinosaurs goes back, in its farthest limits, some 200 million years, the story of the men behind the dinosaurs goes back only a century and a half. The details of this story are well known, and while most of these details are by their nature of concern only to the specialist, many of them are of more general interest. Details of this latter sort compose a very human document, a document that helps us to understand the progress of the long hunt for dinosaurs and of dinosaurian studies during the hundred and fifty years that have elapsed since a dinosaur was first scientifically described. It is proposed in this book to tell some of the story of that long hunt and of the many studies that have revealed to us the world of dinosaurs, and particularly to tell something of the men who have engaged in these interesting pursuits. It is a story in which the men behind the dinosaurs will be of paramount importance, but a story in which the dinosaurs will be a constant center of attention, because the men were above all interested in the dinosaurs. It is the story of Men and Dinosaurs.

This book is a companion piece to the book *Dinosaurs*, which appeared a few years ago.[1]

---

[1] Edwin H. Colbert, *Dinosaurs: Their Discovery and Their World* (E. P. Dutton and Co., Inc., New York (1961), xiv, 300 pp.

At this place it is a great pleasure to express my indebtedness to many persons and institutions, for help received during the preparation of *Men and Dinosaurs*. My grateful acknowledgments to them are hereby set down:

To the Director of The American Museum of Natural History, for the privilege of using pictures under the control of this institution.

To Miss Marlyn Mangus of The American Museum of Natural History for assistance in checking references, and to Mr. Gilbert Stucker of the same institution for information concerning Earl Douglass.

To the authorities of the British Museum (Natural History) for permission to reproduce certain illustrations under their control.

To Dr. Theodore White of Dinosaur National Park, and to the National Park Service, for permission to use photographs under their control.

To Dr. Loris S. Russell of the Royal Ontario Museum, for making available to me the galley proof of his valuable paper entitled "Dinosaur Hunting in Western Canada," and for his reading and criticism of Chapter 7 of this book. To the Geological Survey of Canada and the National Museum of Canada for furnishing me with certain photographs in their files, and for permission to use them.

To Drs. John Ostrom and Elwyn Simons of Yale University for help concerning the work of Marsh, and for illustrations from the files of Yale Peabody Museum, and permission to use them.

To Dr. Frank Westphal of the Paläontologisches Museum und Institut of Tübingen University, for information concerning the work of that institution, and for photographs and permission to use them.

To Dr. Charles M. Sternberg, now retired from the National Museum of Canada, for photographs, and especially for his careful reading and criticism of Chapter 7 of this book.

To Dr. Bernard Krebs of the Freien Universität, Berlin, and especially to Dr. Werner Janensch of Berlin, now retired, for the loan of negatives taken by Dr. Janensch on the Tendaguru expeditions.

To Mr. William B. Wallis, Publisher of the *Vernal Express*, for the loan of the picture of Earl Douglass.

To Dr. A. Rozhdestvensky and Professor I. A. Efremov, of the Paleontological Institute, Academy of Sciences of the USSR, Moscow, for pictures of the Russian expeditions to Mongolia, and for permission to use them.

To Dr. Natascha Heintz of the Norsk Polarinstitutt, Oslo, for permission to use pictures of the expedition to Spitzbergen.

And of course I am greatly indebted to the many paleontologists of former years who wrote accounts of their work in field and laboratory, as well as of the work of their colleagues. The various sources from which much of the information set forth in this book was obtained are listed in the Bibliography. The manuscript was most ably transcribed by Mrs. John Minerly.

Finally I wish to express my appreciation to the Museum of Northern Arizona, and to the various members of its staff, for providing me with a winter refuge and facilities by means of which most of the work on this book was accomplished.

EDWIN H. COLBERT

1967

CONTENTS

ILLUSTRATIONS

LINE DRAWINGS

THE GREAT DINOSAUR HUNTERS and Their Discoveries

CHAPTER 1

THE FIRST DISCOVERIES

EARLY GLIMMERINGS

In the third decade of the nineteenth century England was a Dickensian land, a land still largely rural, with cities that were only beginning to grow into endless, dreary miles of brick and stone, and skies that perhaps were showing only the first thin black clouds from primitive, clanking factories. Yet in spite of these forerunners of a crowded age to come, it was a land very different from the England of today. There was a delightful lack of urban sprawl, of car-congested highways, and of roaring planes overhead. There were not even railroads. And there were no dinosaurs.

This is not quite correct. There were dinosaurs, but no one was acquainted with them. Perhaps dinosaurs had been seen, but certainly they had not been recognized; indeed, recognition was out of the question, because in those days of coaches and inns the idea of dinosaurs had not as yet been born in the mind of man. Dinosaurs were as unknown as were electric lights. Before they could be known, there were some discoveries to be made, and some concepts to be realized.

As a matter of fact some discoveries already *had* been made across the sea, on the North American continent, but they were discoveries without significance at the time because no one seems to have had the slightest inkling as to what they meant. For instance, a large bone, said to be a "thigh bone," was found near Woodbury Creek in Gloucester County, New Jersey, and a report on it was presented to the American Philosophical Society in Philadelphia on October 5, 1787, by Dr. Caspar Wistar, a very competent anatomist and one of the early scientific men of North America, and by Timothy Matlack. Unfortunately, there was no publication of this discovery, and the whereabouts of the fossil is unknown. There is good reason to believe that this was the bone of a large dinosaur, probably one of the duck-billed hadrosaurs, since the site of its discovery is within those Upper Cretaceous deposits of the New Jersey coastal plain that have yielded various remains of hadrosaurian dinosaurs. Indeed, this may have been the first dinosaur ever to be collected, yet it cannot be rated as a true discovery because no verification as to the nature of this fossil was made, nor can it be made.

Again, it would seem likely that William Clark, one of the two leaders of the famous Lewis and Clark expedition to explore the upper Missouri River, described a dinosaur bone in his journal for Friday, July 25, 1806. The description is interesting, not only as a record of a possible early discovery of a dinosaur but also because of its unorthodox (one is tempted to say quaint) spelling. It is here quoted:

"dureing the time the men were getting the two big horns [mountain sheep] which I had killed to the river I employed my self in getting pieces of the rib of a fish which was Semented within the face of the rock this rib is (about 3) inches in Secumpherence about the middle it is 3 feet in length tho a part of the end appears to have been broken off (the fallen rock is near the water—the face of the rock where rib is is perpendr—4 i[nche]s lengthwise, a little barb projects I have several pieces of this rib the bone is neither decayed nor petrified but very rotten. the part which I could not get out may be seen, it is about 6 or 7 Miles below Pompys Tower in the face of the Lar [boar]d Clift about 20 feet above the water" (Clark, quoted in Simpson, 1942a, pages 171–172).

Pompey's Pillar, as it has subsequently been designated, is on the south bank of the Yellowstone River, below Billings, Montana, in an area where there are outcrops of the Hell Creek formation, of late Cretaceous [1] age, a horizon from which numerous dinosaur bones have been collected. Consequently it would seem probable, particularly because of the dimensions of the bone that Clark described, that his discovery was of a dinosaur bone, not of a fish. But again, as in the case of the specimen from New Jersey, no verification is possible, and so this discovery has no standing in the history of paleontology.

Once again, and again in North America, fossil bones were discovered in the red sandstones of the Connecticut Valley by Solomon Ellsworth, Jr., in 1818, and were recorded in 1820 by Nathan Smith, in *The American Journal of Science*, as possibly the remains of human beings. Fortunately, these bones are still available in the Yale Peabody Museum, and have been identified as the bones of the Triassic dinosaur *Anchisaurus*. Since these fossils can be reexamined and studied in the light of modern knowledge, there is no hesitation in listing them among the first known remains of dinosaurs to be discovered, even though at the time their significance was not recognized. The same may be said of the fossil footprints of dinosaurs from the Connecticut Valley, found by Pliny Moody in 1800 and attributed to "Noah's raven." More of them later.

WILLIAM BUCKLAND AND *MEGALOSAURUS*

It is possible that there were still other discoveries of dinosaur bones in other parts of the world at about this time, if not even before, un-

---

[1] The Mesozoic era, the middle age of earth history as revealed by the fossil record, is made up of three geologic periods, these being, from oldest to youngest, the Triassic period, the Jurassic period, and the Cretaceous period. Sediments that accumulated during these periods in rivers and lakes and along the shores of seas, and in which the remains of dinosaurs were buried, are now preserved as rocks—sandstones, shales, and limestones. The fossil bones of dinosaurs are therefore found in these Triassic, Jurassic, and Cretaceous rocks.

The earliest and most primitive dinosaurs lived during the Triassic period, dating back to almost 200 million years ago. The dinosaurs proliferated during the Jurassic period, at which time many of them became giants. They reached the final climax of their evolutionary development in the Cretaceous period, at which time they would seem to have been more numerous and more varied than at any stage in their long history. The dinosaurs became extinct at the close of the Cretaceous period, somewhat more than 60 million years ago. Much use will be made of the names Triassic, Jurassic, and Cretaceous in this story.

Figure 1. A chart of geologic time

ERA	PERIOD	DURATION	THE DINOSAURS	THE LOCALITIES	THE MEN
Cenozoic	Quaternary	2.5 m.y.°	Mammals—successors of the dinosaurs		
	Tertiary	65 m.y.			
	Cretaceous	65 m.y.	Extinction of dinosaurs	Europe	Nopcsa, Huxley, Seeley
			Climax of the dinosaurs	New Jersey Red Deer River	Leidy, Hawkins The Sternbergs, Brown
				Judith River	Cope, C. H. Sternberg
			Increase in diversity of the dinosaurs	Argentina	Ameghino, von Huene
				Mongolia	Andrews, Granger, Efremov, Rozhdest-vensky
			New directions of dinosaurian evolution	Spitzbergen	Heintz, Lapparent
				Southern England	Buckland, Mantell, Owen
				Bernissart	Dollo
sozoic			Wide distribution of giant dinosaurs	Como Bluff	Marsh, Williston, Reed, Lakes
				Canyon City Bone Cabin	Cope, Lucas Osborn,

Era	Period	Duration	Event	Location	Researchers
	Jurassic	45 m.y.	The appearance of giant dinosaurs	Carnegie Quarry Howe Quarry Tendaguru	Brown, Douglass, Holland, Gilmore Brown Hennig, Janensch
	Triassic	45 m.y.	Early dinosaurs	Southern Germany Connecticut Valley New Mexico South Africa	von Huene Hitchcock, Marsh, Lull Cope, Baldwin Broom and successors
			The first dinosaurs Precursors of the dinosaurs	South America	von Huene and others
Paleozoic	Permian Carboniferous	45 m.y. 80 m.y.	Early reptiles Amphibians		
	Devonian	50 m.y.	Fishes with lungs		
	Silurian Ordovician	40 m.y. 60 m.y.	The first fishes		
	Cambrian	100 m.y.	Early life		

°millions of years

recorded and hence unknown to posterity. But for the first discoveries and *descriptions* of dinosaurs (although at the time the fossils were described only as the remains of large extinct reptiles, the concept of dinosaurs being still a matter of future paleontological development) we must turn to the England of the early 1820's, the England introduced at the beginning of this chapter, and particularly to two Englishmen of that time, Dean William Buckland and Dr. Gideon Mantell. These were the men—Buckland, a cleric and a professor at Oxford University, and Mantell, a medical practitioner in southern England—who made the initial discoveries and descriptions in a long and complex chain of finds and studies that eventually were to people an ancient world, a world that existed ages before the advent of man, with the numerous and interesting reptiles that we call dinosaurs. Buckland and Mantell were the pioneers of a new branch of science, who lived at a time when science was something less than formal. They were the men who, all unknowing, because they were pioneers, opened a past world of huge dimensions to the view of modern man, a world that within a century and a half has enlisted the interests and energies of numerous men of science, and has appealed to the curiosity and the sensibilities of untold millions of people on all of the continents. It was a small beginning, as most beginnings are small, but the results have been large and spectacular, as have been many results in scientific development, and the end is far beyond our present horizons.

William Buckland was a divine and a geologist, a man of religion and of science, combining two careers and a variety of interests in a manner not unusual to the nineteenth century. Since formal scientific knowledge and practice were going through the early stages of their development in those opening years of the last century, careers in science generally were developed "from scratch" by men who had backgrounds of book knowledge, which usually meant men trained as ministers, as doctors, or as lawyers. Ministers, who then often enjoyed a solid foundation in the classics, in languages, and in philosophy, were, if intelligent and of inquiring mind, well prepared for forays into new fields of knowledge. Buckland was only one of several nineteenth-century theologians who made distinctive contributions to an infant science in an age of awakening intellectual development.

William Buckland was born at Axminster in 1784, the son of a minister. As a boy in a religious household, he showed a strong interest in the natural sciences. At what today we would consider a tender age, he became a scholar of Corpus Christi College at Oxford University, where in 1804 he attained the status of Bachelor of Arts. In 1809, by now a fellow of the college, he was admitted into holy orders.

At the university he became especially interested in chemistry and mineralogy, but more particularly in geology, a science that then was truly in the formative stages of its development. He devoted himself at the outset of his professional life to a study of the geology of Britain, especially to the development and sequence of sedimentary rocks in that sea-girt isle, and to the fossils contained within these rocks. In 1813 Dr. John Kidd, the teacher of mineralogy at Oxford, resigned from his post, and Buckland was immediately appointed as reader in mineralogy, a position that would correspond more or less to an assistant professorship at a modern American university. So great was the interest generated by his lectures that six years later a position in geology, the first of its kind, was established by the university and endowed by the Treasury, and Buckland became its first incumbent. At about this same time, in 1818, at the age of thirty-four, he was elected to the Royal Society, and a few years later, in 1824, he was chosen as President of the Geological Society of London.

In 1825 he married Mary Morland, an excellent lady who, in addition to her wifely duties, assisted him for many years in his literary labors. In his later years he was made a trustee of the British Museum, and in 1848 he was awarded the Wollaston Medal of the Geological Society of London. His scientific accomplishments were indeed many and important.

And what of his theological life? During all the years of geological research and writing, and of teaching, in which fields he attained great renown, he advanced from one ecclesiastical position to another, including the deanery of Westminster. One would suppose that a man of such accomplishments, and of such high position in the world of learning and religion, would have been a figure of imposing gravity, a man of great decorum and probity, behaving with the dignity that should accord with his station.

Not so; Dean Buckland was one of those many delightful eccentrics who seemed to have flourished with vigor and in considerable numbers in Britain during the nineteenth century. He managed to make his life exciting and unusual, to say the least, and things were always happening around him, wherever he might be. It certainly must have kept his family and associates amused and wide awake.

On his honeymoon in Palermo, Italy, in 1826, he was less than impressed by some bones exhibited as the remains of St. Rosalia, and promptly identified them as belonging to a defunct goat. He had engraved on the handle of his umbrella "Stolen from Dr. Buckland." He undoubtedly must have at times astonished his students; at least it is recorded that at one of his lectures he grasped the skull of a hyena and shouted at the undergraduates, "Who rules the world?" After which he gave the answer himself to this rhetorical and unexpected question: "The strongest . . . the great ones eat the less, and the less, the lesser still."

The Buckland household in Christ Church, Oxford, was indeed a remarkable menage. It was here that Buckland's son, Frank, grew up, and it was here that a clergyman from Devonshire called, bringing some "curious fossils" for identification.

When he produced his treasures, Dr. Buckland called his son, who was playing in the room, "Frankie, what are these?" "They are the vertebrae of an ichthyosaurus" lisped the child, who could not yet speak plain. The dumbfounded clergyman returned home crestfallen.

Frank Buckland's tutor, Walter Stanhope, has left a memorable account of one of his experiences in the Buckland domicile:

"One evening when I was devoting an hour to coaching him up for his little-go, I took care to tuck up my legs, in Turkish fashion, on the sofa for fear of a casual bite from the jackal which was wandering around the room. After a while I heard the animal munching up something under the sofa, and was relieved that he should have found something to occupy him. When our work was finished, I told Buckland that the jackal had found something to eat under the sofa. 'My poor guinea-pigs', he exclaimed; and sure enough, four or five of them had fallen victims.'

"The most splendid animal in the Buckland menagerie was the bear, Tiglath Pileser. He was six months old when he entered Christ Church, where he lived in a corner of a court beside Fell's Buildings. He was provided with cap and gown, and in this costume went to wine parties. Tig took part in the proceedings of the British Association at Oxford in 1847, and in cap and gown attended the garden party given in the Botanic Gardens. He was visited by Lord Houghton (then

Monckton Milnes), who tried to mesmerize Tig in a corner. At first the bear was furious, then gradually yielded to the influence and at last fell senseless on the ground. Of this remarkable meeting Sir Charles Lyell wrote:

" 'In the evening we had an immense party at the Botanic Gardens. Young Buckland had a young bear dressed up as a student of Christ Church, with cap and gown, whom he formally introduced to me and successively to the Prince Canino (Charles Buonaparte), Milne Edwards, and Sir T. Acland. The bear sucked all our hands and was very caressing. Amid our shouts of laughter in the garden by moonlight, it was diverting to see two or three of the dons, who were very shy, not knowing for fear their dignity was compromised.'

"Eventually the Dean of Christ Church ordered the bear to leave the College and he went to live in the Buckland house at Islip. Here he sometimes rode out on horseback with his master, and here it was that he went into the village grocer's shop and was 'devouring the sugar and sweetstuff, and terrifying the shopwoman out of her wits'. 'After this', says Bompas, 'the bear developed such a proclivity for the sweetstuff shop, to the damage of the woman's nerves and his master's pocket, that in November 1847 he was sent to the Zoological Gardens, where he died some time after. . . . ' " (*Antiquity*, 1966, page 85.)

As may be seen from these few highlights, Dean Buckland was an accomplished and many-sided man who received wide recognition early in his career and who, because of his numerous and unusual activities through a long and busy life, continued to be recognized and acclaimed in many ways as the years passed by.

The recognition was justly deserved. After making an early beginning as a geologist, he maintained a high level of activity for the rest of his days, and his geological interests were varied. His first great published work was *Reliquiae Diluvianae, or Observations on the Organic Remains contained in caves, fissures, and diluvial gravel attesting the Action of a Universal Deluge,* first appearing in 1823. Thirteen years later there appeared his book *Geology and Mineralogy,* the Bridgewater Treatise, so called because, together with other volumes written to exhibit the "power, wisdom, and goodness of God, as manifested in the Creation," it had been provided for by the will of the Earl of Bridgewater. This durable work went through several editions, and was widely read. Beyond these works, for which Buckland became widely known to an intelligent lay public as well as to his scientific audience, he published papers on the structure of the Alps, on Pleistocene or ice-age fossil mammals discovered in England, on quartz, on the geology of several regions in Britain, and on the fossil reptiles of the Mesozoic rocks of southern England. He was an early and ardent supporter of the idea of widespread continental glaciation during the Pleistocene Epoch of the last million years in earth history, as originally proposed by Louis Agassiz upon the basis of evidence displayed in central Europe.

Among Buckland's many accomplishments, his work on fossil reptiles concerns us at this place, especially his description of *Megalosaurus*,[2] one of the first two dinosaurs to be made known. This description appeared during the year 1824, in the *Transactions* of the Geological Society of London, and was entitled "Notice on the Megalosaurus or Great Fossil Lizard of Stonesfield." Although this was the original description of *Megalosaurus*, it was not the first use of the name in a publication, because one James Parkinson, in a work which he called "An introduction to the study of fossil organic remains," had cited *Megalosaurus* without a description, merely stating that it was from the calcareous slate of Stonesfield and was housed in the Oxford museum. Evidently several parties had an interest in this ancient reptile, for Parkinson acknowledged the help of the Reverend W. D. Conybeare, one of the pioneer geologists of England, as did Buckland, in his description of the fossil. Indeed, there is reason to think that the name for this reptile may have been coined, or at least suggested, by Conybeare, because Buckland remarked that "I have ventured, in concurrence with my friend and fellow-labourer, the Rev. W. Conybeare, to assign to it the name of *Megalosaurus*." One may say that the scientific birth of *Megalosaurus* was complicated, somewhat clouded, and a bit obscure.

But there was nothing doubtful about Buckland's description, set forth in several pages of text, and illustrated by five large lithographic plates. Here, exhibited to the view of the reader and beholder, was

---

[2] *Megalosaurus* is a genus of dinosaurs. All scientifically described animals and plants, fossil and recent, belong to genera (the plural of genus) and species. The generic name, such as *Megalosaurus*, indicates a category that may include several species, such as *Megalosaurus cuvieri* (named in honor of the great French anatomist and paleontologist Georges Cuvier), and *Megalosaurus insignis* (a name indicating a supposed attribute of this species). Species are included in Genera, Genera in Families, Families in Orders, Orders in Classes, and Classes in Phyla. These are the hierarchies of classification, in increasing order of magnitude.

the evidence of a gigantic reptile that lived at a time when the earth was younger, and in many respects very different from what it now is. The description was based upon several bones—a portion of a lower jaw, some vertebrae, part of the pelvis, a piece of shoulder blade, and several bones from a hind limb. As fossils go, this is pretty good evidence—excellent material for the time at which it was discovered.

Buckland placed *Megalosaurus* within the "order of Saurians or Lizards," and was then properly astonished by the great size of this extinct "lizard." Thus: "From these dimensions as compared with the ordinary standard of the lizard family, a length exceeding 40 feet and a bulk equal to that of an elephant seven feet high have been assigned by Cuvier to the individual to which this bone [the thigh bone or femur] belonged." So, from these words it appears that there was still another scientific midwife participating at the entrance of *Megalosaurus* into the paleontological world, none other than the great Baron Georges Cuvier of Paris, founder of the science of comparative anatomy and the doyen of early-nineteenth-century paleontologists. Cuvier showed his skill and insight when he assigned dimensions to *Megalosaurus;* as we now know, this dinosaur is about thirty to forty feet in length, and in life it may very well have weighed about as much as an elephant of moderate size.

Continuing with his comparisons, Buckland noted that Gideon Mantell of Lewes had in his collection a femur, discovered in the Tilgate Forest near Cuckfield, that "when entire, must have equalled in magnitude the femur of the largest living elephant." It was, indeed, a giant. (Quotations from Buckland, 1824.)

Megalosaurus had large blade-like teeth set in sockets, *not* adhering to the bone of the jaw as is the case among lizards. Buckland noted this important diagnostic feature, yet he failed to appreciate its importance. For it gave unassailable proof that *Megalosaurus* was not a gigantic lizard; it was a gigantic reptile with socketed teeth, such as are possessed by the crocodiles, yet it was not a crocodile, either—Buckland was sure of that. In short, *Megalosaurus* was something new, a reptile the like of which had never before been imagined. (The realization of this fact was not to come for many years, not until Buckland was well along in middle age, and not to Buckland, but to another Englishman, Richard Owen, of whom something will be said farther on in this story.)

This ancient reptile, so different from any animal in the previous

Figure 2. The carnivorous dinosaur *Allosaurus,* a North American counterpart of the European dinosaur *Megalosaurus.* Buckland's dinosaur, when alive, would have looked very much like this. Restoration by Lois Darling

experience of man, was soon accepted by the scientific community and by the world at large. By the time the nineteenth century had run half its course, *Megalosaurus* had become widely known, as we can see from some of the opening sentences of Charles Dickens' *Bleak House,* published four years before Buckland's death in 1856:

". . . Implacable November weather. As much mud in the streets as if the waters had but newly retired from the face of the earth, and it would not be wonderful to meet a Megalosaurus, forty feet long or so, waddling like an elephantine lizard up Holborn Hill". (Dickens, 1852, page 1).

GIDEON MANTELL AND *IGUANODON*

To Dean Buckland, the cleric, the discovery and description of long-extinct reptiles formed but one facet in the life of a man of many interests. To Gideon Algernon Mantell, the physician who discovered and described *Iguanodon,* the second known dinosaur in terms of priority of publication, extinct reptiles formed the center of his particu-

ABOVE. *Plate 1*. Gideon Algernon Mantell in Brighton, 1837. Behind him is the femur, the upper bone of the hind leg, of *Iguanodon*, and the comparable bone of the modern lizard *Iguana*. BELOW. *Plate 2*. Some of the teeth of *Iguanodon* that were studied and described by Mantell

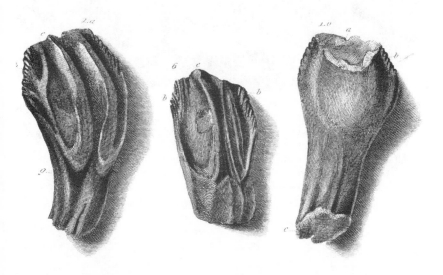

Plate 3. Dean William Buckland

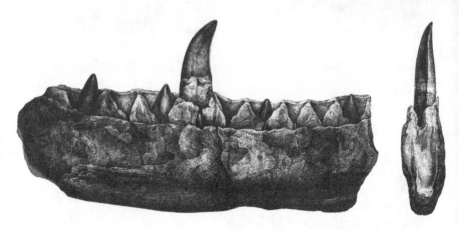

ABOVE. *Plate 4.* A portion of a lower jaw of *Megalosaurus,* described and named by Buckland. RIGHT. *Plate 5.* Richard Owen, the first man to make extensive studies of different kinds of dinosaurs; the first man to realize that dinosaurs should be set apart from modern reptiles. He invented the word *Dinosauria.* From a caricature that appeared in *Vanity Fair*

ABOVE. *Plate 6.* The Crystal Palace of London, after it had been re-erected in its extensive grounds at Sydenham. Victorian sightseers are looking at the models of dinosaurs constructed by Waterhouse Hawkins under the supervision of Owen. These interesting models, still to be seen at Sydenham, demonstrate the Owen-Hawkins interpretation of *Megalosaurus* (pair at left) and *Iguanodon* (pair below and right of bridge)

Plate 7. A rare old photograph of Joseph Leidy, founder of the science of Vertebrate Paleontology in North America. He is posing proudly with a leg bone of *Hadrosaurus*, the Haddonfield, New Jersey, dinosaur, the first dinosaur skeleton found in North America

Plate 8. Interior of the "Paleozoic Museum" in Central Park, New York, a Victorian edifice of cast iron and glass that was planned but never built. On the left are seen dinosaurs as envisioned by Waterhouse Hawkins—inoffensive hadrosauri being attacked by toothed carnivores. In the background are various extinct mammals that lived long after the Age of Dinosaurs

Plate 9. Interior of the "Appleton Cabinet" at Amherst College, with the exhibit of Triassic dinosaur footprints collected by Edward Hitchcock

Plate 10. Dinosaurs are not always found in wild and distant deserts. A view of Bernissart, Belgium, underneath which, in the dark tunnels of a coal mine, was discovered the famous accumulation of *Iguanodon* skeletons

Plate 11. A skeleton of *Iguanodon bernissartensis,* as it was found in the coal mine at Bernissart, Belgium. Faulting of the earth's crust separated the skeleton into three displaced blocks

Plate 12. A skeleton of *Iguanodon mantelli,* as it was found at Bernissart

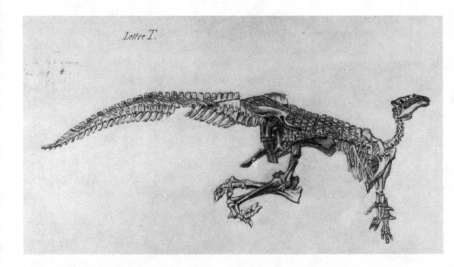

Plate 13. Louis Dollo, who devoted much of his adult life to the study of *Iguanodon*

Plate 14. A skeleton of *Iguanodon* from Bernissart, being set up in 1880 in the medieval Chapel of St. George, near the Royal Palace in Brussels. At that time the chapel served as a workshop for the museum

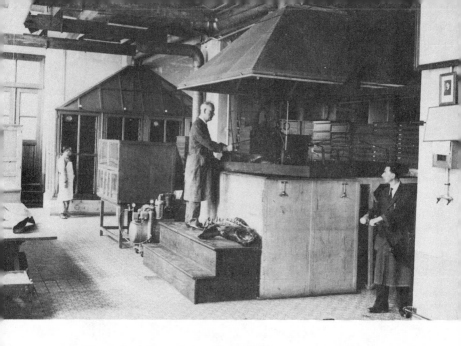

Plate 15. One way in which to preserve dinosaur bones. This elaborate installation was made at the museum in Brussels, for the purpose of impregnating with shellac the thousands of fossil bones from Bernissart

Plate 16. A herd of dinosaurs. Skeletons of *Iguanodon* from Bernissart, as displayed in the Brussels museum, the Institut Royal des Sciences Naturelles de Belgique

ABOVE. *Plate 17.* "Fairfield," the boyhood home of Alfred Drinker Cope. BELOW LEFT. *Plate 18.* The two houses on Pine Street, Philadelphia, used by Cope as a research center. BELOW RIGHT. *Plate 19.* Cope at his desk in the Pine Street house

Plate 20. Como Bluff, Wyoming, as painted in watercolor by Arthur Lakes. This view, from the east, shows Bill Reed in the foreground, and, far in the background, an early train of the Union Pacific Railroad

BELOW LEFT. *Plate 21.* Arthur Lakes, many years after he made the sketch of Como Bluff. BELOW RIGHT. *Plate 22.* Othniel Charles Marsh, hammer in hand, in the field with of the Yale College expedition of 1871

Plate 23. A watercolor sketch by Arthur Lakes, showing E. Kennedy and Bill Reed with dinosaur bones, at Quarry 10, Como Bluff, Wyoming

Plate 24. A self-portrait in watercolor of Arthur Lakes (standing) and his assistant in February, 1879, at Quarry 12, Como Bluff, Wyoming. Lakes entitled this picture "Pleasures of Science"

Plate 25. The house that Marsh built for himself at New Haven, Connecticut

Plate 26. An early portrait of Samuel Wendell Williston, Marsh's assistant who was instrumental in developing the quarries at Como Bluff, Wyoming, and Garden Park, Colorado. Williston later became a world authority on fossil reptiles, first at the University of Kansas, and subsequently at the University of Chicago

Plate 27. Exposures of the Cretaceous Judith River beds, near the Missouri River, in Montana. The figure in the center of the picture gives some idea of the scale and rugged character of these exposures, so diligently explored by Cope and Charles H. Sternberg

Plate 28. The steamer *Josephine* on the upper Missouri River, just before it started downstream with Cope and his Judith River collection on board

ABOVE LEFT. *Plate 31*. Friedrich von Huene at an early stage in his long career as a student of dinosaurs

ABOVE RIGHT. *Plate 32*. Friedrich von Huene today, standing in front of some of his beloved ichthyosaurs

LEFT. *Plate 33*. Franz Baron Nopcsa in Albanian costume, and obviously well armed

lar universe, and everything else was of secondary importance. There were several reasons for this.

One reason was his innate, restless intellectual curiosity. Another was the driving energy within a frail body, which kept him at his appointed tasks for more hours of the day than the average man likes to think about. Still another was the fact that during the first part of his life he lived in southern England near the South Downs, where the Ouse River flows southward across the Weald to the Channel, and where in many a low cliff or roadside cut Cretaceous fossils are to be found. The fossils were there; Mantell was always ready to go and search for them, and his curiosity about them was such that he had to learn as much about them as he could. Such were the ingredients that made Mantell, a slender man with an intense look in his long face, and a singleness of purpose in his enthusiastic mind. The purpose—once he became established in life—was the study of fossils from the South Downs, and particularly the fossil bones of ancient reptiles.

Gideon Mantell was born in 1790 in the little city of Lewes, which is not far distant from the seacoast resort of Brighton, and in Lewes he grew up. He spent many happy hours in the country around Lewes, and as is typical of bright, sharp-eyed boys, he saw much and learned much of the world around him. In his world there were fossils. In later life he recalled these early days. "Here, when a school boy, my curiosity was strongly excited by the petrified 'rams' horns' and 'oak', so abundant in the solid masses of stone in the neighbouring quarries, and which daily came under my notice, in my rambles around the town" (Mantell, quoted by Spokes, 1927, page 2).

While still hardly more than a boy, he became apprenticed to a Lewes surgeon, and in time became a practicing medical man, first with his mentor, James Moore, and subsequently by himself. He was married to a rather handsome young woman, Mary Ann Woodhouse, in 1816, and in the interval between 1818 and 1827 they had four children, two boys and two girls. In 1818 Mantell bought a fine town house in Lewes—Castle Place—and there set himself up in medical practice.

But life at this time was not by any means all medicine with Mantell. He had a large and arduous practice, and one wonders how he managed to find time for other activities—but he did. He made many calls in the country by horse and carriage, and frequently he walked from one patient to another. And always on his rounds he had both eyes trained on the side of the road, and the landscape beyond, in search of fossils.

So we see him on a fine spring day in the year 1822, out in the country, driving to the house of a patient, with his wife accompanying him. They stopped at a house, and while Dr. Mantell was inside with his patient, Mrs. Mantell wandered up and down the road, enjoying the beautiful day and the delicious spring air. Suddenly she saw something shining in a piece of stone—part of a rock pile that had been placed by the side of the road for road repairs. She picked up the piece of rock and saw that it contained fossil teeth of strange form. All unwittingly she had made the first discovery of the dinosaur *Iguanodon* and had thus started a series of events that were to affect her own life profoundly, that were to decide much of the future career of her husband, and that were to loom large in the early history of paleontology. Of course, she showed the specimen to her husband when he came out of the house, and then and there things began to happen.

Mantell was no novice at paleontology; in fact he had already been engaged for several years, during every moment he could snatch from medical duties, in the study of the fossils found around Lewes. In this very year of 1822 he was to publish a large volume, *The Fossils of the South Downs*. It should be added that Mrs. Mantell was not exactly a novice either, because Mantell's monograph was embellished with 42 plates in which 364 separate figures of fossils, all drawn by her, were shown. But these fossils were all primarily the remains of invertebrate animals, of ancient seashells; the fossil teeth were something quite new and different.

The story of Mantell and this first *Iguanodon* has been told more than once; it will be told here once more. Excited by the teeth that his wife had found, he returned time and again for further searches in the region, which is known as the Tilgate Forest, and where in those days there were some rock quarries, worked for road metal. As a result of diligent efforts by Mantell, and especially of the help he received from alert quarrymen, additional fossils came to light. The newly found teeth were quite unlike any other fossil teeth that had been discovered in the strata of Tilgate Forest, and Mantell was more than a little bit baffled by them. He suspected that they might be the teeth of a colossal reptile, some bones of which had already been unearthed in these same sediments. But how was he to solve this puzzle, dug out of the earth and now confronting him? Let us hear some of the first details of the story from Mantell himself:

"Soon after my first discovery of bones of colossal reptiles in the strata of Tilgate Forest, some teeth of a very remarkable character particularly excited my curiosity, for they were wholly unlike any that had previously come under my observation; even the quarrymen accustomed to collect the remains of fishes, shells, and other objects embedded in the rocks, had not observed fossils of this kind; and until shown some specimens which I had extracted from a block of stone, were not aware of the presence of such teeth in the stone they were constantly breaking up for the roads.

"The first specimen that arrested my attention was a large tooth, which from the worn, smooth, and oblique surface of the crown, had evidently belonged to an herbivorous animal; and so entirely resembled in form the corresponding part of an incisor of a large pachyderm ground down by use, that I was much embarrassed to account for its presence in such ancient strata; in which, according to all geological experience, no fossil remains of mammalia would ever be discovered; and as no known existing reptiles are capable of masticating their food, I could not venture to assign the tooth in question to a saurian.

"As my friend Mr. (now Sir Charles) Lyell was about to visit Paris, I availed myself of the opportunity of submitting it to the examination of Baron Cuvier, with whom I had the high privilege of corresponding; and, to my astonishment, learned from my friend that M. Cuvier, without hesitation, pronounced it to be an upper incisor of a rhinoceros.

"I had previously taken this tooth, and some other specimens, to a meeting of the Geological Society in London, and shown them to Dr. Buckland, Mr. Conybeare, Mr. Clift, and other eminent men who were present, but without any satisfactory result: in fact I was discouraged by the remark that the teeth were of no particular interest, as there could be little doubt they belonged either to some large fish allied to the *Anarhicas lupus,* or wolf-fish, the crowns of whose incisors are of a prismatic form, or were mammalian teeth obtained from a diluvial deposit. Dr. Wollaston alone supported my opinion that I had discovered the teeth of an unknown herbivorous reptile, and encouraged me to continue my researches.

"And as if to add to the difficulty of solving the enigma, some metacarpal bones which I soon discovered in the same quarry, and forwarded to Paris, were declared to belong to a species of hippopotamus. Subsequently a dermal horn or tubercle from the same stratum was declared by competent authorities to be the lesser horn of a rhinoceros; and Dr. Buckland, with the generous kindness which marked his character, wrote to guard me against venturing to publish that these teeth, bones, and horn, were found in the 'Iron-sand formation,' with which the Tilgate beds were then classed, as there could be no doubt they belonged to the superficial diluvium: and as the upper beds of the conglomerate in which these first specimens were found was only covered by loam and vegetable earth, there was no clear stratigraphical evidence to support a contrary opinion" (Mantell, quoted in Spokes, 1927, pages 20–21).

Mantell was no man to be discouraged or put off by such eminent authorities as Cuvier, Buckland, and Clift. He *knew* he was right; he *knew* that the strange teeth and bones from Tilgate Forest had been found in place in the rocks and that they were not animal remains of comparatively recent geological age, washed into the sites at which they were found. He *knew* he had the relics of some great reptile hitherto unknown, so he continued his paleontological detective work.

Therefore he took the bones and teeth to London, to compare them with specimens in the Hunterian Museum at the Royal College of Surgeons, in those days the great anatomical repository for animals of all kinds, large and small. There, with the help of William Clift, the curator, he poked through drawer after drawer containing reptilian bones and teeth, but found nothing like the specimens from Tilgate Forest. Perhaps this would have been the end of his search (although it is a pretty safe guess that Mantell, being the man he was, would have persevered until he came up with some sort of a solution to his problem) except for one of those chance happenings that seem to enter so frequently into the story of scientific discovery. Fortunately, as subsequently proved, a young man by the name of Samuel Stutchbury was that day at the Hunterian Museum, and when he saw the strange teeth from Tilgate Forest, which were shown to him by Mantell and Clift after their fruitless search through the collections, he at once saw a resemblance to the teeth of an iguana, a lizard from Central America that he had been working on. He showed the iguana to

Mantell, who immediately realized that here was the clue he had been looking for. The fossil teeth were very much like gigantic iguana teeth!

So it was that in 1825 a paper by Mantell appeared in the *Philosophical Transactions* of the Royal Society of London, entitled "Notice on the *Iguanodon,* a newly-discovered Fossil Reptile, from the Sandstone of Tilgate Forest, in Sussex." The name of the new reptile had been suggested to Mantell by the Reverend W. D. Conybeare, the pioneer English paleontologist who, it may be recalled, had a hand in the naming of *Megalosaurus,* and it means "iguana tooth." The enigmatic teeth from the Tilgate Forest, which for three years had caused so much discussion and differences of opinion, had at last become something real—the petrified evidence of a reptile that now had a name.

Baron Cuvier, who had been so magnificently mistaken in his identification of the fossils, admitted his error, and stated his revised opinion in these freely translated words:

Figure 3. First reconstruction of the skeleton of *Iguanodon* by Gideon Mantell. He obviously based this drawing upon the skeletal anatomy of a large modern lizard; the idea of a giant reptile completely different from any living reptiles was yet to be born. Note that he placed the spike-like thumb on the nose, like the horn of a rhinoceros—a misconception that was to persist for many years

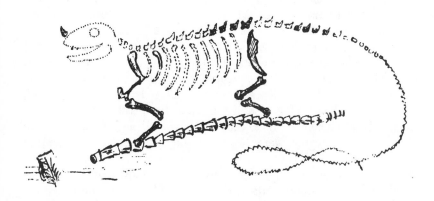

"Do we not have here a new animal, an herbivorous reptile? And even as among the modern terrestrial mammals it is within the herbivores that one finds the species of the largest size, so among the reptiles of another time, then the only terrestrial animals, were not the greatest of them nourished on vegetables? Time will confirm or reject this idea. If teeth adhering to a jaw would be found, the problem might then be resolved."

In these perceptive remarks by Cuvier we see the first adumbration of a new concept—the concept of reptiles of a type hitherto unknown, inhabiting the world in a past age, and living lives different from the lives of modern reptiles. Remember, there was then no such thing as a dinosaur in the mind of man, and indeed almost a generation would go by before the word *dinosaur* was to be coined by Richard Owen. Yet Cuvier managed to point out two common dinosaurian characters in his brief sentences, namely, the large size of these extinct reptiles and their herbivorous diet. It is true that not all dinosaurs were giants and that not all of them were plant eaters, but the great majority of these extinct animals were gigantic herbivores, and thus were different from the reptiles of today. The idea of dinosaurs had made its appearance, and although not formalized with a name, characteristically it did spring from the fertile and well-informed brain of Baron Cuvier, the greatest anatomist and paleontologist of his age.

There were now two extinct reptiles of gigantic size known and described from southern England—*Megalosaurus,* obviously a predatory animal with large, sharp teeth, and *Iguanodon,* evidently a plant-eating animal with expanded, rather flattened teeth. From these two bits of evidence it seemed completely logical to expect more fossils and more new animals in the Cretaceous sediments along the Channel coast. A knowing eye and continued application were needed, and Dr. Mantell was the man to supply these ingredients, so necessary to the successful fossil hunter. To an ever-increasing degree the Cretaceous fossils of the South Downs, and especially the fossil teeth and bones of the great ancient reptiles, occupied his mind and his time. To an ever-lessening degree were his days and his thoughts devoted to medicine.

He had become a figure of considerable renown in Lewes. His home was a museum of sorts, and many people visited him to see the miscellaneous collection of large and curious bones and other fossils that he had gathered together. Furthermore, he was actively corresponding with eminent geologists in England and in other countries; at about this time, for example, he established an exchange of letters with Professor Benjamin Silliman of Yale College that was to continue through the remainder of his life. As a first citizen of Lewes he was among those particularly active in the entertainment of King William and Queen Adelaide when they visited the city in 1830.

But Lewes was beginning to feel a bit small to Dr. Mantell; he wanted a larger and more cosmopolitan center in which to display his fossils, and a larger and more sophisticated audience for his words and thoughts. Consequently in 1833 he moved to Brighton, accompanied by his wife, his four children, his household goods, and his fossils. There he took a house at Number 20, The Steine, in a fashionable part of the town, in which to establish his fossils, his family, and himself, with the drawing room converted into a museum. And here he spent the next eleven years of his life.

What attracted Mantell to Brighton? Although larger than Lewes, it was still what the English are so fond of calling a "provincial" town, a far cry from London (only forty miles to the north), in those days the center of the English-speaking world. But Brighton was then a rather aristocratic seaside resort, frequented by the nobility, and a place very dear to the heart of the king. Here, Mantell thought, in a town conveniently close to the fossil beds, he could obtain noble, even royal, patronage for his efforts. And he could establish a socially elect and lucrative medical practice.

Alas! His high hopes for a brilliant and satisfying life in Brighton never truly materialized. His medical practice there was disappointing, certainly in part because it was his secondary interest. His plans for scientific support from wealthy patrons never got very far. True enough, he did obtain some substantial help from the Earl of Egremont, even to the tune of a thousand pounds to found a Sussex Scientific Society, but this did not attract other enthusiastic patrons to his side. Life was increasingly hard and tense for him and his family (he was without doubt a difficult man to live with), so that there were severe strains within the Brighton home. This is not exactly surprising, when one learns that as early as 1835 his collection of fossils occupied almost the whole of Number 20, The Steine. So far as Mantell was concerned, his family would have to accommodate itself as best it could to his ubiquitous and precious fossils. So far as Mrs. Mantell was concerned, the family did have certain rights, and there ought to be limits as to how far one should be discommoded by a lot of old bones.

The clue to Mantell's rather unhappy situation at this time of his life is, of course, to be found in Mantell himself. For he, like Buckland, was an eccentric of the first order. But whereas Buckland would seem to have been a rather genial eccentric, Mantell was an intense, morose, hypochondriacal man, wholly engrossed in his fossils. The differences between the two men who first described dinosaurs are apparent in their households. Buckland, as we have seen, had a most unusual home, filled with jackals and rollicking bears that lived with the family in a sort of continuous sideshow atmosphere. Mantell, too, had an unusual home, but it was filled with fossil bones, each precious beyond words. One may imagine that the various Mantells must have been sternly adjured to tiptoe through the rooms of the house, moving with caution lest they collide with and damage the priceless specimens. Buckland's home was a menagerie; Mantell's was a museum.

Today Mantell might be a crochety university professor, free to devote most of his thoughts to his fossils, and with a design for living that would keep these fossils in the university museum and out of the living room. But as things were in his day, he was trying simultaneously to live two incompatible lives—one as a physician and one as dedicated paleontologist—and to live them within the confines of his home. To him the fossils were supreme; medicine and the family were relegated to the outer fringes of his life.

THE MAIDSTONE *IGUANODON*

Such a pattern of life eventually was bound to go awry, yet in spite of troubles and difficulties this was for the time being a period of accomplishment. Mantell continued to collect fossils.

In 1834 a partial skeleton of an *Iguanodon* was found at Maidstone in Kent, some forty miles to the northeast of Brighton. Cuvier had asked for "teeth adhering to a jaw" to establish definitely the nature of *Iguanodon*, since heretofore there had been no undoubted association of teeth and bones. The Maidstone specimen was the answer to his request. It did not produce a jaw, but it did have at least a tooth positively associated with the bones, so that now some idea could be gained as to what sort of animal *Iguanodon* might have been, particu-

larly as regards size and proportions. For Mantell it was a truly exciting discovery!

The Maidstone *Iguanodon* came to light in a quarry that fortunately was owned by one W. H. Bensted, a lively and rather unusual
man of his time. In addition to owning and operating the Maidstone
quarry, Mr. Bensted belonged to a "Society of Gentlemen" at Maidstone, named "The AMICI," the meetings of which were devoted to
"literary improvements and mental research." This society once published a volume of contributions by its members, including several

Figure 4. The Cretaceous herbivorous dinosaur *Iguanodon,* first described by
Gideon Mantell. Restoration by Margaret Matthew Colbert

poems by Mr. Bensted, dedicated to flowers and summer skies, as well as an account of his work on the Maidstone specimen. This last piece is an interesting firsthand description of the discovery of the *Iguanodon* at Maidstone; a few paragraphs are quoted below:

"In February, 1834, a portion of one of the lowermost strata in the above quarry, having been blasted, a quantity of some remarkable substance, resembling petrified wood, was observed in the stone. On inspecting a large fragment which had been reserved for me, I at once, perceived, that it was a fossil bone belonging to an animal of great magnitude.

"I immediately searched for other portions and succeeded in finding many more fragments, some of which had been scattered and blown by the gunpowder to a considerable distance. I now felt that I had an object of great interest, and my gratification was much increased, as by degrees, I found myself enabled to fit the various fragments together.

"I erected a temporary shed over them and with mallet and chisel, cleared away the surrounding stone; following the outline of the bone until I had brought to view portions of the skeleton of an extraordinary animal, which had been buried in the bowels of the earth probably in the earliest ages of its existence."

According to the list of materials found at Maidstone, presented at the end of Bensted's paper, a considerable array of bones made up this particular *Iguanodon*. These included various elements of the hind limbs and feet, some parts of the forelimbs, some vertebrae and rib fragments, and a portion of a tooth. Bensted concludes his paper by saying:

"These valuable relics are now at Brighton in the Museum of Dr. Mantell, who is preparing to publish a paper on the subject. From the well known talent and experience of that gentleman, this will doubtless be a highly interesting production" (Bensted, quoted in Swinton, 1951, pages 266, 271).

Incidentally, one sentence in Bensted's paper quoted above is of especial interest by virtue of the fact that it is an early description of a technique of collecting fossil reptile bones. Bensted worked with "mallet and chisel"—an obvious method for exposing and extracting the bones from their surrounding rock matrix, but whether he took any pains to attempt to treat the fossils with preservative materials is not recorded; probably he did not. In those early days fossils were dug out of the ground, often by very crude methods, chiseled free from the rock, and glued together (as was almost inevitably necessary) as best as could be managed. Sophisticated techniques for extracting bones whole and preserving them against the effects of the atmosphere were to come many years later, as we shall see.

Bensted's statement that the "valuable relics" were in Gideon Mantell's Museum leaves certain things unsaid. There were to be some journeys and some negotiations, before Mantell finally got his hands on the fossils.

Of course, the news of Mr. Bensted's unusual discovery quickly spread far and wide, and inevitably it was described after a fashion in the London papers. Many people came to Bensted's house to see his large and interesting fossil bones, but no one could tell him what kind of animal he had found. So Bensted wrote to Mantell, describing the fossil as best he could, and in due course of time Mantell made a journey to Maidstone to examine the specimen. On June 4 Mantell made the following entry in his Journal, the rather extensive diary that he kept during most of his adult life:

"Called on Mr. Saull, and left London with him outside the Maidstone Coach: after a pleasant journey arrived at Maidstone after five. Put up at the Mitre: so soon as we had refreshments went to Mr. Binsted and saw the fossil bones: they are of the lower extremities of Iguanodon: a magnificent group. Visited the quarry where they were dug up. Went to bed very late" (Mantell, quoted by Swinton, 1951, page 263).

Here we see the dedicated fossil hunter. Not for him a restful evening after a coach ride from London, with examinations of the fossils and a visit to the quarry scheduled for the morrow. He must see everything immediately, and at this pleasant duty he spent the hours of a long summer evening, where in England at the time of the midsummer solstice there is light in the sky until nine or ten o'clock. Mantell obviously was enthusiastic about the bones, because before the summer had ended he was bending his efforts toward the acquisition of the fossils for his museum:

"August 14th.—Another week has worn away: am better but not well. Mr. Binsted the owner of the Maidstone Iguanodon refused my offer of £10 for it; he had been offered £20 and required £25. My *very very* kind friends Horace Smith and Mr. Ricardo took upon themselves to obtain it if possible and present it to me; they therefore mentioned their wishes to Mr. Anderson, Wagner, Sir J. Hunter and several other friends, all of whom concurred in their opinion and this very evening the two Mr. Binsteds arrived with the specimen and it is safely deposited in my house: now for three months hard work at night with my chisel; then a lecture! I must do something to merit such kindness" (Mantell, quoted by Swinton, 1951, page 272).

Thus did Gideon Mantell acquire the Maidstone *Iguanodon,* an event that was quaintly celebrated in the volume of The AMICI society:

> "Our young Geologist, who found
> These monstrous Bones deep underground
> And sent his parcel, not a light one,
> To his enlightened Friend at Brighton;
> Imagined, perhaps, like those who send
> The marbles of almighty Greece
> Here, to some Antiquarian friend,
> They'd make a famous *Mantel-piece*."
> (Swinton, 1951, page 273)

There is a modern epilogue to the story of the Maidstone *Iguanodon,* now a part of the Mantell collection in the British Museum. Not many years ago the town fathers of Maidstone decided to incorporate their famous dinosaur in the civic coat of arms, and made application to the College of Arms to this end. Their request was granted, as attested in the citation of 1949:

"I the said Garter Principal King of Arms do by these Presents further grant and assign to the Borough of Maidstone the Supporters following that is to say:—On the dexter side an Iguanodon proper Collared Gules suspended therefrom by a chain Or a scroll of Parchment—" (Swinton, 1951, page 276).

It is good to see an "Iguanodon proper" take his place alongside the griffens, wyverns, and other ornate beasts that for so many centuries have displayed their strange anatomical forms on the crests of our European predecessors.

To supplement the excitement of the Maidstone *Iguanodon,* there was, for Mantell, the satisfaction of having a book, *The Wonders of Geology,* published in 1838. Thus he could review these few years in Brighton with a sense of some accomplishment. Nevertheless troubles and disappointments seemed to outweigh accomplishments. In order to help himself along, he finally and reluctantly decided to sell his "Museum" to the British Museum. He hoped for £5,000, but he could not quite realize this, and finally, in 1838, the collection went to London for £4,000. With the money, or part of it, he bought a medical practice at Clapham, and moved once again.

He had now left the scene of his fossil collecting, and his later life was, in a sense an anticlimax. In many respects it makes a sad story. His domestic troubles came to a head in 1839; his wife and his children eventually left him; and he spent his last years very much alone. In 1841 he suffered a severe injury to his spine in a carriage accident, and from this he never fully recovered. He moved once again, in 1844, to London, where he spent the remaining few years of his lonely life. There were some compensations, even in those last years. He was active in the Royal Society, and in 1849 he was awarded this society's

Figure 5. The city of Maidstone, England, emblazons its civic coat of arms with an *Iguanodon*

Gold Medal, in spite of strong opposition from Sir Richard Owen, at this time Mantell's bitter rival and adversary. He died in 1852.

These are a few incidents in the career of one of the first dinosaur hunters. His was an up-and-down life, with many disappointments, but with certain solid rewards. Perhaps his life was destined to be so varied, with such a mixture of successes and failures, partly because of his prickly personality and partly because he was a scientist before science was a profession, and a student of dinosaurs before dinosaurs were generally known.

The dinosaurs may be regarded as Mantell's monument; he discovered one of the first two dinosaurs identified, and certainly he presented the first adequate scientific description of a dinosaur. By the door of Mantell's house in Lewes there is a brass plate to commemorate his residence there, and beneath his name on the plate is the simple phrase "He discovered the Iguanodon."

CHAPTER 2

DINOSAURS COME TO LIFE

RICHARD OWEN AND THE DINOSAURIA

William Buckland and Gideon Mantell made the first discoveries; Richard Owen looked at these discoveries as well as several later ones with a very perceptive eye, and created the concept of the dinosaurs. It required a perceptive eye and an analytical mind, and in addition a broad knowledge of reptilian anatomy, for this step to be taken when it was taken. Owen had the necessary attributes. Let us look at the man.

Richard Owen, eventually Sir Richard, born in Lancaster, England, in 1804, was at the age of sixteen apprenticed to a surgeon and apothecary in that city. Four years later he became a medical student at the University of Edinburgh, and a year after that he transferred to St. Bartholomew's Hospital in London, where he completed his medical education. If Owen had been an ordinary young man, he would at this stage in his life have begun his career as a medical practitioner, but he was far removed from being an ordinary type of person. As a student he had become much interested in anatomical research, and because of his interest and ability in the study of anatomy he was made an assistant to William Clift (whom we met in the first chapter), the Conservator of the Museum of the Royal College of Surgeons. In 1836, at the age of thirty-two, he was appointed Hunterian Professor in the Royal College of Surgeons; in 1849 he succeeded Clift (whose daughter in the meantime had become Mrs. Owen) as Conservator, and in 1856 he became Superintendent of the Natural History Division of the British Museum. In this post, which he held until his final years, he performed signal service to science and to Britain; he had long had the vision of a separate national Museum of Natural History, and thanks in large part to his efforts he saw the vision grow into reality. A large building inspired by Owen's sketches was erected in South Kensington, designed in the shape of a vast Victorian railway-terminal-Gothic structure, to provide the housing that was needed for collections that had become crowded beyond endurance at the British Museum in Bloomsbury. This accomplishment, which would have been the substance of a career for many a man, was only an incident, albeit a large one, in Owen's life. Owen is remembered primarily as the great pioneer anatomist and paleontologist of England, the "English Cuvier," as he was termed during his lifetime by some of his admirers.

The designation was an apt one, for Owen truly carried on and developed the science of comparative anatomy, which had been founded by Cuvier. Indeed, Owen as a young man visited Paris and met Cuvier, who was then an old man, and the meeting made an influential impression on the energetic and talented anatomist from London. Owen went on to study diligently and widely, and to publish profusely in the field of anatomy. He became a leader of British science, so that even as a comparatively young man his opinions were widely sought and his words were widely accepted. He was a personal friend of Queen Victoria and her large Royal Family, and on many occasions he instructed them at the palace in the wonders and complexities of nature. So highly did the Queen regard him that in 1852 she presented him with a home, Sheen Lodge in Richmond Park, where he lived with his family for the rest of his life.

It would be an unusual person indeed who would not be affected by such honors and blandishments. By his middle years Owen was very sure of himself, very opinionated, and very rigid in his scientific thinking. He considered himself infallible. He could not adapt himself to the changes in the scientific climate that were brought about by the publication of Darwin's *Origin of Species* in 1859, and to the end of his days he was an antievolutionist. Consequently, his unique position in the scientific world declined after the middle of the century. Although honored by royalty and by the government, he was challenged by brilliant younger men—by Thomas Henry Huxley and by Richard Flower, who were to become famous zoologists, as well as by others—and he could not meet their challenge. So he ended his days as a sort of shadow of his former self, a somewhat bitter old man whom the world had passed by. Yet he could think back to a life of immense public service and of many outstanding accomplishments, a life that in its earlier aspects had been filled with excitement.

Some of this excitement was owing to the discovery of great fossil reptile bones in the Mesozoic rocks of southern England. Owen was somewhat younger than Buckland and Mantell, but knew them both, and was involved, intellectually if not physically, with their early discoveries. In fact, Owen became interested in fossil reptiles at a rather early stage in his career, so that by 1841 he was describing them in his own right. In that year he named two extinct reptiles that later were to be designated as dinosaurs; an early form, *Cladeidon*, from Triassic rocks, and a gigantic swamp dweller, *Cetiosaurus*, from the Jurassic Oxford clays.

But in the interval between Buckland's *Megalosaurus* and Mantell's *Iguanodon*, and the two fossils described by Owen, several other fossil reptiles (which also were to be recognized as dinosaurs) had been discovered and described. These were: *Hylaeosaurus*, an armored reptile from the Wealden of southern England, described by Mantell in 1832; *Macrodontophion*, with a name that is something of a jawbreaker, found in the European Jurassic, and described by a gentleman with the jawbreaking name of Zbarzevski in 1834; two primitive forms, *Thecodontosaurus* and *Palaeosaurus* from the Triassic sediments of England, described by Riley and Stutchbury in 1836; and *Plateosaurus*, an ancestor of later giants, from the Triassic of southern Germany, described by Meyer in 1837. Thus, all in all there were nine genera of Mesozoic reptiles known in 1841, which, as was later realized, were not the gigantic lizards that had been envisioned by

Buckland and Mantell. These were reptiles deserving separate and special consideration, and three of them, *Iguanodon, Megalosaurus,* and *Hylaeosaurus,* were the objects of careful scrutiny by Owen.

In the busy years prior to 1841, Owen had prepared extensive catalogues of the collections in the Royal College of Surgeons Museum, while during this same time he enjoyed the privilege of dissecting those animals that had died at the gardens of the Zoological Society —the famous Regents Park Zoo. Consequently he acquired an enormous knowledge of comparative anatomy, the knowledge that ensured to him most unequivocally his position as the English counterpart to and successor of Cuvier. With his background of information on reptiles, living and fossil, Owen had come to understand at this time that the bones of certain Mesozoic reptiles being unearthed with ever-increasing frequency in southern England and on the Continent could not be included within the families or even the larger categories, the orders, under which modern reptiles are classified. These were not the bones of ancient lizards or crocodiles or other reptiles of the kind that inhabit the world today.

As Owen wrote, many years later, "Every specimen accessible in 1840, of Megalosaur, Iguanodon, Hylaeosaur, having been examined and compared by me. . . ." the conclusion was reached that these bones represented reptiles belonging to a large group that had long since vanished from the earth. For this group Owen coined the name *Dinosauria*—from the Greek *deinos,* meaning terrible, and *sauros,* meaning lizard. (One must not be confused by Owen's choice of a Greek word meaning "lizard" when he devised the name for this group of reptiles; the Greeks did not always have a word for everything, so Owen chose the term that etymologically was the nearest thing he could get. Perhaps it is permissible to extend the original meaning of the Greek word, and think of *sauros* in this connection as meaning "reptile".) The name was proposed by Owen at the meeting of the British Association for the Advancement of Science, convened at Plymouth in 1841. It was published in 1842 in the *Proceedings* of the association.

"The combination of such characters, some, as the sacral ones, altogether peculiar among Reptiles, others borrowed, as it were, from groups now distinct from each other, and all manifested by creatures far surpassing in size the largest of existing reptiles, will, it is presumed, be deemed sufficient ground for establishing a distinct tribe or suborder of Saurian Reptiles, for which I would propose the name of *Dinosauria*" (Owen, 1842, page 103).

In this manner Owen added a word to the language of science, a word that, suitably modified in various ways, is now also a part of numerous common languages throughout the world. At the same time he introduced new dimensions into the understanding of ancient life on the earth. Although Owen's concept of a single large group of dinosaurs has since been altered (for it is now clear that the dinosaurs belong to *two* distinct orders of reptiles, as will be discussed more fully in some subsequent paragraphs), his invention of this word, with all of the connotations that go with it, was a great step forward in the interpretation of past life. Now, having come to the year 1841, we can talk about dinosaurs.

Owen and his contemporaries could talk about dinosaurs too, in the years following 1841; their trouble was that they still did not have a large body of fossil evidence on which to base their discussions. As we have seen, nine genera had been described at the time Owen proposed that a new group of reptiles of this particular sort, to be known as dinosaurs, should be recognized. During the decade and a half after the creation of the Dinosauria, four additional genera of such reptiles were discovered in Europe, and described. It was not an impressive array of fossils, but it did begin to indicate some of the features and limitations of those great reptiles that ruled the Mesozoic continents. The massive and sometimes gigantic bones, showing quite a range in variety and form, thus indicating numerous adaptations for different modes of life, strongly impressed Owen, and led him to speculate in his mind as to what some of these ancient animals might have looked like, if their bones were to be covered with muscle and skin. Owen labored under the handicap, which he could not appreciate, of not knowing as much as he thought he knew about the dinosaurs. But he was not deterred. He went ahead to create the vision of dinosaurs in their native haunts, and although the vision was distorted it was a beginning. In paleontology, as in other branches of science, and for that matter in other branches of human endeavor, something is better than nothing, and it is well to do something with that something. If men were to wait for complete knowledge before attempting anything, such as the restoration of animals that lived in past ages, little would be accomplished. Owen used the facts that were before him, and upon the basis of his anatomical knowledge he brought to life, for the first time, some of the dinosaurs.

THE CRYSTAL PALACE DINOSAURS

Owen's vision came into very solid form in 1854, when the famous Crystal Palace, originally erected in Hyde Park, London, for the first of the world's fairs, the great exhibition of 1851, was dismantled and moved to Sydenham, one of the more peripheral sections of the metropolis. Here the Crystal Palace was reerected in spacious grounds, and in these environs some of the animals of an ancient world were restored—in three dimensions and at full size. Professor Owen was in charge of the project, in which he collaborated with a most competent and imaginative sculptor, Mr. Waterhouse Hawkins. Numerous life-size models of extinct animals, dinosaurs, ichthyosaurs, plesiosaurs, ancient amphibians and crocodiles, and various mammals that lived after the dinosaurs had become extinct, were made by Hawkins of concrete, under Owen's watchful eye, and these when completed were placed among the trees and shrubbery of the Sydenham grounds, where they still may be seen. It was a big undertaking, and Owen spent a large part of the year 1854 at this task.

Perhaps the most famous of Owen's dinosaurian restorations was that of *Iguanodon*, of which two models in different poses were made by Hawkins, while *Hylaeosaurus*, like *Iguanodon* a dinosaur originally described by Mantell, was also restored, admittedly upon very slender evidence. *Iguanodon* was envisioned as a four-footed beast with a horn on its nose—a sort of dinosaurian rhinoceros. (We now know that this dinosaur was a characteristic biped, walking on strong hind limbs, with handlike front feet, having on each thumb a strong spike, the spike that formed the nose horn in the Owen-Hawkins model.) The work on *Iguanodon* was long and arduous, and as has been told elsewhere more than once, a dinner party was held within the body of the reconstructed dinosaur as it neared completion. Professor Owen sat at the head of the table, which appropriately placed him in the head of the dinosaur, while Hawkins and twenty other dignitaries banqueted in crowded proximity within the sides of the animal. It was an auspicious occasion, for it heralded the near-completion of a thoroughly successful undertaking with long-lasting results.

His supervision of the reconstructions made by Waterhouse Hawkins marked a climax, but certainly not an end, to Owen's search for dinosaurs. Indeed, the search continued for the remainder of his life. It was a search prosecuted not in the out-of-doors, but in the quiet atmosphere of the laboratory, because Owen was never in any true sense a "field man." He did not tramp through the countryside, nor did he clamber over cliffs and banks to look for fossil bones. Neither did he sit for long hours in the rocky confines of quarries, helping to dig out slabs of rocks containing the petrified remains of extinct animals. This was not his métier, for he was not a geologist or even, in the strict sense, a paleontologist. As has been said, Owen was an anatomist, and during much of his life a public figure of considerable importance, a man who by predilection and circumstances hardly had the time to be out wandering across hill and valley, tracking down to their original resting places the fossils on which such a considerable part of his reputation was based. In a way this was too bad; perhaps if he had ventured into the field to collect some of his fossils with his

Figure 6. A contemporary published drawing, showing the models of prehistoric animals, as constructed by Waterhouse Hawkins under the direction of Richard Owen, and exhibited on the grounds of the Crystal Palace at Sydenham, near London. The two reptiles with horns on their noses are *Iguanodon;* the one with the long head and heavy shoulders is *Megalosaurus.* The names on the rock strata indicate the succession of Mesozoic rocks, as then known, in southern England. See Plate 6

own hand, there would have been an added dimension to his work and to his thought. But such firsthand methods of acquiring fossils were outside Owen's sphere. Instead he devoted much of his life to the description of fossils discovered and collected by other men, fossils not only from Britain but also from other parts of the world as well, especially mammal-like reptiles from South Africa and gigantic flightless birds from New Zealand. His discoveries were made in London, and they were many.

Owen was a prodigious worker in various branches of anatomy, and through one decade after another he published, each year, ten or twelve or perhaps fifteen or more scientific contributions—papers, monographs, and occasional books. He turned his attention to fossils of all kinds, animals without backbones as well as the vertebrates. In an even greater measure he studied and described the anatomical features of an amazing variety of modern animals. There were more general works, too, as well as philosophical discussions and syntheses of lesser studies. Consequently his work on dinosaurs was but a fraction of his interests, yet this work went on through the years, and resulted in much important new knowledge.

In 1854, the year of the work on the Crystal Palace models, he named the Triassic dinosaur *Massospondylus*. Then in 1858 he published a study of *Hylaeosaurus*, the dinosaur first described by Mantell, while during this same year there was another paper by him on everybody's old friend, *Iguanodon*. In fact Owen's interest in *Iguanodon* lasted through later years, so that he contributed several subsequent studies on this interesting dinosaur. In these later years he brought into the world some hitherto unknown dinosaurs as well. Such were *Scelidosaurus*, a plated dinosaur that he described in 1859 and 1861, and *Omosaurus*, another plated type, a stegosaurian, described in 1877 with some extended accompanying remarks on the "Life and Affinities of Dinosauria." *Cetiosaurus* and *Bothriospondylus*, giant swamp-dwelling sauropods, were described in 1875. In 1883 he published a study of the skull of that original dinosaur, *Megalosaurus*. Thus his deeds on behalf of the dinosaurs never flagged. He was one of the great early leaders in those broad fields of dinosaurian studies that today have grown to such earth-encompassing proportions.

Yet in spite of the probing studies by Owen, in spite of his insight and his efforts, the dinosaurs were, at the middle of the nineteenth century, still an ill-defined and slightly understood agglomeration of ancient reptiles. Owen had "created" them; but because of the paucity of fossils at that time, neither he nor his contemporaries had been able to enlarge them to any considerable degree beyond the bounds of their first definition. The structural limits of the dinosaurs were not yet known, and therefore they could not be very satisfactorily defined or even always recognized.

THE CONNECTICUT VALLEY FOOTPRINTS OF EDWARD HITCHCOCK

This is nicely illustrated by the career of Edward B. Hitchcock, a New England divine of some note, for many years the president and professor of Natural Theology and Geology of Amherst College. He was the man who collected and described innumerable dinosaur footprints from the Triassic rocks of the Connecticut Valley, without ever knowing that they were dinosaur footprints. To his dying day Hitchcock supposed that he had unearthed the tracks of ancient birds. For this he can hardly be blamed. Today, with the benefit of a century of hindsight, we realize that the earliest dinosaurs were very birdlike in many ways, especially in the structure of the feet, and this was what misled Hitchcock.

There is a reason for this. Birds, which may with considerable justification be looked upon as "feathered reptiles," are descended from the same ancestral reptilian stock as were the dinosaurs; birds and dinosaurs represent divergent evolutionary branches from certain Triassic reptiles known as thecodonts. Consequently they show numerous resemblances in their anatomical structure, a fact dramatically emphasized to the student of dinosaurs every time he has chicken for dinner. Is it any wonder, then, that Hitchcock spent many years of his very active life in the search for what he thought were ancient bird tracks?

These tracks had been seen and noted in the Triassic rocks of the Connecticut Valley since the beginning of the nineteenth century, at which time they were often referred to as the footprints of "Noah's raven." Hitchcock became interested in them as early as 1835, and from that date until the end of his life they occupied much of his attention. Back and forth across the valley he conducted the search for tracks, summer after summer, and as the years progressed the collection grew. It grew, in fact, to such a degree that in time a museum, the "Appleton Cabinet," was built at Amherst for the footprint collection. This museum, so named because it was made possible largely by funds left to Amherst according to the will of Mr. Samuel Appleton of Boston, was a graceful building of neoclassical style, then so popular among American architects, and its entire lower floor was devoted to the collection of footprints. Hitchcock had his materials in remarkable abundance, and from these prints in the rocks he reconstructed the Triassic life of the Connecticut Valley according to his own interpretation. The interpretation naturally was one that drew a picture in which birds, large and small, were the most numerous of the prehistoric denizens living in an ancient New England:

"It is no idle boast to say, that I have devoted much time, and labor, and thought, to these mementos of the races that, in the dawn of animal existence in the Connecticut valley, tenanted the shores of its rivers and estuaries. Whatever doubts we may entertain as to the exact place on the zoölogical scale which these animals occupied, one feels sure that many of them were peculiar and gigantic: and I have experienced all the excitement of romance, as I have gone back into those immensely remote ages, and watched those shores along which these enormous and heteroclitic beings walked. Now I have seen, in scientific vision, an apterous bird, some twelve or fifteen feet high,—nay, large flocks of them,—walking over the muddy surface, followed by many others of analogous character, but of smaller size. Next comes a biped animal, a bird, perhaps, with a foot and heel nearly two feet long. Then a host of lesser bipeds, formed on the same gen-

---

Figure 7. Some dinosaur tracks look very much like bird tracks. The footprints of a Triassic dinosaur from the Connecticut Valley

eral type; and among them several quadrupeds with disproportioned feet, yet many of them stilted high, while others are crawling along the surface, with sprawling limbs. . . . Strange, indeed, is this menagerie of remote sandstone days; and the privilege of gazing upon it, and of bringing into view one lost form after another, has been an ample recompense for my efforts, though they should be rewarded by no other fruit" (Hitchcock, 1848, pages 250–251).

Hitchcock published this in 1848, thirteen years after he had begun his study of the Connecticut Valley tracks. Beyond the interest to us of this passage because of its delineation of the supposed birdlife of the prehistoric Connecticut Valley are the remarks indicating the pleasures of paleontology. These words of Hitchcock should be emphasized here, because the romance of the ancient scene as envisioned in the mind's eye, and as he says, "the privilege of gazing upon it, and of bringing into view one lost form after another" constitute strong motives that have led men to the search for fossils ever since the days of the Renaissance. Remember Hitchcock's words when thinking of Mantell and of Owen, and of the many men who came after them, some of whose stories will be told in these pages.

Ten years later there was published Hitchcock's monumental work *Ichnology of New England*, printed by the State of Massachusetts, a large quarto volume of 220 pages and 60 lithographic plates. Many of the tracks described and figured in this book were considered by the author to represent lizards, turtles, amphibians, and what he called "marsupialoid animals," but the numerous three-toed tracks were still, in his view, the footprints of birds. He regarded them as belonging to two groups, the "pachydactylous, or thick-toed birds," and the "leptodactylous, or narrow-toed birds." As we now know, of course, these represent accordingly the tracks of comparatively large, heavy Triassic dinosaurs, and those of relatively small, light dinosaurs. But our knowledge, based upon a greatly augmented fossil record, was still not available to Hitchcock. Fossil footprints so closely analogous to the tracks of modern birds must represent ancient birds; such was the logic of his argument, which at that time was beyond reproof.

In 1864 Edward Hitchcock died. But during his final years, through times of failing health, he continued his work on Connecticut Valley fossil footprints with remarkable persistence and devotion. Thus he completed a volume of no mean proportions, supplementary to his great *Ichnology*, embodying results from discoveries that had been made since 1858. This final achievement of his long fossil hunt was published in 1865; the preface, addressed to Governor John A. Andrew of Massachusetts, was dated December, 1863, shortly before Hitchcock's death. And in this last of his quite substantial contributions to our knowledge of fossil footprints, he still peopled the Connecticut Valley of Triassic times with birds.

In 1861 a discovery had been made in the lithographic limestone quarries of Solnhofen, Germany, that might possibly have suggested to Hitchcock the error of his conclusions; instead it reinforced him in his supposition that many of the Connecticut Valley tracks were those of birds. The discovery in Germany was of the first skeleton of *Archaeopteryx*, the oldest known fossil bird, and a bird about which there can be no doubts, because with the skeleton are the imprints of feathers in the fine-grained limestone. Although *Archaeopteryx* has feathers, and is consequently a bird by definition, the skeleton is in many respects very reptilian. Moreover, this fossil, together with specimens subsequently discovered, occurs in Upper Jurassic rocks, many millions of years younger than the Upper Triassic rocks of the Connecticut Valley. Since this very primitive, almost archtypical bird is no older than the late Jurassic, one might suspect that the Triassic footprints would represent animals earlier and more primitive than any birds, in other words, reptiles. We have long known this to be so.

But Hitchcock seized upon the discovery of *Archaeopteryx* as evidence to support the birdlike nature of the three-toed tracks he had described. He compared *Archaeopteryx*, a skeleton with imprints of feathers, with his genus *Anomoepus*, based upon prints of the hind feet, with occasional forefoot prints and marks made by the tail, and decided that a close relationship was to be seen between the fossils from Germany and New England. Certainly the hind footprints of *Anomoepus might* have been made by a primitive bird very similar to *Archaeopteryx*, and the tail marks associated with the *Anomoepus* tracks *might* have been made by an *Archaeopteryx*-like bird, although Hitchcock was worried by the fact that the *Anomoepus* marks were very narrow, and not what might be expected from a long, feathered tail. He did, however, find other marks in the Connecticut Valley sandstones that he thought might have been made by birds with long tails. Another particularly worrisome point was the problem of the front feet. The prints show that *Anomoepus* had five rather short fingers in the hand, which does not correspond very well with the three greatly elongated wing fingers of *Archaeopteryx*.

"This [the forefoot print in *Anomoepus*] certainly looks more like the fore foot of a lizard, and still more like that of some mammals, than the fore arm of a bird; and it is difficult to conceive how it could have been used as an organ of flight, though possibly it might have been employed for prehension" (Hitchcock, 1865, page 29).

It was a difficulty, yet in spite of this seeming anomaly, Hitchcock clung to the idea that the prints of *Anomoepus* had been made by a bird.

"If we can presume that the Anomoepus was a bird, it lends strong confirmation to another still more important conclusion, which is that all the fourteen species of thick-toed bipeds which I have described in the Ichnology, and in this paper, were birds. . . . new examinations brought new facts to light, and the history of the Solenhofen [1] fossil added others, until it appears to me, we may now with more confidence than ever, maintain the ornithic character of these animals" (Hitchcock, 1865, pages 32–33).

With these thoughts in his mind Hitchcock died, unaware of the fact that he was in a sense the first man to discover and describe North American dinosaurs. Although he had failed to realize the significance of many of the Connecticut Valley footprints, he had brought them together in great numbers and had seen to their safe housing and preservation; moreover, he had described them in detail and had illustrated them faithfully. These were his contributions to the search for dinosaurs, and for his long and devoted work he will be gratefully remembered during years to come.

JOSEPH LEIDY AND *HADROSAURUS*

Even though Hitchcock had described and classified literally thousands of dinosaur footprints during his years in the Connecticut Valley, the presence of dinosaurs in North America was still unrecognized at the midpoint of the nineteenth century. The misconception of bird tracks in the Connecticut Valley still held, and as yet no bones had been described as dinosaurian in form and relationships. Then, in

[1] This spelling of the locality, used by Hitchcock, is very common in the literature. The correct spelling today is Solnhofen.

1856, the first Western Hemisphere dinosaurs were described by Dr. Joseph Leidy, of Philadelphia. Nor did he stop there; he continued his studies of dinosaurs for some years afterward, and among his works the descriptions of *Hadrosaurus,* the first dinosaur known in North America from at least a partial skeleton, were especially important. Leidy was, in effect, the man who introduced the New World to dinosaurs.

To consider the man, Joseph Leidy was born in Philadelphia in 1823, the son of an industrious and prosperous hatter of German descent. Although Leidy's father had little formal education, he was a man of uncommonly good sense who was most anxious that his son should have a good education. He was generous to the best of his ability in supporting his son through the formative years. Leidy's mother, also of a German family, was a woman of intellect and education. When Joseph was but a year and a half of age, his mother died, leaving behind four small children, of whom he was the third. He was raised by a kind and understanding stepmother. There is an interesting coincidence here between the childhood years of Leidy and of his two younger contemporaries, Marsh and Cope, for, as we shall see, they too were made motherless when very small boys, and they too were raised by stepmothers.

Leidy had a good preparatory training at a private school, where as was typical of the day Greek and Latin were the prime subjects for study. But Joseph had an intense interest in the natural world, and so he spent many hours wandering through the fields and woods outside Philadelphia, even at times playing the truant from school. As a young man he received an education in medicine at the University of Pennsylvania, receiving his degree of doctor of medicine at what would now be considered the premature age of twenty-one. He attempted to practice medicine for two years after his graduation, but at this he dismally failed. His was an inquiring mind; he was a scholar, not a practitioner.

Leidy had very early in his career developed an interest in anatomy, and had demonstrated unusual skill in the art of dissection. It was thus almost inevitable that he should become a student of anatomy, and a teacher. Having abandoned the practice of medicine in 1848, Leidy spent a brief session as demonstrator of anatomy at the Franklin Medical College. He soon progressed from this appointment to a position at the University of Pennsylvania, where he spent much of the rest of his life, first as an assistant to the professor of anatomy, and within a few years as professor in his own right.

At this time in his career, Leidy had become a close friend of Spencer Fullerton Baird, of the young Smithsonian Institution. Baird had made arrangements for Leidy to accompany an expedition to the western territories in 1852, to collect fossils. But on the eve of his departure, Dr. Horner, the professor of anatomy at the university, became seriously ill, and Leidy was informed that it was quite essential for him to remain in Philadelphia to carry on Dr. Horner's work at the university. Dr. Horner's illness was fatal, and the problem of his successor was immediately raised. Baird wrote to Leidy: "Do not leave Philadelphia until you have settled the professorship. Do not worry about the fossil bones; they will all be sent to you anyhow."

And thus Leidy missed an opportunity to explore the western fossil fields. He was appointed to the professorship, and from that time on the press of duties prevented him from venturing into the field in search of fossils. He studied many dinosaur fossils, it is true, but they were usually fossils collected by other men.

Leidy's work on fossils is but one indication of the breadth of his research interests. In addition to being a paleontologist and an eminent anatomist (he wrote a medical textbook on human anatomy), he was a student of modern mammals and reptiles, of snails and sponges and other invertebrates, and in addition he was a renowned pioneer in protozoology and parasitology. He had an extensive knowledge of botany, and he was a mineralogist of ability, lecturing on that subject at Swarthmore College, and assembling an outstanding collection of minerals and gems.

Because of these wide interests in natural sciences, Leidy became associated with the Academy of Natural Sciences of Philadelphia at an early stage in his career. He served the academy faithfully and well throughout his professional life—as a scientist studying the collections in the academy, as a member of the board of trustees, and finally as president. Indeed, the name of Leidy was so inseparably interwoven with the name of the academy that he became a sort of patron saint of the institution. Today a bronze statue of Leidy, larger than life, stands in front of the academy, facing Logan Circle.

In some ways Joseph Leidy in America paralleled Owen in England. Both men were trained in medicine and both were teachers. Both men were the leading anatomists of their day. Both men had interests that went far beyond medicine and indeed far beyond man, to include all the other classes of backboned animals and many of the invertebrates as well. But the parallelisms in the professional lives of Leidy and Owen did not extend to their private lives. Leidy was about twenty years younger than Owen, yet there was more than an age difference to mark them apart, for Leidy had none of Owen's arrogance and self-esteem. Leidy was a man of calm dignity, of genuine modesty and friendliness of spirit that went well with his great accomplishments as a scientist. All who knew him spoke of his gentle nature, and he was widely beloved. Truly the strong placidity of the inner man was reflected in his outward appearance, for he was a person of distinguished aspect. One additional point of interest is the fact that in contrast to Owen, Leidy embraced Darwin's theory of the origin of species, immediately after the publication of the epoch-making book in 1859. Leidy was married at the age of forty; there were no children.

In 1855 Dr. Ferdinand Vandiveer Hayden, one of the early scientific explorers of the territories west of the Mississippi River, collected some fossil teeth of Cretaceous age near the confluence of the Judith River with the great Missouri, in what is now Montana. These he submitted to Dr. Leidy when he returned to Philadelphia after his explorations of that year, and Leidy published short descriptions of them in March of the following year. Two of the teeth Leidy designated as *Palaeoscincus* and *Troödon* and indicated them as being "lacertilian." The other teeth, several in number, were named *Trachodon,* a "herbivorous lacertilian reptile allied to the *Iguanodon,*" and *Deinodon,* a reptile resembling *Megalosaurus.* The evidence was pitifully scant, yet Leidy, with his perspicacious eye, correctly saw the relationships of these scattered teeth; he saw the resemblances of certain of them to European fossil reptiles that had by this time been classified as dinosaurs. Such was the recognition of dinosaurs in North America.

These first bits of evidence were fragmentary indeed, but within two years a discovery was made, figuratively in Dr. Leidy's backyard, that was to provide very solid evidence for dinosaurs in North America. This was the unearthing of the partial skeleton of the dinosaur *Hadrosaurus,* mentioned above.

It all began with Mr. William Parker Foulke of Philadelphia, who was enjoying the summer and autumn of 1858 at Haddonfield, New

Jersey, across the Delaware River from Philadelphia, and at no great distance from the city. Mr. Foulke learned that one of his neighbors, Mr. John E. Hopkins, had discovered twenty years previously some fossil bones while digging Cretaceous marls on his farm. These bones, which from the description by Mr. Hopkins were plainly vertebrae, were said to have been of large size, and numerous. At the time they had been carried away by various visitors, and unfortunately Mr. Hopkins could not in 1858 remember the names of the people who had appropriated the fossils as souvenirs. He was certain that no skull

Figure 8. The skeleton of a Cretaceous duck-billed dinosaur, a close relative of *Hadrosaurus,* as reconstructed by Professor Othniel C. Marsh of Yale. This drawing, made perhaps thirty years after Leidy first described *Hadrosaurus,* is correct in all its essential characters. It demonstrates the advances in knowledge that had been made, the result of the collecting of complete skeletons, during the three decades after the first dinosaur skeleton had been discovered in North America

had been found, nor any leg bones or other skeletal parts of size; the fossils were all vertebrae.

Seeing that Mr. Foulke was very much interested in the prospects of something unusual and interesting in the ground, Mr. Hopkins gave him permission to dig on the farm. It took some time and trouble to locate the old marl pit, which in the meantime had all but disappeared because of slumping and filling, but finally one of the workmen who had been employed two decades earlier thought that he remembered its location, in the bed of a narrow ravine.

A group of experienced diggers was hired, and a new excavation was begun at the edge of the old pit. After considerable digging the workers came upon a deposit of bones, many of them of large size. Dr. Leidy and Mr. Isaac Lea of Philadelphia were informed of the exciting discovery, and of course they visited the location. It was decided to continue with the digging as long as the weather would permit, and so the project was carried on through the month of October. Very little in addition was found, only a few stray bones. However, interest had been aroused, and one of the workmen continued to poke about, not at Haddonfield, but at other pits south of the town. His efforts were rewarded; he found bones and teeth of a crocodile, of the same age as the dinosaur bones that had been excavated at the Hopkins farm. Leidy and Foulke also made excursions around the countryside, and they too located fossil crocodile bones that had been found some years earlier in a pit south of Haddonfield. But there were no more dinosaur remains forthcoming.

Leidy first described the bones from Haddonfield in December, 1858, and proposed the name *Hadrosaurus foulkii* for them. Subsequently he described the fossil in detail. Leidy pointed out that *Hadrosaurus* was closely allied to *Iguanodon*, which two years earlier, it may be recalled, he had indicated to be the case with *Trachodon*, one of those dinosaurs known from teeth collected along the Judith River. But whereas *Trachodon* was represented by a few teeth, *Hadrosaurus* consisted of nine teeth, a fragment of a lower jaw, a series of twenty-eight vertebrae, bones of the fore and hind limbs and the hind feet, and the bones of the pelvis (which are very important to students of dinosaurs). Here was the first adequate evidence on which to reconstruct a picture of an American dinosaur, and this Leidy did, with the skill and insight of an accomplished anatomist. These are some of his remarks, made in the preliminary description of *Hadrosaurus:*

"The great disproportion of size between the fore and back parts of the skeleton of *Hadrosaurus*, leads me to suspect that this great extinct herbivorous lizard may have been in the habit of browsing, sustaining itself, kangaroo-like, in an erect position on its back extremities and tail." Leidy was correct on every point in this trenchant sentence. He pictured *Hadrosaurus* in the pose that we now know was proper for this type of dinosaur, in decided contrast to Owen's misinterpretation of the pose of the closely related *Iguanodon*. But then Leidy allowed conventional caution to get the better of his first judgment, and in the next sentence he presents the alternative interpretation. "As we, however, frequently observe a great disproportion between the corresponding parts of the body of recent and well known extinct saurians, without any tendency to assume such a position as that mentioned, it is not improbable that *Hadrosaurus* retained the ordinary prostrate condition, progressing in the manner which has been suspected to have been the case in the extinct batrachian of an earlier period, the *Labyrinthodon*." In thus backtracking from his first statement Leidy was not entirely wrong. It is evident that *Hadrosaurus* and related dinosaurs probably did go down on all fours at times, just as do modern kangaroos, but their characteristic pose was bipedal, as Leidy so shrewdly observed in his first sentence. Then he went on to describe most correctly in modern terms the environment of *Hadrosaurus* and the circumstances of its burial:

"*Hadrosaurus* was most probably amphibious; and though its remains were obtained from a marine deposit, the rarity of them in the latter leads us to suppose that those in our possession had been carried down the current of a river, upon whose banks the animals lived" (Leidy, 1858, pages 9–10).

With these words a dinosaur, *Hadrosaurus*, came to life in North America, in the mind of Leidy, just four years after a related dinosaur, *Iguanodon*, had come to life in Britain at the hands of Richard Owen and Waterhouse Hawkins.

THE PALEOZOIC MUSEUM IN CENTRAL PARK

Ten years later this same *Hadrosaurus* was to come to life in a more material way, and through the efforts of none other than Waterhouse Hawkins, the man who had reconstructed *Iguanodon*. It all came about because the City of New York had a great new park, the now world-famous Central Park, with an ambitious man, Mr. Andrew H.

Green, in charge of it. Mr. Green was Comptroller of the Park—today he would be called the Park Commissioner.

On May 2, 1868, Waterhouse Hawkins, who was then in the United States, received the following letter from Mr. Green:

"DEAR SIR:

"Recognizing the interest that has long attended your restorations of the forms of extinct animals in Europe, the Commissioners of the Central Park have thought that a similar work in the direction of reconstituting the phenomena of the ancient epochs of this continent would be of equal scientific value, and of especial interest in an educational point of view.

"The admitted advantages of an exhibition of a rehabilitated animal over one showing the mere remains of its fossil frame, are not to be questioned; and as this improved method of bringing before us creatures of a past age is chiefly due to your skill and scientific labors, the Commissioners of the Park are desirous to make at least a commencement in this direction, if they can feel assured of your cooperating interest, and supervising skill and advice.

"It gives me great pleasure in their behalf to propose to you to undertake the resuscitation of a group of animals of the former periods of the American continent.

"Should your engagements be such as to admit of your entering upon this work, that will so well supplement your previous achievements in the same department, I think I may promise you the sympathy and support of the scientific men of this country, and that museums and collections of fossil treasures, public and private, will be freely opened for such examinations as you may desire to make in the prosecution of this interesting undertaking.

"With great respect,
"ANDW. H. GREEN,
"Comptroller of the Park"

Hawkins, obviously delighted with an opportunity such as this, replied favorably, with alacrity, and in the orotund phraseology so generally used by Victorian letter writers:

"DEAR SIR:

"I have received your favor of May 2d, proposing on behalf of the Commissioners of the Central Park of New York, the restoration of a group of ancient fossil animals in the grounds under their control, where art has already accomplished so much for public pleasure and improvement.

"The interest in the remains of ancient animal life which Geology has revealed within the last century is world wide, and almost romantic in its influence upon the imagination, and I quite agree with you that there can hardly be a question as to the advantage of representing these remains, clothed in the forms which science now ventures to define.

"The restorations which were committed to my charge in the Crystal Palace Park at Sydenham, were the first efforts of the kind ever attempted, and their acknowledged success, both in commanding the cordial approval of scientific men, and also a large measure of public appreciation, encourages me to hope that a similar enterprise may meet with equal favor on this side of the Atlantic.

"In regard to the educational value of those restorations to which you are pleased to refer, I would say, that if it was marked and most decisive in England, notwithstanding that their situation was several miles from London, where they were only accessible through a charge for admission, it may be assumed that the benefits will be greatly enhanced, where the animals, conspicuously placed in your grand Park, would be freely open to all. Nor do I fail to recognize the eminent advantages which result from that higher condition of popular intelligence for which this country is pre-eminently distinguished.

"Your kind intimation that I may expect the favor and sympathy of the scientific men of the United States in carrying out this work is very gratifying to me, as I came among you a stranger scarcely expecting to resume my former labors, under such auspicious circumstances, in a foreign country, while my experience of the most hospitable kindness, and a general interest manifested in those subjects to which I have devoted my life, confirms your assurance that the aid and support I so greatly need will be generously accorded.

"Sincerely appreciating this flattering evidence of your confidence, I accept the proposal, and am prepared to enter at once upon the preliminary steps of the undertaking.

"With the highest consideration,
"I am, dear sir,
"Yours faithfully,
"B. WATERHOUSE HAWKINS

(Both letters are extracted from the *Twelfth Annual Report of the Commissioners of the Central Park,* 1868, pages 132–134.)

Hawkins lost no time in getting the project under way. He accepted Mr. Green's proposal on the ninth of May, and on the eighteenth he was engaged by the commissioners. There followed a consultation between them, with the resulting decision that Hawkins "should attempt to reproduce the original forms of life inhabiting the great Continent of America, rather than repeat the European forms that had been already illustrated in the Palace Park at Sydenham, in England" (*Twelfth Annual Report,* 1868, page 135).

Waterhouse Hawkins accordingly spent the summer and autumn months at the United States National Museum in Washington, at the Philadelphia Academy of Natural Sciences (where the partial skeleton of *Hadrosaurus* was kept), and at Yale University, studying fossils. A large workshop was erected in Central Park, assistants were hired, and he went to work.

In the meantime the Park Commission proceeded with plans for the erection of the "Paleozoic Museum," which was to be a Crystal Palace type of cast-iron and glass structure with a great arched roof, located within the park near Eighth Avenue (or as it is now termed, Central Park West), opposite Sixty-third Street. Work was begun on the foundation of this building, while grandiose visions arose within the minds of all concerned. Thus, the *Report* of the park commissioners for 1869 had this to say:

"The great group of ancient animals formerly living during the secondary geological epoch on the continent of America, now being modeled and restored to the natural size and the appearance of the animal as in life, by Mr. Hawkins, for the Central Park, consists of the gigantic *Hadrosaurus* of the exact dimensions (one twenty-six feet, the other thirty-nine feet, long), as proved by the fossils described by Dr. Joseph Leidy in the 'Smithsonian Contributions to Knowledge, No. 192'; also models of Laelap's Aquilunguis' fossils, described by Cope, together with the aquatic '*Elasmosaurus* and *Mosasaurus*'" (*Thirteenth Annual Report,* 1869, page 28).

Laelaps is the carnivorous dinosaur generally designated as *Dryptosaurus.*

These dinosaurs, together with various other extinct creatures found on the North American continent, were to repose on a sort of island in the center of the museum, surrounded by appropriate tropical greenery. It would have been an imposing restoration of Mesozoic and later life, although a bit overblown.

Unfortunately for Waterhouse Hawkins and his dreams, the entire scheme foundered in mid-course. Those were the days of the infamous Tweed Ring in New York City, and the Paleozoic Museum, together with Mr. Green and Hawkins, became the victims of some

---

Figure 9. A drawing by Edward Drinker Cope to show what *Dryptosaurus (Laelaps)*, a close relative of *Megalosaurus*, might have looked like in life—according to Cope

sinister political machinations. Central Park was made part of an enlarged Department of Public Parks, externally a seemingly innocent and logical coordination of facilities, internally a plan to supplant Mr. Green and his commission by some Tweed henchmen. The Paleozoic Museum was abandoned, its foundation was demolished, Hawkins was dismissed, and the molds and casts for his models were buried somewhere in the southern part of Central Park.

Hawkins was understandably bitter. He immediately went to Philadelphia, where he made a cast of the skeleton of *Hadrosaurus*, based upon the bones available, plus a liberal use of Hawkins' ideas as to what the missing bones should be like. This cast was for many years exhibited in the Academy of Sciences of Philadelphia, and although in many respects it contained many inaccuracies, it none the less came closer to what a dinosaur of its type should be like than did the model of *Iguanodon*, created in 1854 under the direction of Owen.

Subsequently, Waterhouse Hawkins spent some time at Princeton University (then the College of New Jersey at Princeton), where he made a series of oil paintings showing dinosaurs and other creatures of the Mesozoic as he envisioned them. These restorations are still in the possession of the university—quaint attempts as seen by modern eyes, but valuable records of what, almost a century ago, the ancient reptiles of North America were thought to have looked like.

Such were some of the early efforts in Britain and in North America to bring dinosaurs to life. Such were some of the attempts to give form to those ancient reptiles first discovered by Buckland and Man-

---

Figure 10. World map, showing the locations of some important and historic dinosaur localities. (1) Southern England and Belgium: Buckland, Mantell, and Dollo. (2) The Connecticut Valley: Hitchcock, Marsh, and Lull. (3) Como Bluff and Canyon City, Dinosaur National Park, Howe Quarry: Marsh, Cope, Douglass, and the Carnegie Museum, Osborn, Granger, Brown, and The American Museum of Natural History. (4) Trossingen: von Huene. (5) New Mexico Triassic: Cope. (6) Red Deer River: the Sternbergs and Brown. (7) Mongolia: Central Asiatic Expeditions, Russian Expeditions. (8) South Africa: Broom and his successors. (9) Tendaguru: Hennig and Janensch, British Expeditions. (10) Argentina: Ameghino, Wichman, and others. (11) Southern Brazil: von Huene. (12) Queensland. (13) Spitzbergen: Heintz, Lapparent

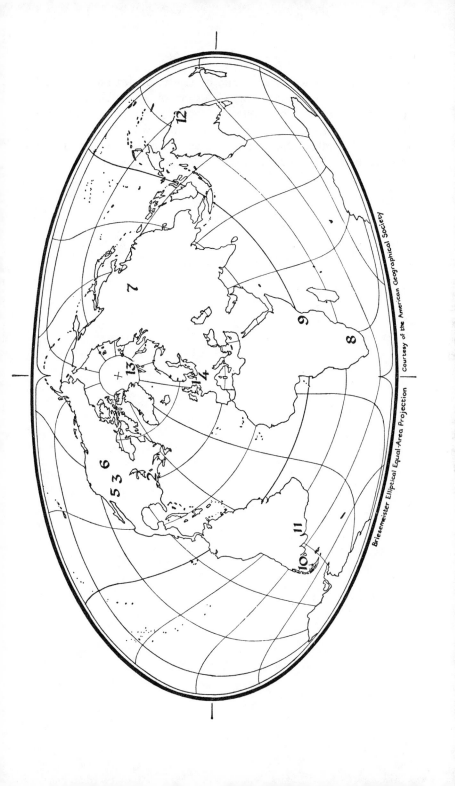

tell, and first defined as dinosaurs by Owen. Such were some of the beginnings of a long and fascinating story of paleontological exploration, deduction, and interpretation, the beginnings that laid foundations for an immense amount of subsequent work by many men in field and laboratory, that through the years has re-created the world of a hundred million years ago, the world of the dinosaurs.

CHAPTER 3

SKELETONS IN THE EARTH

THE IGUANODONTS OF BERNISSART

The years 1877 and 1878 are notable in the history of the search for dinosaurs because they marked the beginning of large-scale discoveries of dinosaur skeletons on both sides of the North Atlantic. In 1877 two bitter rivals on the American paleontological scene during the latter part of the nineteenth century, Othniel Charles Marsh and Edward Drinker Cope, made the first of their collections of gigantic skeletons from the Upper Jurassic beds of Colorado and Wyoming, collections that were to accumulate during the next decade to astound the world of science and astonish the man in the street. And in 1878 a remarkable concentration of *Iguanodon* skeletons was encountered a thousand feet below ground in a Belgian coal mine at Bernissart, near the French border.

It would seem that some fossils had been seen at Bernissart in 1877, but evidently not much significance was attached to them. But in 1878, some coal miners while developing a new gallery in the Fosse

Sainte-Barbe, a mine belonging to a company named the Charbonnage de Bernissart, encountered numerous large fossil bones at a depth of 322 meters, or 1,046 feet. Because of the difficulties under which the men worked—in a small tunnel at a great depth underground, and with very dim light to guide them—it would appear that they had picked their way right through one skeleton and had almost completely destroyed it before they were aware of its presence. For this they can hardly be blamed; such things have occurred more than once above ground and in full sunlight. The miners told the managers of their discovery, no doubt with many excited words and gestures, and the men in the front office, notably the director of the mine, M. Gustave Fages, informed the Musée Royal d'Histoire Naturelle de Belgique in Brussels of the find. The museum immediately dispatched P. J. van Beneden, one of the noted Belgian paleontologists of that day, to the scene, to explore and evaluate the situation. Dr. van Beneden reported the bones to be those of *Iguanodon*, obviously present in great numbers. The situation was remarkable, to say the least, and time did not diminish its dimensions.

Indeed, these dimensions increasingly impressed the men who were surveying the various aspects of the discovery, and soon it was evident that an undertaking of major proportions was in the making. Accordingly M. Gustave Arnould, the engineer at the mine, requested that expert technical help for excavation of the bones be made available in the person of M. De Pauw, the man in charge of the museum laboratory. M. De Pauw went to Bernissart, where, "adopting the life of a miner," he spent three years directing the arduous and painstaking work of digging out the skeletons. Fortunately, he had the help of trained assistants, as well as much aid furnished by the officials of the

Figure 11. A schematic section, showing the formations at Bernissart, Belgium. Note the fosse, or shaft, indicated by a vertical line, joining the two horizontal galleries, one at 322 meters, the other at 356 meters below the surface. The skeletons of *Iguanodon* were encountered where these galleries cut through the Cran du Midi. From a drawing made at the time of the discovery of the Bernissart iguanodonts

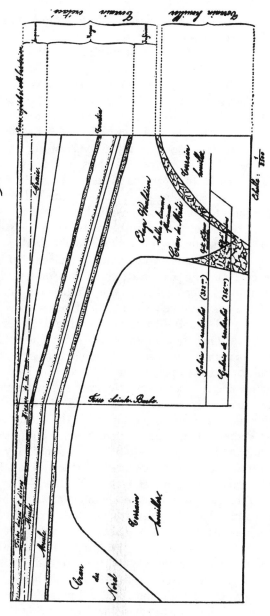

Coupe générale Nord-Ouest Sud-Est (Bernissart).

mine, who made their resources available to ensure the safe recovery of the fossils for the museum.

It was a herculean task. A second and lower tunnel had been driven parallel to the first one, this time at a depth of 356 meters, or 1,157 feet, and again bones were encountered. Thus it could be seen that the fossil boneyard was evidently one of gigantic proportions, especially notable because of its vertical extension through more than a hundred feet of rock. This was most unusual. The bones were not contained within the regular stratified beds of the coal mine, but rather were deposited in unstratified clays that cut *through* the layered shales and coals. In short, the fossils were within a *cran*, a deep pit or filled fissure, extending down through the sediments. Did this remarkable concentration of bones through such a depth of sediments signify a long period of time during which many dinosaurs died and were buried in accumulating muds? One might think so, but careful work by M. De Pauw and his assistants would seem to indicate that within the coal mine of Bernissart there was preserved an ancient ravine—a narrow, deep gully in the Cretaceous landscape, into which, within a comparatively short span of years, many iguanodonts had slipped and fallen and died, to be buried in deep deposits of mud brought in by flooding waters after heavy rains. The painstaking digging and mapping that were done in the mine revealed this detail in an ancient landscape; it was possible to delineate the banks of the Cretaceous ravine, and to discern the inwash of sediments that had filled it—all quite distinct from the regular layers of coal and shale that were being mined far beneath the surface of the earth. Certainly such an unusual deposit of dinosaur skeletons must be approached with understanding, and must be carefully and systematically excavated if meaningful results were to be obtained. Needless to say, M. De Pauw and his assistants worked under great difficulties—in cramped positions and with the rather feeble illumination available from the miners' lamps of those days. Nevertheless they carried out their long task with admirable skill and originality. Careful surveys and measurements were maintained during the progress of the work, and the positions of the bones in the deposit were recorded. Blocks of coal shale containing bones were taken out and numbered, so that they could be reassembled in the laboratory. All possible precautions were taken to preserve the fossils against breakage during the excavations and during their journey back to Brussels, and they were treated to prevent deterioration in the air. This latter problem was a very large one, because the bones of the Bernissart iguanodonts, like so many fossils that are preserved in coal deposits, suffered from "pyrite disease," the effect of iron sulfide in the fossils, which on exposure to air causes a breaking down of their surfaces. The problem was not immediately solved, but in subsequent years, thanks to increased knowledge and improved equipment, it was possible to give additional treatments to the fossils, ensuring their preservation to this day.

The bones were originally prepared and the first skeletons were mounted in the romantic setting of the fifteenth-century Chapelle Saint-Georges in Brussels, once an oratory belonging to the palace of the Princes of Nassau, which just before the turn of the present century was used as a laboratory by the museum. Here, beneath Gothic arches where robed monks and nobles had gathered, and perhaps on more than one occasion had exchanged fearful tales of dragons, were now set up skeletons of the real dragons of antiquity, the dinosaurs that had inhabited Belgium in a far-distant age. The preparation of the Bernissart iguanodonts occupied a quarter of a century, with results that were magnificently impressive.

The iguanodonts of Bernissart were not preserved as an indiscriminate pile of bones, as so frequently is the case in fossil deposits, but rather were for the most part remarkably well articulated, the remains showing animals in the positions in which they had been buried. The first skeleton was mounted in 1883, and at the end of the century five skeletons were to be seen in the Royal Museum, then newly completed. Today the impressive array of iguanodonts in Brussels is made up of eleven standing skeletons, with twenty additional complete and partial skeletons, recumbent on the base of the display. It is a group of dinosaurs of one kind, unique in the world.

The discovery of the Bernissart iguanodonts helped to open a new era in the understanding of these ancient reptiles, an era in which interpretations were to be based not upon single teeth or a few isolated bones, but upon complete skeletons, and as in this case, upon a magnificent series of skeletons of one species. Thus materials were made available for penetrating studies and significant conclusions that could be tested by repetition—which is the criterion of the scientific method. In the case of the Bernissart iguanodonts, and of dinosaurs in Europe for that matter, this new era of study and interpretation was inaugurated by Louis Dollo.

LOUIS DOLLO, STUDENT OF *IGUANODON*

Louis Dollo, a man of solemn appearance, with a heavy, drooping moustache, was born in Lille, France. He attended the university there, where he completed a degree in civil engineering in 1877. Although an engineer by early training, and although he had a short career in industry, he was especially interested in geology and zoology, subjects he had studied assiduously during his university years. Moreover, he was as a young man influenced by the work of the Russian paleontologist Vladimir Kowalevsky, and he worked in close association in Brussels with the German anatomist Paul Albrecht. Why was he in Brussels? He had gone there in 1882 to study the iguanodonts, the excavations of which were then coming to an end and the laboratory work on which was then under way in earnest. His studies were elegantly conducted and significant; and because it was apparent that Brussels was to be the place where he would develop his career, he became a Belgian citizen in 1886, to continue for many years his research on *Iguanodon*. In 1891 he was named Conservator in the Museum, and in 1909 Professor of Paleontology at the University of Brussels.

During these years he labored mightily, taking only one leave of absence from the museum, a visit to Brittany in 1906. He devoted himself completely to his studies of *Iguanodon*, to supervising the technicians in their work of cleaning and preparing the fossils, to directing the mounting of the skeletons, and at the same time to delving into other facets of paleontology. To say that he worked hard is to state it mildly. For example, the year 1887 saw the publication of the quite incredible total of 94 scientific papers by Dollo. Some of these were mere notes, it is true. But many of them were substantial studies, each of which must have required much time in preparation. Although exceptional, this was not an isolated year of high production in Dollo's early scientific life, because his papers in the years preceding and following 1887 can be numbered by the dozens and the scores. Dollo was indeed a prolific thinker and writer, a man whose thoughts poured out in great profusion. Many of his ideas were of exceptional originality.

Although he did venture into the field, Dollo was not a man who particularly enjoyed going out to study the geology of hill and valley, or to collect the fossils that were eroding from the ground. He was a student of almost monastic habits, a retiring man who sought the seclusion of his laboratory, closeted for long hours with his fossils and spending these long hours making notes and writing manuscript. Yet in spite of the hours and days and weeks thus spent, his papers are unusual for conciseness and brevity. He had no love for long publications, either those written by himself or by others. Once, in response to a question concerning the progress of a certain project, he said: "I am not close to the end of my work; it is not as yet sufficiently brief." Dollo's ideal was to trim and cut, so that many of his writings are of almost telegraphic style, frequently with every paragraph numbered. This, it would seem, harked back to his mathematical training, and to his preoccupation with order.

Another preoccupation was with synthesis, and at this Dollo exercised great skill. He was not a mere describer; he attempted to gather together the isolated facts of paleontology and to unite them into meaningful statements. He developed theories, even what some later paleontologists have called "laws."

Dollo's first note on the iguanodonts of Bernissart appeared in 1882, and from then until the end of the century he brought out a series of technical papers elucidating new facts and new interpretations concerning these famous dinosaurs. And yet, in spite of his industry and application, he never published a great definitive monograph on *Iguanodon*. It was just not in his nature to devote his talents to such a large and confining task. Instead he published twenty-seven papers on Bernissart fossils, nineteen of them devoted to dinosaurs. His contributions to what had by now become almost a discipline of "iguanodontology" were therefore of the utmost importance.

The iguanodonts of Bernissart revealed to Dollo the answers to many questions about dinosaurs that heretofore had been discerned but dimly, if at all. Here were complete, articulated skeletons, allowing for interpretative study with a minimum amount of supposition and interpolation, and with the possibility of checking on details from one skeleton to another. It was the sort of situation that even a modern-day dinosaurian student dreams about and all too seldom realizes. It was a situation whereby Dollo could almost literally wallow in a profusion of well-documented fossil bones. He made much of his opportunities.

The large suite of fossils gave him the chance to study variability and age differences within one or two dinosaurian species. As a result of his studies Dollo decided that there were actually two species in the Bernissart deposit, an idea that had originated with G. A. Boulenger, a noted authority on living and extinct reptiles. There were, according to this view, a large species, *Iguanodon bernissartensis,* named after the locality at which it was discovered, and a smaller one, *Iguanodon mantelli,* named in honor of that extraordinary Briton, Gideon Mantell, who may be regarded as the patron saint of all iguanodonts. Dollo showed that distinct anatomical differences separated the two, and, moreover, that they had been found at different levels, an argument that generally looms large in the thinking of fossil hunters. Other students have felt that the iguanodonts of Bernissart are very probably of a single species; that the anatomical differences are probably those separating the two sexes, and that the differences in levels are to be accounted for by the accumulation of the carcasses in a narrow, deep ravine, as was previously mentioned.

However that may be, the anatomical details of these completely articulated Bernissart iguanodonts left no doubt in Dollo's mind as to the bipedal pose in these ancient reptiles, a point that, it may be remembered, had been raised by Joseph Leidy in 1858. Actually, the reality of bipedalism in the iguanodonts had been reiterated and firmly emphasized by Thomas Henry Huxley, Darwin's brilliant disciple, in 1868 and in subsequent years, after Leidy's tentative suggestion had been put forward but before Dollo entered upon his dinosaurian studies. Huxley had pointed out not only the bipedal pose of these dinosaurs but also their remarkably birdlike characters, and at the same time their rather close relationships to the crocodilians. All these features were confirmed by Dollo as he studied the Bernissart skeletons. Dollo also showed quite conclusively that the great bony spike, which Owen had thought was a nose horn, and which he had so restored in the Crystal Palace models, was in fact the base for an enormous spike or claw on the thumb, obviously a weapon for offense and defense. In addition, Dollo solved the problem of the complex succession of teeth in these plant-eating dinosaurs, thanks to the numerous skulls and jaws with which he could make comparative studies, back and forth. He discovered, too, that *Iguanodon* had a remarkable lattice-like arrangement of ossified tendons crossing the vertebrae in the rear portion of the skeleton, an arrangement (which we now know is common in many of the plant-eating dinosaurs) that must have added great strength and no little amount of stiffness to the tail. Dollo studied these curious bony structures, and during the course of his studies he devoted considerable attention to the musculature in the iguanodont dinosaurs. He was able to analyze in detail the manner in which the immense muscles for locomotion were attached to the pelvis, to the tail, and from thence to the hind limbs.

Nor did his study of the soft anatomy in this dinosaur end with an analysis of the musculature. He gave his attention to the problem of feeding, and came to the conclusion that *Iguanodon* had a long and prehensile tongue, somewhat like the tongue of a giraffe—a conclusion, by the way, that need not be accepted today. One day King Leopold of Belgium visited Dollo, and said to him: "You have given much study to giant animals. I would like to tell you what I think, and if it is something foolish, please forgive it. For it is not my business to be concerned with such questions, and I consider that each man should confine himself to his own specialty. I think that the iguanodonts were some sort of giraffes."

To which Dollo replied, "Yes, Sire, but they were *reptilian* giraffes, because they were scaled animals as are typically all reptiles, and not furred animals as are the mammals. Moreover, like the giraffes they searched for their food among the leaves of trees" (translated from Casier, 1960, page 63).

This illustrates very simply an important aspect of Dollo's scientific work—his interpretation of the life and habits of extinct animals. He was indeed the creator of what he called ethological paleontology— the study of the relationships of ancient animals to their environments. This study has many aspects. So far as the Bernissart iguanodonts are concerned, these included the careful description of the skeleton and its interpretation as a living mechanism, the study of those animals associated with the iguanodonts, the study of the plants as well, the analysis of the sediments in which the skeletons were buried as a key to meteorological and other conditions prevailing at the time the great dinosaurs were alive, the interpretation of the manner in which the skeletons were positioned within their burial ground as some indication of how they may have died and have been entombed, and various other aspects of the large problem. Several of these subjects were studied by Dollo, as the basis for his interpretations of how the Bernissart iguanodonts lived, and the kind of world they lived in. As we have seen, he was especially active in reconstructing the dinosaurs—not only in placing their skeletons in proper poses

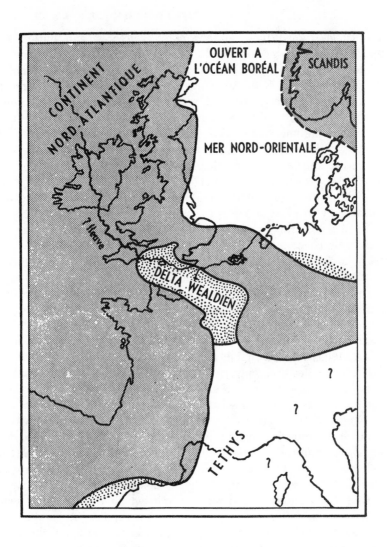

Figure 12. A paleogeographic map, adapted by Casier from Willis, showing the extent of continents (shaded) and oceans (unshaded) in early Cretaceous time, when *Iguanodon* and *Megalosaurus* roamed across an ancient North Atlantic continent. Note the Weald delta, extending from the English Channel coast southeast through northern France and Belgium, with its outlet in the ancient Tethys Sea

and learning how the bones moved in relation to one another but also in reconstructing the muscles that gave power to the skeleton and the integument that protected the muscles. He also described other animals that lived with the iguanodonts, especially the reptiles—crocodiles and turtles, and the frogs of that ancient time. Upon the basis of Dollo's work other students have added knowledge as to the insects and plants, the nature of the sediments, and the circumstances of burial, so that today we can reconstruct the ancient scene in Bernissart in considerable detail.

Briefly the scene may be envisioned about as follows. In early Cretaceous time, somewhat more than 100 million years ago, a portion of northern France, Belgium, and southern England constituted a large delta that opened from a northern continent into the great Tethys Sea, a transverse shallow ocean that stretched across southern Europe and through Asia. It was a delta in a tropical environment, with a lush cover of ferns over the ground, above which rose the forms of numerous pines and other trees. Insects were in the air, crocodiles, turtles, and frogs in the ponds and rivers of the delta. And dominating the landscape were the gigantic iguanodonts, feeding upon the abundant vegetation with which they were surrounded.

But the peaceful, browsing iguanodonts did not have the world all to themselves, because in this land were the giant predators, the megalosaurs, which made their living off of the big plant-eating dinosaurs. Against these active carnivores, powerful of limb and body, and equipped with savage teeth and claws, the iguanodonts could protect themselves in part, but not completely. Perhaps the sharp beak that formed the front of the skull and jaws could be used for biting, but as pitted against the long jaws of the megalosaurs, studded with scimitar-like teeth, it was comparatively ineffectual. Probably the long spike on the thumb was a weapon of sorts, but it had to be used in opposition to the sharp claws of the hands and feet of the megalosaurs. As Dollo showed, the muscles of the tail were of immense power, so that the tail could be used as a great flail, for striking down an adversary. Iguanodonts may have used this method of defense to hold off their attackers. Finally, *Iguanodon* could retreat to the water and swim away, thus escaping trouble rather than trying to fight back. And probably this happened very often.

Such was the life of the iguanodonts of Bernissart. As for their deaths, there have been various theories to account for the remarkable accumulation of skeletons in one burial place. Dollo noted that these were all the skeletons of adult animals—seemingly there were no youngsters in the lot. Moreover, according to Dollo, it would appear that the animals perished suddenly and collectively. "The Iguanodons of Bernissart were perhaps the old individuals that had withdrawn to this place to die, and were covered by floods that probably occurred frequently," said Dollo. The more agile animals, he thought, would have escaped. Here again is an example of Dollo's mind at work. He required facts, in this instance numerous skeletons of adult animals in a deep fissure, but once the facts were in hand he did not hesitate to develop original theories to explain them. This particular theory of Dollo's, put forward to explain the concentration of *Iguanodon* skeletons at Bernissart, need not be accepted, but it must be recognized for its originality.

The work on the fauna of Bernissart was, as much as anything, Dollo's monument. He began his studies at a time when dinosaurs in Europe were known largely from bits and fragments. At the end of his career (he died in 1931), man's acquaintance with the dinosaurs had been extended to include the details of excellent skeletons, numbered in the hundreds—perhaps in the thousands—from all over the world. He indeed witnessed the growth of dinosaurian studies from a modest beginning to a vast body of knowledge. For this we owe much to Louis Dollo, who brought to life the iguanodonts of Bernissart.

MARSH AND COPE

We now cross the Atlantic and go back to the year 1877, the year that marked the first tentative discoveries of *Iguanodon* bones at Bernissart, and the beginning of dinosaurian discoveries on a large scale in North America. Which brings us to those arch rivals mentioned at the beginning of this chapter, Marsh and Cope. These two able, energetic, and self-centered men hunted, dug up, and described dinosaurs on a scale hitherto unprecedented, and in the course of their work became involved in one of the most bitter personal feuds in the history of science. Their contributions to the knowledge of dinosaurs were truly vast; their quarrel was of large dimensions but petty, and unfortunately scientific objectivity and consuming mutual hatreds were so intertwined in the lives of these two men that it is difficult to review their careers and keep the many cross currents of excellent, often brilliant research separate from erosive backbiting and violent rivalry. Cope and Marsh are all too frequently remembered for their monumental feud, a fight that involved many other people, not a few of them quite against their wills. Yet in spite of their epic row, which colors much of the story of vertebrate paleontology in North America during the last three decades of the nineteenth century, they are none the less remembered also for their great contributions to the history of life as based upon fossil evidence. Among these contributions their work on dinosaurs takes a prominent place.[1] The beginning of the story takes us for the moment several decades back of the year 1877.

Othniel Charles Marsh was born in Lockport, New York, in 1831, the son of Caleb Marsh, a rather inept farmer from New England. When Marsh was three years old, his mother died. He consequently lived a mixed and perhaps a confused boyhood, spent partly with his father, partly with a stepmother, partly with uncles and aunts. As a teen-age boy he had collected fossils under the tutelage of an engineer working on the Erie Canal at Lockport, one Colonel Ezekial Jewett. These fossils struck within him an inner spark of sorts, yet all in all he seemed to be a most ordinary young fellow, reaching the age of twenty without a show of much ambition or much direction to his life.

Then for him there was a sudden change. In 1852 he came of age, and received a settlement from the proceeds of his mother's dowry, which had been given her by her brother, his uncle, George Peabody. With this money in hand Marsh entered Phillips Academy, Andover, where he graduated as an ancient of twenty-five among teen-agers. And while he was at Phillips he was extended a generous helping hand by Uncle George, a man of fabulous wealth and high position, who loomed in the background just as in a Victorian romance. The credo of George Peabody was "Education: a debt due from present to future generations," and in keeping with this sentiment he assumed the responsibility for Othniel's further schooling.

How did it happen that such a wealthy and generous patron was associated with the penniless Marsh family? The story of George Peabody, a sort of Horatio Alger epic translated into real life and furnished with numerous embellishments, should be mentioned here. George Peabody was born in 1795 in Danvers, Massachusetts, one of

[1] See: Osborn, 1931; Plate, 1964; Schuchert and Le Vene, 1940.

eight children in a family as destitute as the Marsh household. His father, a cordwainer and farmer, died when George was sixteen years old, leaving a legacy of debts and a mortgaged home. Young George was working for an older brother in a dry-goods shop when his father died, and to add misfortune to tragedy, the shop was shortly thereafter destroyed in a fire. George was on his own.

He worked as an itinerant peddler; he served briefly in the War of 1812; and after that he formed a partnership with one of his military companions, Elisha Riggs, the two of them establishing a business as importers and merchants. Peabody had the golden touch. The firm of Riggs and Peabody prospered and grew with astonishing rapidity, and within a few years became the firm of Peabody, Riggs and Co., with offices in several of the large eastern cities.

During this time George Peabody made several business trips to Europe, one result being that he grew extraordinarily fond of London. In 1837 he established his residence in London, and lived there for the rest of his life, although he always retained his American citizenship. He soon became one of the leading bankers of London and a very influential man in that world capital. In 1845 a Boston merchant, Junius Spencer Morgan, became Peabody's business partner, and this was the beginning of the great house of Morgan.

Peabody, who remained a bachelor, was always very conscious of the struggles of his early childhood and his lack of formal education. So in his middle and later years he turned much of his attention and his resources to the support of good works. He established Peabody institutes for the promotion of learning and culture in seven American cities; he built model homes for poor working people in London; he set up the Peabody Education Fund, for the purpose of reviving education in the defeated southern states after the Civil War (the George Peabody University in Nashville is an outgrowth of this); he contributed to the care of sick and wounded of the Union armies during that war; he endowed several chairs in schools and colleges in the eastern states; and he gave the founding endowments for three museums—the Peabody Museum of Salem, devoted largely to maritime history; the Peabody Museum of Harvard, devoted to anthropology; and the Peabody Museum of Yale, devoted to natural history, this last established, as we shall see, as a result of the persuasive arguments of his nephew, Othniel Marsh.

In his later years Peabody had been honored by many citizens, universities, learned and philanthropical groups and government representatives in both America and Britain. Queen Victoria had a special miniature portrait of herself painted for him. He died in London, in 1869. He was buried with great ceremony in Westminster Abbey, but his remains rested there for only a brief time. The family wished to have the body brought home, so it was placed on board the newest British ship of war, H.M.S. *Monarch,* and with pomp and circumstance was transported to the United States.

In 1856 Marsh wrote a letter to his Uncle George, expressing his gratitude for the help that had been given him at Phillips Academy, and asking permission to enter Yale College. George Peabody, impressed by his nephew, promised support for Marsh's college training.

Six years were spent at Yale, where, because of his maturity (he must have seemed like something of a graybeard to his fellow students), he was variously known as "Daddy" or "Captain." After Yale, Marsh journeyed to Europe to study, thanks again to the kindness of George Peabody. He used his time in Europe, which amounted to several years, to good advantage, studying at the universities in Berlin and Breslau, visiting museums and making excursions into the field. And in England he visited Uncle George for a purpose. Marsh already was showing considerable ability as an organizer; he persuaded Mr. Peabody to give a generous endowment to Yale for a new museum at which he was to be an endowed Professor of Paleontology. Thus Marsh returned to Yale in 1865 as a professor with no teaching duties and no salary, but with a comfortable income available for the rest of his life, supplied by his cooperative and farsighted uncle. He could devote himself completely to fossils, and he did, even to the point of never taking a wife. He consequently became a very self-centered and suspicious man, a hard person to live and work with, who became increasingly difficult as he advanced in age, in position, and in status.

Status meant a great deal to Othniel Charles Marsh, who at middle age had risen very high in the world since those days when he was a farm boy, living by the side of the Erie Canal. At the time of his late mature years he was widely hailed not only for the famous museum at Yale University, for which he was primarily responsible, but also for the immense collections of fossils, dominated by the skeletons of huge dinosaurs, that he had gathered together to fill its halls and storerooms. He was a professor in a great university, and an acknowledged authority on extinct reptiles and mammals, known throughout the world from his 270 scientific publications. He was truly a leader in the scientific community of North America, and a respected man of science in Europe. For ten years he served as the first Vertebrate Paleontologist of the United States Geological Survey. For twelve years he served as president of the National Academy of Sciences, the highest scientific body of the United States. By reason of both of these positions he wielded great authority in scientific affairs within and without government circles. And finally, on a more personal level, he lived the life of a very proper Victorian gentleman, occupying a large and imposing brownstone house of eighteen rooms, which he built for himself in New Haven. Here he entertained many of the great people of his day, from abroad and from many parts of this country. And on his frequent trips to New York he was often seen in various fashionable clubs. Marsh could indeed look back upon his accomplishments with much satisfaction.

Edward Drinker Cope was born in 1840 and grew up at Fairfield, the family home, which is now well within the city limits of Philadelphia. His father, Alfred Cope, was a devout and wealthy Quaker shipowner who had given up his business interests for a life devoted to philanthropic activities. Cope's mother died when he was three years old, just the same age at which the little Marsh boy lost his mother. Here the parallel to Marsh's boyhood ends. Cope grew up in a well-ordered household, where he received much attention from his elders, especially a loving and understanding stepmother who came into his life when he was eleven years old. He was a precocious child, and at an early age took more than a schoolboy's interest in the world of nature, particularly in animals, living and extinct. At the age of six he was making rather sophisticated notes concerning the skeleton of an ichthyosaur that he saw in the Philadelphia Academy of Sciences, including some remarks about the development of the bony sclerotic plates in the eye socket of this ancient seagoing reptile!

His boyhood was spent at the large and gracious home at Fairfield, set in spacious grounds given over to well-tended lawns, shrubbery, and gardens, and at the Westtown School, a Quaker institution that is still flourishing. When he reached the status of a teen-ager, his summers were spent on a farm, where his father hoped he would develop an interest in what were then modern agricultural methods. But Cope was more interested in the snakes and the frogs that shared the farmland with him than in corn and potatoes—so interested, in fact, that he applied himself seriously to the study of these animals, as well as of birds and other forms of life. By the age of eighteen he had published his first scientific paper. Compare his early start as a professional naturalist with the early career of Marsh, who at the age of twenty had hardly found himself and who did not publish his first scientific contribution until he had reached the ripe age of thirty!

Cope, like Marsh, spent several years in Europe as a young man, where he studied at museums and universities, and acquired a prodigious knowledge of backboned animals, recent and fossil. This interlude in Cope's young life took place during the Civil War, and it saved Cope the embarrassment of trying to avoid military service, for, albeit a pugnacious individual, he belonged to a family having strong and sincere beliefs in the principles avowed by the Society of Friends. (It might be added, parenthetically, that Marsh's first trip to Europe was also during a part of the Civil War, but although willing he was unable to serve in the army because of trouble with his eyes.)

Cope returned to the United States in 1864, joined the faculty of Haverford College, a noted Quaker seat of learning, and the next year married his cousin Annie Pim. His sojourn at Haverford was short; in 1867 he moved with his wife and a baby daughter, Julia, to Haddonfield, New Jersey, where it will be remembered the skeleton of *Hadrosaurus* had been excavated in 1858. There he could live the life of a man of independent means, with the facilities of the Academy of Natural Sciences of Philadelphia not far away. This allowed Cope to devote all his attention to his studies, at which he was a master in three fields—modern fishes, modern amphibians and reptiles, and fossil vertebrates of all classes—and this he did with prodigious energy and a touch of true genius. For example, in 1864, the year of his return to America, he published five scientific papers; in 1870 there were thirty-nine, and in 1872 his contributions numbered fifty-six, and so on for the rest of his life. His bibliography includes the incredible total of about 1,400 published works, many of them of great importance.

An independent career was the type of life for which Cope was suited, because although a very friendly man of sunny disposition, he was much too much of an individualist to fit easily within the framework of institutional life. This was to be the pattern of his life for most of his days. In 1875 Alfred Cope died, and Edward Drinker, then aged thirty-five, inherited a considerable fortune. Invested wisely, the money would have allowed Cope to live comfortably for the remainder of his life, with a considerable sum left over to support his scientific activities. But he must try to swell his fortune by investments in mining stock, and in the end he lost virtually everything he had. His final days were spent as a salaried professor at the University of Pennsylvania.

Although Cope in some respects did not cut so large a public figure as did Marsh, his own accomplishments, as judged in the perspective of time, are much greater than those of his adversary. In his last years Cope lived very simply, as compared with the ostentation of Marsh. His final days, spent on a plain cot in a crowded room of his Pine Street house in Philadelphia, a room bulging with books and specimens, are in decided contrast to Marsh's declining years, spent in his eighteen-room mansion. But Cope left a legacy of scientific accomplishment that will long be remembered.

It has already been said that he was the author of some 1,400 papers, books, and monographs, an output of publications that staggers the imagination. Moreover, this was all the work of Cope's own hand—he never had a corps of assistants to do his scientific spadework. And as has also been said, these publications established Cope as a world-renowned authority on the backboned animals. As a posthumous tribute to Cope's genius, the scientific journal of the American Society of Ichthyologists and Herpetologists (in plainer language, the organization of those scientists interested in fishes, amphibians, and reptiles) was named *Copeia*. Thus Cope stands on an eminence of his own making as a sort of patron saint for those men who study the "lower" vertebrates; moreover, he is certainly regarded by vertebrate paleontologists as one of the founders of their science in North America. Much of this recognition of Cope as a great genius in the annals of American science came after his death. So to the Quaker naturalist, looking back over a lifetime, and not a very long one at that, of great accomplishments and of soul-searing disappointments, the world must have seemed to have given grudging recognition to all that he had done.

In 1895, two years before his death, however, he was accorded a signal honor by being elected president of the American Association for the Advancement of Science. It was recognition greatly deserved, accorded by the scientists of North America to a great man.

In 1868, shortly after Cope had moved to Haddonfield, Marsh came there to visit him, and the two men spent a friendly week together in the field, poking around in the Cretaceous marls of New Jersey. But by the following year they were at swords' points, and their enmity and hatred built up, year after year, for the rest of their lives. What had caused it all? Many things, for the most part of little consequence. Both men were individuals of independent means, and being free from the necessity of making those daily adjustments that are the lot of most men they both lacked a certain amount of perspective in the field of human affairs. They were both possessive and ambitious to an unusual degree; each man wanted what he wanted, and when he wanted it. Neither was overly scrupulous when the other man stood in his way. It all added up to inevitable trouble between them.

COMO BLUFF

With this diversion for the purpose of outlining some of the background of Marsh and Cope, we now return to the year 1877. By one of those coincidences that seem to have occurred at intervals in the lives of the two rivals, two schoolmasters in the spring of that year found gigantic bones in Colorado, and sent word of their discoveries to the two now bitterly antagonistic paleontologists. There were complications.

One of these schoolmasters was Arthur Lakes, a graduate of Oxford University who had gravitated to the West when it was truly wild and woolly. Lakes had discovered some huge bones in a hogback ridge forming a line of foothills bordering the Front Range of the Rocky Mountains, near Morrison, Colorado. He informed Marsh, and shipped some of the bones to him. He also sent some of the fossils to Cope for examination. Here indeed was a situation that could lead to paleontological fireworks.

Marsh, not knowing that bones had been sent to Cope, forwarded one hundred dollars to Mr. Lakes, and asked him to keep the discovery a secret. It was too late. Cope already had received the bones and was describing them for publication by the American Philosophical Society. But before Cope's article had gone to press, he received a letter from Lakes asking that the bones be sent on to Marsh. This must have seemed to Cope like a devilish combination of insult and injury, and one can only imagine the towering rage that he must have felt, but there was nothing he could do. Marsh had in the meantime concluded some very firm arrangements with Mr. Lakes, especially through the intermediary efforts of Professor Benjamin Mudge of the Agricultural College of Kansas, whom Marsh retained as one of his field collectors.

The triumph of Marsh over Cope was short-lived. The other schoolmaster, Mr. O. W. Lucas, had found gigantic bones at Garden Park near Canyon City, Colorado, in the Morrison formation, the same geologic horizon in which Lakes was collecting his specimens at Morrison (the locality for which the formation was named), and had sent these to Cope. Thus began a long and fierce struggle between the two rivals to accumulate the bones of North American dinosaurs. It was a private war, carried on with all the resources at the command of the two adversaries, often with comic-opera overtones.

Time has added a certain amount of color to all aspects of the Cope-Marsh feud, including their rivalry in the search for and the description of dinosaurs, but even without the growth of the story through the years to sometimes larger than life dimensions the bare facts are incredible enough. The tale has many aspects, some of interest, others of the routine type that accumulate during the progress of all long-range projects, and a full presentation of them would lead the reader through such a maze of details that he probably would find himself more than a little confused, perhaps even bored. So let us be reasonably brief.

The discoveries near Canyon City by Mr. Lucas pleased Cope beyond measure, but they made Marsh very unhappy, indeed. The trouble was one of size and preservation. The bones from the Garden Park locality were, it seemed, frequently considerably larger than those from the Morrison hogback, and the materials were more complete than the specimens that were being excavated by Mr. Lakes. It seemed to Marsh as if Cope might win the race for bigger and better dinosaurs.

But the turn of fortune, which had favored Cope, now swung back toward Marsh. One day during that summer a rather mysterious letter came to Marsh. It came from two gentlemen in Wyoming, "Harlow and Edwards," who informed Marsh of gigantic bones that they had found. They wished to sell these fossils to him, he being, in their words, "well known as an enthusiastic geologist, and a man of means."

Marsh asked Harlow and Edwards to ship the bones to New Haven, and in return promptly sent a check for seventy-five dollars to them, only to be informed that they could not cash it. He also sent his assistant and collector, Samuel Wendell Williston (subsequently to become one of the great paleontologists of his day) to investigate the discovery. Williston soon cleared up the mystery of why Harlow and Edwards could not cash the check; with a passion for secrecy that must have afforded Marsh a great deal of satisfaction (for he was a most secretive man so far as fossils were concerned) they had not used their right names. They were in truth Mr. W. E. Carlin and Mr. W. (Bill) H. Reed, who labored for the Union Pacific Railroad, and they had found their fossils at Como Bluff, a long east-to-west ridge in southern Wyoming, paralleled in this region by the steel rails. Williston was tremendously impressed by the find. He wrote to Marsh that the bones "extend for *seven* miles and are by the ton. . . . The bones are very thick, well preserved, and easy to get out." And in a following letter he wrote that "Canon City and Morrison are simply nowhere in comparison with this locality both as regards perfection, accessibility and quantity" (Plate, 1964, page 190; Ostrom and McIntosh, 1966, page 9).

Williston's first letter to Marsh, written shortly after he had arrived at Como, was dated November 14, 1877. He was so excited by what he saw along the bluff, and by the possibilities for future work there that in addition to writing he also wired Marsh, urging him to draw up an agreement with Reed and Carlin as soon as possible. In the meantime Williston was all pins and needles—he lived in daily apprehension that the news of the great deposits of bones along Como Bluff, presently known only to himself, Reed and Carlin, and a few others, would leak out and that this would bring some of Cope's men on the run to the locality. Evidently he communicated to Marsh a real sense of his own feelings of urgency, because on November 17th, only three days after that first letter from Williston, Marsh drew up in his own hand an agreement for Reed and Carlin to sign. According to this agreement, the two men were to work exclusively for Marsh for at least a year, and to do their best to keep all other collectors out of the region. Just how they were to accomplish this latter on land they did not own was not stipulated—but such was the charge given them by Marsh. For this they were to receive each ninety dollars a month. Marsh furthermore stipulated that it would be his right to keep one or more "superintendents" at Como Bluff to oversee the work being done by Reed and Carlin. Though the two ex-railroad men did not care for this last provision, they accepted the agreement. As time was to prove, the appointment by Marsh of superintendents over Reed and his associates was to cause a great deal of trouble. The bone diggers in the course of their work resented the presence of Williston in their midst, and subsequently, as we shall see, Bill Reed objected most forcefully to the activities of Arthur Lakes, who, on orders from Marsh, eventually transferred his operations from Morrison to Como Bluff.

Reed and Carlin had collected a truly incredible amount of huge bones during that summer of 1877 before they became bound to Marsh, and they continued to work and collect great masses of bones afterward—through the bleak months of winter. Williston, who stayed with them for a time, wrote to Marsh on November 30th, in reference to one choice specimen, "The small saurian I have not yet sent and cannot for a few days till the snow blows off so that *we can find it*" (Ostrom and McIntosh, 1966, page 12).

As an example of the difficulties of work in those winters, Arthur Lakes reported several years later, in 1880:

"Collecting at this season is under many difficulties. At the bottom of a narrow pit 30 feet deep into which drift snow keeps blowing and fingers benumbed with cold from thermo between 20 and 30 below zero and snow often blowing blindingly down and covering up a bone as fast as it is unearthed" (Ostrom and McIntosh, 1966, page 32).

Williston soon had to leave Como Bluff because of ill health, but Reed continued to dig, with the help of a paid assistant (Carlin having made a trip east for various reasons). Thus we find Reed writing in his inimitable style to Williston in March of 1878:

"I had the worse time finding a good quary that a man ever had but now I wish you wer here to see the bones roll out and they are

Figure 13. The skeleton of *Stegosaurus*, one of the Jurassic plated dinosaurs from Como Bluff, as restored by Marsh. This drawing, like Marsh's other reconstructions of dinosaur skeletons from western North America, is remarkably accurate, and demonstrates the fullness of knowledge that was attained by the discovery of complete skeletons

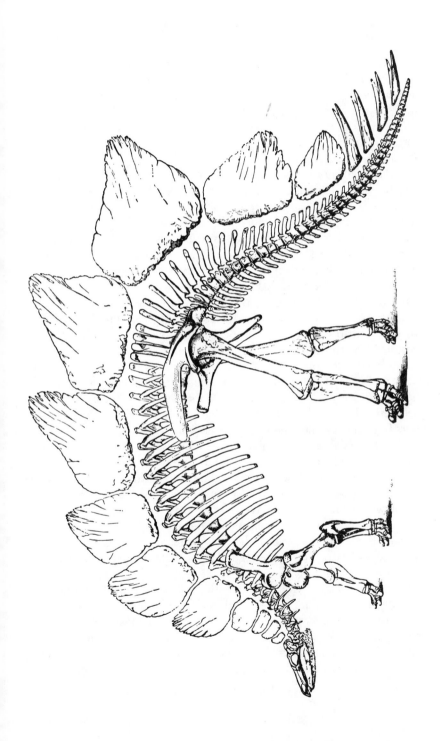

beauties to I think this quary eaqual no. 1 for good bones and quanity it outcrops for X80 feet length there is more than one animal it would astonish you to see the holes we have dug since we left no. 3. I think I took up ten tons of bones" (Ostrom and McIntosh, 1966, page 14).

The work at Como Bluff went on, year after year, summer and winter. This massive and continuous effort makes a fascinating story, the details of which could be continued through many pages of text. Fortunately, the story has recently been told in detail and with authority, and need not be repeated here. (See Ostrom and McIntosh, *Marsh's Dinosaurs: The Collections from Como Bluff.*) Suffice it to say that a little band of Marsh collectors labored through the seasons in the Como Bluff quarries, digging out ever-increasing masses of dinosaur bones to ship back to New Haven. The composition of the bone-digging parties kept changing from year to year. Men came and went, but always Bill Reed, who had given up the joys of the railroad to work for Marsh, remained as the key figure in this long and complicated project. He had been a professional big-game hunter, employed by the railroad to furnish fresh meat for the workmen, so he was accustomed to an outdoor life. Moreover, he was a practical type who could handle the problems of a large-scale excavation and the attendant problems of living in camp in a no-nonsense way. On the whole he managed his assistants well, except for Mr. Lakes. Lakes was hired separately by Marsh, and therefore he was not strictly subject to orders from Reed. Marsh had sent Lakes from Morrison to Como in order that his skill and knowledge might be used in the great excavations that Reed was conducting, but Reed did not always appreciate Lakes' efforts. Lakes liked to sketch the fossils as they were being dug out of the ground, and he liked to make field notes and descriptions, all of which subsequently have proved to be very valuable. But Bill Reed thought that Mr. Lakes should be wielding a pick and shovel during those intervals when he was instead wielding a pen or a watercolor brush. On his side, Lakes considered Reed as a rather uncouth character.

Between 1877 and 1883 Reed with various assistants worked continually at the Como quarries, while Lakes, who had been ordered by Marsh to work separately, after that first year of bickering and quarreling with Reed, spent the winter of 1879–1880 elsewhere in the Como diggings. Through the years there was quite a roster of men who dug for Marsh at Como, and thanks to this team of trained exca-

Plate 34. The *Plateosaurus* Quarry at Trossingen, in southern Germany. This picture gives some idea of the size of the quarry

Plate 35. Excavating the *Plateosaurus* Quarry

Plate 37. Plateosaurus, as restored by G. Biese and showing von Huene's concept of the environment in which this dinosaur may have lived and died

ABOVE LEFT. *Plate 38*. Richard Swann Lull in 1902, out to explore western fossil fields. ABOVE RIGHT. *Plate 39*. Lull, fifty years later, in his office at Yale University

Plate 40. Some of the Triassic dinosaur tracks from the Connecticut Valley, to which Lull gave so much attention

Plate 41. Henry Fairfield Osborn, with rifle; William Berryman Scott, with pistol; and Francis Speir in the center—three young men who explored the Bridger Basin of Wyoming in 1877

Plate 42. Osborn with Barnum Brown (left) excavating a skeleton of the dinosaur *Diplodocus*, in 1897, at Como Bluff, Wyoming

Plate 43. Four dinosaur hunters in 1895. Left to right: O. A. Peterson, for many years with the Carnegie Museum of Pittsburgh; Jacob Wortman, Walter Granger, and Albert Thomson, all of The American Museum of Natural History

Plate 44. The Bone Cabin site when it was first discovered. The ground here is covered with large fragments of dinosaur bones

Plate 45. The Bone Cabin Quarry in an early stage of its development. In the foreground are excavated dinosaur bones in their plaster bandages. The rude cabin in the rear was built to serve as a semipermanent base during the years that the Bone Cabin Quarry was being worked

Plate 46. Paleontologists from The American Museum of Natural History applying plaster bandages to gigantic dinosaur vertebrae at the Nine Mile Quarry, Como Bluff, Wyoming. Left to right: Richard Swann Lull, who spent most of his professional life at Yale University; Peter Kaisen, who for many years worked in the field with Barnum Brown; William Diller Matthew, who did some work on dinosaurs but who was especially noted as an authority on fossil mammals

Plate 47. Hauling dinosaur bones from Bone Cabin to the railroad, in the days when horsepower was supreme

ABOVE. *Plate 48*. Earl Douglass of the Carnegie Museum, at work in 1909 at the great dinosaur quarry that later was to become Dinosaur National Monument. Here he is seen standing in front of the partially exposed skeleton of *Diplodocus*—one of the great discoveries in the history of dinosaur hunting. He has reason to smile. BELOW. *Plate 49*. The first bones discovered at the Carnegie Museum dinosaur quarry being viewed by Elder "Dad" Goodrich, who assisted Douglass in 1909

Plate 50. The house that Douglass built—facing the Green River, with its back to the hills in which was located the Carnegie Museum dinosaur quarry

Plate 51. Public transportation in Utah, as photographed by Earl Douglass circa 1910. Off for a trip from Vernal

Plate 52. Making the first cut at the Carnegie Museum Quarry. The stratum bearing dinosaur bones is on the left side of the cut

Plate 53. Digging for dinosaurs—winter. Carnegie Quarry

Plate 54. Digging for dinosaurs—summer. Carnegie Quarry, showing exposure of the dinosaur-bearing stratum on the right side of the cut

Plate 55. The Carnegie Quarry. The men are preparing to haul out a bandaged and boxed bone by means of a sled or stoneboat. Note the packaged bones ready to be removed from the quarry. Note also the dinosaur-bearing cliff in the background, with painted guidelines to help in mapping the positions of the bones as they were exposed

Plate 56. Charles W. Gilmore, of the United States National Museum, a noted authority on dinosaurs, who described many of the fossils from the Carnegie Quarry

Plate 57. Renewed work at the Carnegie Quarry, after it became Dinosaur National Monument. This picture nicely illustrates the upended strata of the Morrison Formation at this locality. The dinosaur-bearing stratum is on the right side of the cut

Plate 58. First steps in exposing skeletons at the Dinosaur National Monument. At the right is a temporary building. Today a permanent building encloses the cliff; and numerous bones and parts of skeletons, in addition to those shown in this picture, are exposed in place

Plate 59. The Howe dinosaur quarry, excavated by Barnum Brown and his party from The American Museum of Natural History. The almost level quarry floor is seen in the center of the picture, to the right of the museum camp. The derrick lifts a photographer high above the quarry, to make pictures of the bone deposit as it is exposed

Plate 60. A picture of the Howe Quarry, giving some idea of the abundance of dinosaur bones in this deposit. Barnum Brown and Mrs. Brown are at the top of the picture; to their right is the shadow of the photographer in his aerial tub. R. T. Bird, who made the chart of the quarry (Figure 28), is seen at the bottom

Plate 61. The beginning of the end at Howe Quarry. Many of the bones have been excavated, bandaged, and boxed. In the background is the Howe ranch house

vators the work was continued unabated, and bones went back to New Haven by the ton.

Of course, the spectacular discoveries made by the Marsh parties at Como Bluff attracted Cope, and his collectors visited this region in 1879 and 1880. Legend has it that there were some impromptu battles waged with fists and rocks when the Cope men appeared in what the Marsh men considered as their own sacred precincts of Como Bluff. But perhaps the legend expresses the inner feelings among the antagonists rather than actual events. It would seem probable that there was a certain amount of glaring back and forth and quite a bit of dissembling when Cope men and Marsh men encountered one another, and that was about the extent of the warfare. Cope and Marsh might hate each other most violently, but there were no compelling reasons why their several assistants should wield cudgels on behalf of their employers.

Some of the encounters with the Cope parties were reported by Reed to Marsh. For example:

"the Cope party was up to 13 [a quarry number] yesterday. they did not come to the quarey but was all around it the went to those big Bones west of the quarey and I started out to see them and they left. . . . I find their tracks all around no. 9 [the famous Quarry 9, from which numerous bones of tiny Mesozoic mammals, contemporaries of the dinosaurs, were collected by the Marsh parties and sent to New Haven] but they have not done any work there" (Ostrom and McIntosh, 1966, page 38).

Certainly the incursions of the Cope collectors were a constant worry to Bill Reed. In one letter he proposed an obvious way in which to control their invasions—a solution that seemingly was never put into effect.

"the C. Party came over there [to quarries 9, 10, and 11] twice to the ridge in front of the quaries and took a look at us and went Back. . . . there is one way in which to keep them away from our quaries and that is to preempt or take the land under the desert act by this act we can pay 25 cents per acre and hold the land three years and then by paying one dolar per acre more get a deed but three years is ample time the least amount we can take is 160 acres if we do this myself and Ashley can take 160 each one at 13 and the other at 9, 10, 11 and that will take the best of the ground" (Ostrom and McIntosh, 1966, pages 37–38).

Cope himself made a visit to Como Bluff in 1879, and at least one member of the Marsh group, Arthur Lakes, indicated in his journal that he was agreeably surprised by Cope's charming manner.

"The monstrum horrendum Cope has been and gone and I must say that what I saw of him I liked very much his manner is so affable and his conversation very agreeable. I only wish I could feel sure he had a sound reputation for honesty" (Ostrom and McIntosh, 1966, page 29).

There were invasions in the other direction too, for the exposures at Garden Park, near Canyon City were a magnet that attracted dinosaur hunters. In 1877, soon after Lucas had made his discoveries near Canyon City, Marsh telegraphed Benjamin Mudge, his trusted field man, to go there and appraise the situation. This Mudge did, and reported back to Marsh that Lucas was obtaining bones in large amounts and of great size, and shipping them to Cope.

Mudge went to work at Garden Park, and soon asked for skilled assistance. So Marsh instructed Williston, who was a superb anatomist, to go to Mudge's rescue. Williston arrived—but was not satisfied with the results of the digging there. He wrote to Marsh: "I am very sorry to find that Cope is getting by far the best lot of fossils. . . . Prof. Mudge thinks we had better work out these than use time in the risk of not finding better. But I *am* going to find better" (Schuchert and LeVene, 1940, page 195).

Alas for Williston's hopes, he never had the chance to search for better fossils in the Canyon City region. After he had been there a few weeks, Marsh decided to abandon the dig, and he ordered Williston to work with Arthur Lakes at Morrison. But not long after Williston had joined forces with Lakes there was a huge rock fall in the Morrison quarry which only by chance did not eliminate the entire party of bone diggers. No one was hurt, but work at the quarry was stopped for the season. Some years later Marsh decided to make a second attempt at Canyon City, and a party under the supervision of still another Marsh stalwart, M. P. Felch, worked the old Garden Park quarries with truly spectacular results.

To return to Como Bluff, which was Marsh's great hunting ground, after six years of constant work in the string of quarries that stretched for miles along the Bluff, Bill Reed resigned in 1883, to go into the business of raising sheep. He turned the direction of the quarries over to E. Kennedy, who had been working with him for several years and

Kennedy, who was an able and accomplished bone digger, proceeded vigorously to continue with the excavation of Como Bluff dinosaurs. All went well for a time, until the appearance on the scene of Fred Brown, another Marsh bone digger, who had previously worked for Marsh at Como Bluff and more recently at the Garden Park locality near Canyon City, and whom Marsh had rehired in 1884 to take charge at Como. Brown was not inclined to submit to Kennedy, and Kennedy was not giving up anything to Brown. And so for a year these two men worked independently—Kennedy, bitterly resentful of Brown's superior authority, at Quarry 9, and Brown in Quarry 13. Meetings between the two men often produced sparks but nothing of a serious nature, except on one occasion, when Brown threatened Kennedy with a brace of revolvers.

From this time on, Kennedy became less and less enthusiastic about the work at Como, and finally he resigned, leaving the entire Como Bluff project in Brown's hands. Brown continued for several years more, to a large extent running a sort of caretaker operation, and finally, in 1889, he left Como. This marked the end of the Marsh diggings along Como Bluff.

COPE IN MONTANA

Although the search for Morrison dinosaurs filled the minds, used the energies, and strained the finances of Marsh and of Cope during those years of the late seventies and the eighties, these two incredible men nevertheless turned their attentions to still other dinosaurs. They had described a world of ancient giants—*Allosaurus, Ceratosaurus, Brontosaurus, Camarasaurus, Amphicoelias, Diplodocus, Camptosaurus, Stegosaurus,* and others that lived in western North America during late Jurassic time. But there were still the Cretaceous dinosaur-bearing beds to be explored, countless miles of rock exposures within which were dinosaurian treasures to be sought out, dug up, studied, and described. With such unknown and untold fossiliferous riches waiting to be exposed to the light of day and the eye of man, neither Cope nor Marsh could entertain thoughts of rival forces being the first to explore new fossil fields and to reap paleontological rewards. Consequently their collectors ranged far and wide in the Cretaceous rocks of the western states and territories.

Cope had been introduced to the Cretaceous dinosaur beds of Mon-

tana in 1876, the year before the big discoveries of Morrison dinosaurs in Colorado and Wyoming. In that year he had gone west to
join Charles H. Sternberg, one of the greatest of the dinosaur hunters
(of whom much more later) in order to explore the Judith River
formation (a name based upon the locality where the formation was
first studied) that is exposed along the upper reaches of the great
Missouri River. Cope met Sternberg and a companion, Mr. Isaac, in
Omaha, and from there they traveled by train and later by stagecoach
to Helena, Montana. Arriving in Helena they found the small frontier
city in a state of high excitement; Chief Sitting Bull and his warriors
had just wiped out General Custer and his command at the battle of
the Little Big Horn. Would it not be dangerous for Cope and his
companions to venture into the field, where Indians, drunk with their
victory, were roaming the plains and uplands? No, said Cope. All the
Sioux warriors were with their chief, to the southeast, and the Judith
River badlands, along the Missouri River, would be empty of Indians
until late in the season, when the Sioux would retreat north before
pressure from United States troops under General Terry. Cope's prediction was correct; he and his little band, Sternberg and Isaac, a
scout and a cook, ventured forth with horses and a wagon, and were
not molested.

They did meet occasional Indians, but such meetings were of the
peaceful sort. On one occasion Cope entertained his redskin guests by
taking out his false teeth, and then popping them back into his
mouth. The Indians were fascinated—they insisted on Cope repeating
the performance time and again, always to their amazement and
mystification.

The work in the Judith River beds was exhausting. The days were
hot and the nights were cold. The topography of this region is rugged,
and the men were worn out by the end of each day with hard
climbing—always in search of dinosaurs. Then at night there were
other hardships. Sternberg recalled them many years later.

"Every night when we returned to camp, we found that the cook
had spent the whole day in cooking. Exhausted and thirsty (all the
water in the Bad Lands being like a dense solution of Epsom salts),
—we sat down to a supper of cakes and pies and other palatable, but
indigestible food. Then, when we went to bed, the Professor would
soon have a severe attack of nightmare. Every animal of which we

had found traces during the day played with him at night, tossing him into the air, kicking him, trampling upon him.

"When I waked him, he would thank me cordially and lie down to another attack. Sometimes he would lose half the night in this exhausting slumber. But the next morning he would lead the party, and be the last to give up at night" (Sternberg, 1909, page 75).

It was on this trip that Cope found the horned dinosaur *Monoclonius,* one of the first of these interesting reptiles to be unearthed and described. He also found the remains of duck-billed dinosaurs.

And it was on this trip that Cope and Sternberg devised an improved method for collecting fossil bones. Hitherto it had been the practice to dig fossils out of the ground in a rather primitive fashion. The rocks containing the bones, and frequently the bones themselves, were usually hacked out with picks and hammers and chisels, very much as had been done by Mr. Bensted, who, it may be remembered, excavated the Maidstone *Iguanodon* in 1834. No matter how carefully this technique of collecting was practiced, there was inevitably a great deal of damage to the brittle fossils. It occurred to Cope and Sternberg that if the bones could somehow be encased, even before they were completely freed from their rock matrix, a great deal of protection between field and laboratory would be afforded to the fossils. So with the materials at hand they improvised. They boiled rice into a thick paste, dipped cloth strips cut from flour bags and burlap bags into the paste, and wrapped the impregnated strips around the fossils. In each instance, when the paste hardened the resulting stiff jacket protected the fossil, particularly against the effect of jarring and torsion. Thus specimens could be shipped back to Philadelphia in much better shape than heretofore had been possible.

It was Marsh and his associates, however, who developed a method for protecting fossil bones that has been almost universally employed from his day to the present time. In 1877 Samuel Wendell Williston, who incidentally had been educated as a medical doctor, was writing to Marsh from the quarry at Canyon City, Colorado, suggesting that the fossils then being collected might be protected by wrapping them with strips of strong paper dipped in flour paste. The method was tried and found to be reasonably successful. During this same year, Arthur Lakes, who was working with the party at Morrison, Colorado, wrote to Marsh:

"The rock is so intensely hard, so destitute of good cleavage and seamed in every direction that it is next to impossible to prevent fractures and not infrequently the seam breaking right across the bone has a tendency to break it up into minute fragments. To obviate this I have occasionally laid on a strong coat of plaster of paris on the outside of the bone to preserve it whilst the rest of the rock was being jarred by the hammer" (Schuchert and LeVene, 1940, page 175).

These first efforts pointed the way. Why not adopt the method that had been developed by medical doctors for setting a broken limb? Enclose a bone, or even a large slab of rock containing a bone or several bones, in a strong jacket formed by dipping porous cloth, such as burlap, in plaster of Paris. The method was adopted and by 1880 was standard practice among the collectors working for Marsh. It has survived to the present time with little change, and by the use of this technique the most brittle and fragile fossils can be collected and transported safely from field to laboratory.

To get back to the Judith River Cretaceous beds, by the end of the summer the collections were completed, and it was time for Cope and his helpers to get the fossils, as well as themselves, out to civilization. It was Cope's intention to proceed with his little party and their horses and wagon, out of the badlands to the banks of the Missouri, there to await a river streamer that would take them downstream. But just before Cope made this move his scout deserted—and took the cook along with him. It seems that on the day of the desertion the scout, on his foray ahead of the party, had spied Sitting Bull's camp, inhabited by thousands of warriors, not far away along the Missouri River. So he and the cook gathered up their blankets and departed, leaving Cope and his two assistants the task of getting the horses and wagon down the steep slopes to the river, at a place where they would be out of range of the victorious and truculent Sioux. They managed it, but it was a hair-raising task.

Once on the shores of the river, it was necessary for Cope and his helpers to get the horses and wagon and their collection to the steamboat landing, and quickly too, because the boat they were meeting was the last one of the season to make the trip down the river. They caught the boat, but in order to do so it was necessary for Cope to purchase an old scow, on which they loaded their effects. They then hitched a long rope to one of their horses on the riverbank, and with much difficulty towed the scow along the river to the boat landing. Sternberg has left an account of their arrival at the boat:

"When about sundown we hove-to under the big steamer, the deck was crowded with passengers watching our approach. Cope was covered with mud from head to foot, and his clothing, with hardly a seam whole, hung from him in wet, dirty rags. He had forgotten to bring along any winter wearing apparel, so, although the nights were quite cold, and the women were clad in fur coats and the men in ulsters, he emerged from the sergeant's tent, whither he had carried his grip, in a summer suit and linen duster" (Sternberg, 1909, page 94).

Those final few days in the Judith River beds had indeed been filled with exciting adventures, but at last Cope was on board with his precious collection.

The year after Cope's explorations in the Cretaceous Judith River beds there came the Morrison strikes, and for a time Cope's attentions were diverted to older and richer fossil fields. But eventually he came back to the Cretaceous, and as late as 1892 and 1893, only a few years before his death, he was searching for duck-billed dinosaurs in the lands of the Sioux Nation. The Indians were quite aware of fossils on their land, and they feared these strange objects. Huge serpents had burrowed in the earth, they said, and had been hunted by the Great Spirit, who had killed them with bolts of lightning, leaving their unholy bones in the ground—objects to be avoided by mere human beings. But Cope went into the forbidden territory to discover and collect an extraordinarily fine skeleton of the Cretaceous duck-billed dinosaur *Trachodon,* as well as a complete skeleton of a horned dinosaur. The opportunities that rose before him for continuing his acquisitions and studies of dinosaurs were indeed bright. In these years he was still a man in his early fifties, exploring with vigor and enthusiasm a virgin fossil field. But fortune, or rather the lack of a fortune, was against the Quaker paleontologist. As has been remarked, Cope during these years had decided to swell the very considerable inheritance from his father by investments in western mines. He invested heavily, and lost heavily, so that just as the chances for making exciting and important discoveries of Cretaceous dinosaurs were within his grasp, he found himself in effect a poor man, and with no institutional funds available for his use. He was literally at the end of his financial rope. And so he necessarily and sadly abandoned what might have been a brilliant program of work on those dinosaurs that had lived at the very end of the Age of Dinosaurs. For him the romantic days of fossil hunting in the wide expanses of western plains, badlands, and mountains had ended. The four years of life that were left to him were spent largely in his crowded study, in a house on Pine Street, Philadelphia, which he had long ago rented to serve as his private museum and laboratory.

MARSH'S CRETACEOUS DINOSAURS

Marsh's introduction to the Cretaceous dinosaurs of western North America had taken place some years before Cope's Judith River expedition of 1876. It should be said that at a comparatively early stage in his scientific career, in 1870, when he was still on reasonably good terms with Cope, Marsh had described a duck-billed dinosaur, *Hadrosaurus minor*, on the basis of scattered bones collected in the Cretaceous coastal plain sediments of New Jersey. Then, in the following year, the skeleton of a small duck-billed dinosaur was collected by a Yale field expedition in the Niobrara chalk beds of Kansas. This specimen was described by Marsh in 1872 under the name of *Claosaurus agilis*.

But the major part of Marsh's work on Cretaceous dinosaurs was in the late eighties and the early nineties, and his contributions were considerable. The activities of his collectors, especially of John Bell Hatcher, who, like Williston, began his career as a Marsh assistant, and then went on to become an outstanding paleontologist in his own right, were concentrated especially in the Upper Cretaceous Lance formation, as it is exposed in the high plains, just to the east of the Rocky Mountain Front Range. Here, in the Denver beds, as they were then called, were the bones that enabled Marsh to open a new chapter of dinosaurian history. Some of the best-known of the Cretaceous dinosaurs were introduced to us by Marsh—the armored dinosaur *Nodosaurus*, the graceful ostrich dinosaur *Ornithomimus*, and various

---

Figure 14. The skeleton of *Triceratops*, a late Cretaceous horned dinosaur from western North America, as restored by Marsh

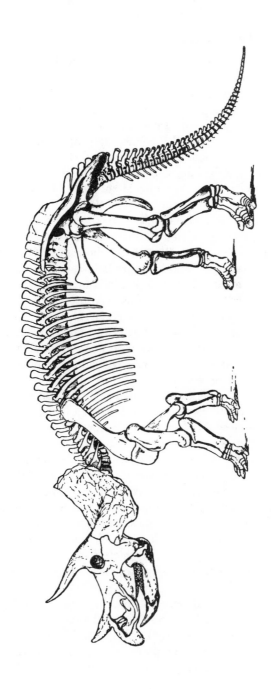

horned dinosaurs, among which *Triceratops* is particularly well known. There is an interesting tale about the discovery and the first description of *Triceratops*.

In 1887 a pair of large fossil horn cores had been sent to Marsh by Whitman Cross, a government geologist who was studying the age of the Denver beds. Marsh had immediately concluded, against the advice of some of his laboratory assistants, that the fossil horns represented an extinct buffalo, and had described them in December, 1888, as *Bison alticornis*. He said that they *must* be of very late geologic age, although Cross was convinced that they had been found in place in Cretaceous sediments.

In this same year, John Bell Hatcher, on his way back east from a collecting trip to the Judith River beds, those same Cretaceous rocks that Cope had explored a dozen years before, saw a large horn core that was part of a gigantic skull embedded in a sandstone concretion, found in a deep canyon in Cretaceous exposures north of Lusk, Wyoming. He wrote to Marsh about this discovery, which served to confirm some suspicions that were already in Marsh's mind with regard to "*Bison*" *alticornis*. The new horn core was sent to New Haven, and lo and behold! it corresponded with the supposed bison horn cores. Marsh immediately retreated from his first opinion; he was now convinced that a new and gigantic horned dinosaur had been found. He sent Hatcher back to Wyoming at the greatest possible speed, and that veteran and accomplished collector soon had in hand the gigantic skull, weighing a ton or more. It went to New Haven to become the first known skull of the now well-known horned dinosaur, *Triceratops*.

Incidentally, this adventure was the beginning of Hatcher's subcareer, if so it may be called, as a collector of horned dinosaurs. During the field seasons of 1889 to 1892, he sent to New Haven the skulls and skeletons of fifty horned dinosaurs. More than thirty of these were skulls, the largest of which weighed three and a half tons. The horned dinosaurs were among the greatest of Marsh's triumphs, and greatly enhanced his reputation as a paleontologist and as a student of the dinosaurs.

The story of Marsh and Cope and the dinosaurs might be continued to great lengths, but perhaps this short and selected account will give some impression of their efforts to obtain and describe these extinct reptiles. Both men spent large parts of their professional lives in the search for dinosaurs—Marsh to a greater degree than Cope. Cope's interests were much broader than were those of Marsh, and dinosaurs were only a part of a wide spectrum of natural-history studies to which this remarkable man devoted the attention of his fertile mind. Marsh's interests were more narrowly limited to fossil reptiles and mammals, and dinosaurs loomed very large in this field. Moreover, Marsh had at his command resources of money and men that were beyond the reach of Cope.

As pointed out above, Cope was an independent worker without institutional connections until his very last years, when he became associated with the University of Pennsylvania. Moreover, he was rather inept in his management of affairs and money. Marsh, in contrast, was a most astute organizer and manager, perhaps what we would today call a "wheeler-dealer," so that he had available the resources of the Peabody Museum at Yale and the United States Geological Survey. Furthermore, Marsh eventually was elected to the presidency of the National Academy of Sciences, much to Cope's disgust, which afforded him a high standing and wide influence in scientific circles.

These differences in connections and resources determined the results of their work on dinosaurs. Cope had the brilliance of mind, but Marsh had the knack of management. Thus to the less able of the two men were given the means for carrying out programs of fieldwork, laboratory preparation, and study of dinosaurs, which by the nature of the materials are laborious and very expensive. In the end Cope had to give up his extensive explorations for dinosaurs because of the cost, while Marsh was able to continue under a full head of Victorian steam, with Yale University and the federal government supplying the power.

Their rivalry, so costly and unnecessary in some ways, perhaps had the effect of spurring Cope and Marsh to efforts greater than either would have attempted had the other man not been in the background. Certainly because of their unprecedented labors in a virgin land they were able to open tremendous vistas of dinosaurian life, views into the past that were heretofore unimagined. Much of what we now know about dinosaurs is the result of the rivalry between Marsh and Cope, resulting in two late-nineteenth-century decades of intensive work in the fossil fields of the West. Of particular value were their collections of *complete* specimens, of whole skeletons instead of bits and pieces.

Before the work of Dollo on the dinosaurs of Bernissart and the work of Marsh and Cope on the dinosaurs of western North America, these great reptiles were at best imperfectly seen. After Dollo and Marsh and Cope the dinosaurs were well documented; described from complete fossil skeletons that gave a picture of the giants of yesteryear, in which the elements of conjecture were reduced to the minimum extent. The labors of these men marked a turning point in the history of research on dinosaurs; their contributions can never be overshadowed.

CHAPTER 4

THE TWO EVOLUTIONARY STREAMS

THE INCREASE OF DINOSAURS

As the nineteenth century drew to a close, man's knowledge of dinosaurs was overwhelmingly advanced beyond what it had been at the midpoint of the century. This was owing, in a large degree, to the remarkable concentration of *Iguanodon* skeletons unearthed at Bernissart, to the even more remarkable quarries developed at Como Bluff, Morrison, and Garden Park, to the explorations in various Cretaceous deposits of western North America, and especially to studies on the dinosaurs from these localities by Dollo, Marsh, and Cope. These three great paleontologists had abundant fossils of dinosaurs available, so that for the first time the bones of the ruling reptiles of the Mesozoic could be studied as integrated parts of once-living animals rather than as bits and pieces of unknown and mystifying beasts. Such overwhelming quantities of fossils were destined to affect greatly the previous concepts as to the nature of the dinosaurs, particularly when these fossils came under the scrutiny of men of great ability. Dollo, Marsh, and Cope were almost literally buried by the tons of dinosaur bones, many of them comprising complete skeletons, that were paraded before their eyes. Theirs was an embarrassment of riches, as a result of which they were unable to probe exhaustively into many of the problems presented by the paleontological riches surrounding them. There simply were not enough days in the year, or years in their respective lifetimes, for these men to comprehend fully the things they had. Nevertheless they were, one might say, three copious fountains of new knowledge concerning dinosaurs, and the facts they spread before the world of science opened broad vistas of life in the past, vistas that were beyond the dreams of their scientific predecessors.

Mantell and Buckland had envisaged the few dinosaurs known to them more or less as great, glorified lizards; they had no background for thinking in other terms. Owen, upon the basis of the still scanty fossil record available to him, was able to see that the gigantic bones being excavated from Cretaceous sediments on the two sides of the English Channel represented reptiles quite unlike any of the reptiles inhabiting the present-day world. Therefore he coined the name *Dinosauria*—the "terrible lizards" to represent what he considered to be a group of extinct reptiles, living in a remotely past age, quite set apart from modern reptiles. In making this proposal in his famous paper read at the meetings of the British Association for the Advancement of Science in 1842, Owen took a great forward step in the understanding of the dinosaurs.

And this brings up a point that should be stressed. The important discoveries of science are not made entirely in the field or in the laboratory. They come in part, and one might say in large part, from the mind of man. The bones of dinosaurs had been weathering out of the earth since time immemorial, but until Buckland and Mantell turned their attention to the earth around them, nobody had seen these bones, at least with any degree of understanding. If such bones had been noted at all, they were generally regarded as unexplained curiosities—or perhaps as the bones of giants. Buckland and Mantell saw these bones as the remains of reptilian giants, and in thinking of reptilian giants they were prone to magnify in their minds' eye some of the animals with which they were familiar. It remained for Owen to create the dinosaurs, and the creation sprang from his fertile and well-informed mind, a mind that could take facts coming to it, and by combining these facts with a vast storehouse of other facts already in the back of that mind, develop a concept that was new to man. It was a concept that was to become so well established in our thinking as to be accepted today, as are accepted the ideas of other worlds in the sky or other worlds in the atom. Truly the discoveries made within the mind are fully as exciting as those made out on the side of a lonely hill beneath the wide sky or in the quiet seclusion of the laboratory.

Let us recall once again the words of Owen, by which he created the dinosaurs:

"The combination of such characters, some, as the sacral ones, altogether peculiar among Reptiles, others borrowed, as it were, from groups now distinct from each other, and all manifested by creatures far surpassing in size the largest of existing reptiles, will, it is presumed, be deemed sufficient ground for establishing a distinct tribe or suborder of Saurian Reptiles, for which I would propose the name of *Dinosauria*" (Owen, 1842, page 103).

This was the basic framework upon which rested the interpretations of their fossils made by Dollo, Cope, and Marsh, and for that matter, the interpretations of other men who in those days ventured into the studies of dinosaurian anatomy and development. At the time it seemed to be an adequate framework, and these three great paleontologists of the late nineteenth century were able to embellish it with many details. For example, before Marsh and Cope began their rival efforts in field and laboratory there were just nine species of dinosaurs known from North America, most of them having been created by their able and amiable predecessor and sometime colleague Joseph Leidy. At the end of their two careers, these men had added 136 new species of dinosaurs to the roster of the ancient ruling reptiles on this continent, Marsh having created eighty species, Cope fifty-six. It should be said that not all these species have stood the test of time. A certain number of them have disappeared, as it has become apparent upon the basis of later studies that Marsh and Cope, in their efforts to outdo each other, every now and then gave more than one name to the same dinosaur. It was an easy thing to do; it is still being done by scholars in systematic biology and paleontology who are working on new materials. Moreover, in the days of Marsh and Cope there was not so much appreciation of the differences between individuals of a species because of growth or of variability or of sex as there is today. So it was that Cope, for example, described three species of a small, early dinosaur from New Mexico upon the basis of fossils that included large and small, old and young individuals of a single species. But even allowing for the errors made by two men who were trying to top each other, the number of new dinosaurs they described was truly prodigious; perhaps no other two men have studied and described as many.

It was inevitable that Marsh and Cope, handling and scrutinizing such vast numbers of dinosaur bones, would soon come to realize that there were dinosaurs and dinosaurs. Some were of gigantic size; some were small. Some were obviously plant-eating animals; some were just as obviously meat eaters. Some were covered with armor; some were not so protected. Therefore both Marsh and Cope devised systems of classification whereby the dinosaurs might be subdivided; each man made his own census of the dinosaurs and tried to indicate how they were related to one another and how they differed. (Dollo did not get himself involved in this question of dinosaurian relationships to the degree that it occupied Marsh and Cope; he was more interested in the study of numerous bones of one dinosaur, *Iguanodon*.)

HUXLEY, DINOSAURS, AND BIRDS

But Marsh and Cope were not the only men who at that time became interested in dinosaurian relationships. True enough, they were the two men who were working at first hand and most intimately with the fossils of these extinct reptiles. But once their studies were published, the new facts set forth in their papers became common knowledge, available for the use of any other person who might feel himself competent to express himself on this particular subject. And two English contemporaries of the American rivals did so express themselves. One was Thomas Henry Huxley—the great Huxley who was Darwin's champion and who became involved in many works, scientific and otherwise, during his busy and productive life. The other was Harry Govier Seeley, a man not so prominent in the public eye as was Huxley, but none the less a most able paleontologist, teacher, lecturer, and writer. As might be expected, the four men, Marsh, Cope, Huxley, and Seeley, had four different systems for classifying the dinosaurs.

Huxley not only was making his name known throughout the world as the aggressive defender of Darwin in the years immediately following the publication of Darwin's epochal work, *The Origin of Species,* but he was also an authority in zoology and paleontology, publishing numerous monographs and papers outlining the results of his research in these fields. He was furthermore an inspiring lecturer and teacher. For example, Huxley published a famous essay, based upon one of his lectures, entitled "On a Piece of Chalk." With a piece of ordinary blackboard chalk in his hand (the natural chalk that formerly was used, not the synthetic crayon of today) he led his listeners, or his readers, on a spellbinding trip into the past, a trip that involved the history of the earth, the development of seas, and the panorama of evolving life. Huxley also was very much involved in social problems, particularly in the standards of education in Britain. Withal he had time to study the dinosaurs, not the least of which were the newly found riches of Marsh and of Cope, and in his active and imaginative mind to realize the larger implications of the fossil bones. Here again, as in the case of Owen's creation of the Dinosauria, we see an exploration by the mind of a man, an exploration of fossil bones as important as the earlier digging up of those bones in the field.

Huxley's contribution to our understanding of the dinosaurs was not to be *the* definitive classification, as we shall see, but it was an important steppingstone in the constant forward progress of scientific knowledge. He accepted Owen's Dinosauria, but he saw this category as including many but not all of the great extinct reptiles living during Mesozoic times. Basing his conclusions upon a consideration of the sum of numerous anatomical features in these ancient reptiles, the teeth, the jaws, the pelvis, the femur, or upper bone, of the hind limb, and the presence or absence of protective armor, Huxley considered that the Dinosauria, including three families, the armored forms, the plant-eating iguanodonts (first described by Mantell), and the meat-eating megalosaurs (first described by Buckland) constituted one moiety of a larger group or order which he named the Ornithoscelida. The other divison of this order he called the Compsognatha, based upon the tiny chicken-sized dinosaur *Compsognathus,* from the Jurassic lithographic limestones of Bavaria.

Thus:

ORNITHOSCELIDA

		Scelidosauridae—armored dinosaurs
Dinosauria	{	Iguanodontidae—iguanodonts, etc.
		Megalosauridae—carnivorous dinosaurs
Compsognatha		*Compsognathus*, the small carnivorous dinosaur from Solnhofen, Bavaria

In erecting the new order, Ornithoscelida (*ornithos*—bird, *scelida* —leg; hence, birdlike legs), Huxley brought out something that either was missed or was not given much attention by those men who had preceded him in the study of dinosaurs. This was the extraordinary resemblances between dinosaurs and birds in the structure of the hind limbs. Indeed, in a paper published two years before his proposal for a new classification of the dinosaurs, Huxley gave particular emphasis to these resemblances:

"There can be no doubt that the hind quarters of the *Dinosauria* wonderfully approached those of birds in their general structure, and therefore that these extinct Reptiles were more closely allied to birds than any which now live." Continuing his discourse, Huxley stressed what he considered the particularly strong birdlike features of the little dinosaur *Compsognathus*, for which reason he set it apart from the other dinosaurs: "Notwithstanding its small size [it was not much more than two feet in length], this reptile must, I think, be placed among, or close to, the *Dinosauria*; but it is still more bird-like than any of the animals which are ordinarily included in that group" (Huxley, 1868, page 311).

Is it any wonder that Professor Hitchcock, who died only a few years before Huxley published these words, thought that the fossil footprints, preserved by the thousands in the Triassic sandstones of the Connecticut Valley, were made by birds? Indeed, so close is the resemblance between the feet in many dinosaurs and birds that it would seem that Huxley himself was not quite sure about the origin of some of the Connecticut Valley tracks:

"And this conclusion [the close resemblance between dinosaurs and birds] acquires a far greater force when we reflect upon that wonderful evidence of the life of the Triassic age, which is afforded us by the sandstones of Connecticut. It is true that these have yielded neither feathers nor bones; but the creatures which traversed them when they were the sandy beaches of a quiet sea, have left innumerable tracks which are full of instructive suggestion. Many of these tracks are wholly undistinguishable from those of modern birds in form and size; others are gigantic three-toed impressions, like those of the Weald of our own country. . . . These bipeds were either birds or reptiles, or more probably both. . . ." (Huxley, 1868, page 312)

Perhaps this account of Huxley's classification of the dinosaurs has become unduly involved with his earlier ideas as to the close resemblances (and relationships) of dinosaurs with birds. As a matter of fact, it is this remarkable resemblance between dinosaurs and birds, particularly in the hindquarters, that provides one very important clue for our understanding of dinosaurian relationships.

THE CLASSIFICATIONS OF COPE AND MARSH

In arriving at his system for classifying the dinosaurs as members of an order Ornithoscelida, the reptiles with legs like birds, Huxley was rejecting an earlier classification by Cope, based upon the relationships of the bones of the ankle to those of the lower leg. Cope's classification, published in 1866, and revised by the same author in 1883, was marked by his splitting of the dinosaurs into *four* distinct orders. These were the armored and the duck-billed dinosaurs and their relatives, placed in one order; the gigantic marsh-dwelling brontosaurs placed in a second order, and the meat-eating dinosaurs, contained within two other orders:

DINOSAURIA
1883

Orthopoda	Armored and duck-billed dinosaurs
Goniopoda	Carnivorous dinosaurs
Hallopoda	Small carnivorous dinosaurs, including *Compsognathus*
Opisthocoela	Gigantic swamp-dwelling dinosaurs

Cope's classification was parallel to but rather different from a system proposed by Marsh in 1878 and 1884. Marsh, too, recognized the dinosaurs as being constituted of four orders, but these orders were of different dimensions than the ones proposed by Cope. (One would hardly expect the two men to have agreed on this problem, any more than they did on anything else.) Marsh separated the armored and the duck-billed dinosaurs, which Cope had combined, and called the two orders the Stegosauria and the Ornithopoda, respectively. He then recognized the giant brontosaurs as distinct, as did Cope, and called them the Sauropoda. Finally, he placed the carnivorous dinosaurs, which Cope had divided between two orders, into a single order, the Theropoda:

DINOSAURIA
    Stegosauria—armored dinosaurs
    Ornithopoda—iguanodonts, duck-billed dinosaurs, etc.
    Sauropoda—gigantic marsh-dwelling dinosaurs
    Theropoda—carnivorous dinosaurs

These names proposed by Marsh, rather than the names proposed by Cope, are still in use for four of the six *sub*orders of dinosaurs recognized today, a fact that must disturb the unquiet spirit of Cope in its eternal sojourn beyond the far banks of the Styx.

HARRY GOVIER SEELEY AND DINOSAURIAN DUALITY

This brings us to Harry Govier Seeley and his classification of 1887. But first let us look briefly at the man.

Seeley was born into an early Victorian family of culture, in which books and music were much prized. This was the environment in which he grew up, an environment that prepared him for Cambridge University. His career at Cambridge was a promising one; while there he became the assistant of Adam Sedgwick, one of the giant founders of geology, the Sedgwick who was Darwin's teacher and who perhaps was more influential than any other man in shaping the career of the young Darwin. When Seeley reached that stage of life at which he wished to break away from a subordinate position, to become something other than a scientific assistant, he was offered a position at the British Museum, as well as a recommendation from none other than Thomas Henry Huxley for a post with the Geological Survey of Britain. But Seeley refused both; he wished to be free of such trammels. For many years he was a more or less independent worker, studying fossils and writing about them, writing books and giving public lectures, at which he was quite successful. Rather late in life Seeley was appointed to a Professorship at King's College of the University of London.

Seeley was an ardent student of fossil reptiles. He was the authority of his day on the flying reptiles of the Mesozoic age, and he did much work on the dinosaurs. He produced a voluminous amount of work on the important mammal-like reptiles of South Africa, during the course of which he went to that then far corner of the earth, to collect fossils, at a time when the making of such collections in South Africa involved considerable hardships and required more than a little stamina. So Seeley knew the fossil reptiles intimately.

And knowing the reptiles as he did, Seeley put his mind to the problem of dinosaurian relationships. He looked at the remains of these ancient reptiles with an insight resulting from much experience, and perceptively and elegantly he solved the problem to which he had addressed himself. If Owen's recognition that the dinosaurs were not magnified lizards, but rather reptiles considerably different from the reptiles that live today, was a first great step toward the proper appreciation of these extinct animals, then Seeley's recognition that the dinosaurs were not a homogenous group or a plexus of three or four orders of reptiles, but rather *two* distinct orders, was a second great step forward toward an understanding of the true nature of dinosaurian relationships.

Perhaps this all seems rather esoteric. What is the difference whether the dinosaurs are all closely related or whether they belong to two separate groups, or three, or four? As remarked above, it is a matter of properly understanding them, a matter the importance of which should not be underestimated. Perhaps an illustration is in order.

In the days of Cuvier, the great French anatomist who lived during the latter part of the eighteenth and the early years of the nineteenth centuries and who, it will be remembered, viewed the first remains of *Iguanodon*, sent to him by Gideon Mantell, with something less than an understanding eye, it was a common practice to lump the elephants, rhinoceroses, and hippopotamuses together as "pachyderms," or thick-skinned mammals. The association of these animals as zoological cousins was made upon an external feature, which we now realize is of secondary importance, a point that was not appreciated by zoologists of Cuvier's generation. Many animals may develop thick skins quite independently; indeed this character is in part a function of size, and large or gigantic animals are almost certain to have heavy skins. We now know that elephants belong in a group of their own, that rhinoceroses are first cousins to horses and tapirs, and that hippos are first cousins to pigs. If we try to bring together the elephants, rhinoceroses, and hippopotamuses as pachyderms, we immediately encounter many problems; their distinctive characters under the skin are so diverse that there is no making of any sense out of such a grouping. In short, we now have an understanding of anatomical characters revealing the true relationships of these animals, making it quite apparent that elephants belong by themselves, that rhinoceroses really show numerous characters in common with horses, and likewise, hippopotamuses with pigs. The zoological relationships of these animals, so grouped, assume a logical pattern.

In a like manner Seeley saw that the dinosaurs were not a single group; but he saw also that the fragmentation of these ancient reptiles into three or four orders of equal status, as based upon the anatomical characters that had been selected by Cope and Marsh and Huxley, was also erroneous. He realized that these men, although circling around the problem, were not quite centered upon it, because they were failing to understand the significance of some of the anatomical characters of the dinosaurs.

Cope, as we have seen, gave particular emphasis to the relation between the ankle and the bones of the lower leg, while Marsh stressed the sum of many features of the anatomy throughout the body. Huxley, who did not divide the dinosaurs into separate orders, realized the basic relationship of these ancient reptiles with birds. Seeley cut through these several lines of evidence and came to the crucial point, namely, that the dinosaurs can be very definitely subdivided into two distinct orders, especially on the basis of the structure of the pelvic girdle. Of course, other characters in the anatomy

---

Figure 15. The pelvic girdles of the saurischian dinosaur *Diplodocus* (left) and the ornithischian dinosaur *Iguanodon* (right) as figured by Dollo. These views of the left side of each pelvis show the ilium (IL), pubis (P) and "postpubis" (PP), ischium (IS), and acetabulum (A), the socket for head of the femur. In the saurischian dinosaur the pubis is a simple bone, extending forward and down; in the ornithischian dinosaur it is a somewhat complex bone with a forward process (P) and a posterior process (PP) parallel to the ischium—as in birds

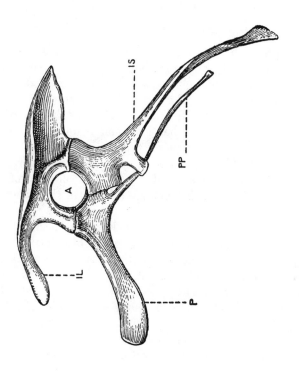

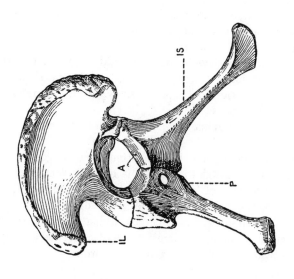

of these reptiles go along with the two types of pelvis to support a twofold division of the dinosaurs, but the pelvis is crucial. And it has proved to be so in the eighty years that have elapsed since Seeley proposed his classification. The proof of the pudding is in the eating, so goes the old saying, and the fact that Seeley's division of the dinosaurs into two basic orders has held and is universally accepted is proof of its validity. It has stood the test of time.

Seeley published his revolutionary concept on dinosaurian relationships in 1887, in a paper entitled "On the Classification of the Fossil Animals Commonly named Dinosauria." And in this paper he made the statement:

"The considerations adduced appear, however, to show that the Dinosauria has no existence as a natural group of animals, but includes two distinct types of animal structure with technical characters in common, which show their descent from a common ancestry rather than their close affinity. These two orders of animals may be conveniently named the Ornithischia and the Saurischia. . . ." (Seeley, 1887, page 170.)

The Ornithischia, so named by Seeley because the pelvis (ischia) is like that in the birds (ornithos), was defined by him by the fact that in the hip girdle the pubic bone (the front lower bone on each side), "is divided, so that one limb is directed backward parallel to the ischium [the back lower bone on each side] as among birds, and the other limb is directed forward." In the Saurischia the pelvis (ischia) may be compared with the pelvis in other reptiles (sauros), and as Seeley stated, "the pubis is directed forward . . . and no posterior limb of the bone is developed." It should be mentioned that Seeley outlined other characters in the pelvis and in the skeleton that accompany these basic differences as shown by the structure and position of the pubic bones.

The order Ornithischia as defined by Seeley contains, in terms of one modern system of classification, Marsh's orders, Ornithopods, or duck-billed dinosaurs, and their relatives, and Stegosauria, or plated dinosaurs, now reduced to the status of *suborders,* and in addition two other suborders not known when Marsh wrote his paper, namely, the Ankylosauria, or Cretaceous armored dinosaurs, and the Ceratopsia, or horned dinosaurs. The Saurischia contains Marsh's orders Theropoda, or carnivorous dinosaurs, and Sauropoda, or giant dinosaurs, now also reduced to the status of suborders.

The several views of dinosaurian classification as proposed by Huxley, Marsh, and Cope, and their relationships to the proved dichotomy of these reptiles, as discovered by Seeley, may be outlined in the following manner. Thus:

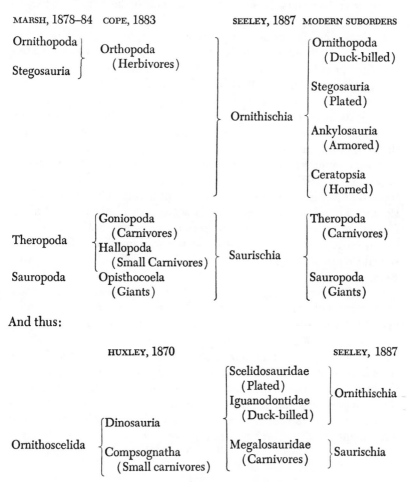

And thus:

A basic classification of the dinosaurs that is obviously a natural one was thereby established, through the acumen and experience of Harry Govier Seeley, and the ground was laid for the modern era of discovery and research on these reptiles. Again, as was previously shown, a discovery was made in the mind of a man, this discovery supplementing and enlarging previous discoveries that had been made by other men who labored in the field with picks and in the laboratory with hammers, chisels, and awls. Such is the nature of paleontology.

In this crucial paper of Seeley's another very perceptive observation appeared, to the effect that there could be no ground for associating the Ornithischia and Saurischia together in one group, unless that group would include in addition the crocodiles, the birds, and certain Triassic reptiles now known as thecodonts. Here again Seeley demonstrated his knowledge of reptiles. We now know that the two orders of dinosaurs do indeed have much in common with the thecodonts, the crocodiles, and the birds, and it should be said with the flying reptiles, or pterosaurs, as well. This is because all these several orders of reptiles, as well as the birds, are descended from a common ancestry—from a primitive thecodont reptile, probably of very early Triassic age. Therefore the dinosaurs show resemblances to the birds, as Huxley so sagely observed, not because they are "intermediate between birds and reptiles" which was the role in which Huxley envisioned them, but because they branched out from a common ancestral stem.

So it was that Seeley was the first man who realized that there were two evolutionary streams of dinosaurian development. Moreover, Seeley saw these two evolutionary streams as but two manifestations of a still larger evolutionary stream pattern, a pattern that included not only the dinosaurs but also their ancestors, the Triassic thecodont reptiles, as well as the crocodiles, the flying reptiles, and the birds, all descended from a common stem. The reptiles making up this complex are the reptiles which are now generally termed as *archosaurs,* and the birds, though set apart from reptiles, are, if you wish, highly modified archosaurian types.

Figure 16. The Jurassic saurischian dinosaur *Ceratosaurus,* from Como Bluff, as figured by Marsh. Note the saurischian pelvis, the birdlike hind limbs, the clawed front feet, the long jaws with teeth around their margins

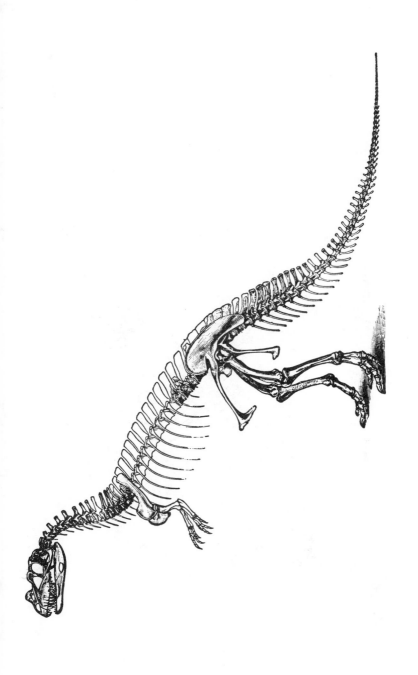

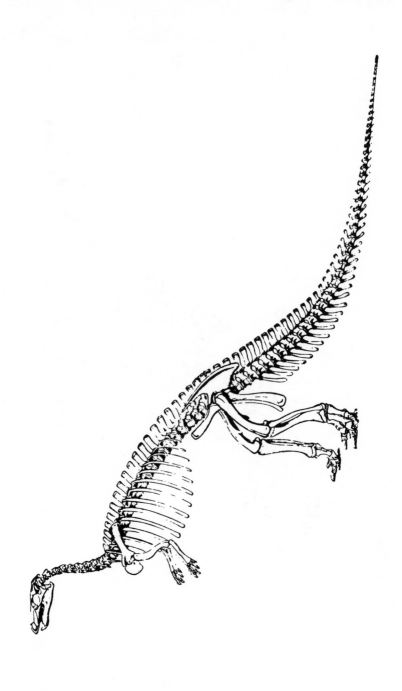

The relationships of the archosaurian reptiles may be shown in the following way:

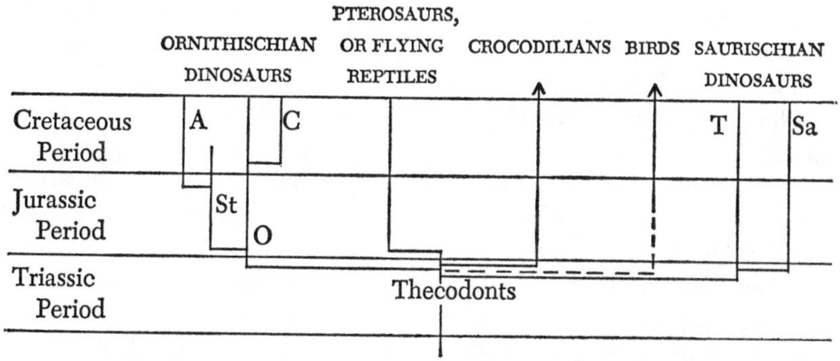

	ORNITHISCHIAN DINOSAURS		PTEROSAURS, OR FLYING REPTILES	CROCODILIANS	BIRDS	SAURISCHIAN DINOSAURS	
Cretaceous Period	A	C			↑	T	Sa
Jurassic Period		St O					
Triassic Period			Thecodonts				

The commonly recognized suborders of dinosaurs are indicated by letters on the above diagram, as follows:

A—Ankylosaurs, or armored dinosaurs ⎫
St—Stegosaurs, or plated dinosaurs   ⎬ Ornithischia
C—Ceratopsians, or horned dinosaurs   ⎪
O—Ornithopods, or duck-billed dinosaurs ⎭

T—Theropods, or carnivorous dinosaurs ⎫ Saurischia
Sa—Sauropods, or giant dinosaurs   ⎭

From this it can be seen that the two streams of dinosaurian evolution are indeed quite distinct.

FRIEDRICH VON HUENE AND FRANZ NOPCSA

In the world of science, as in the other worlds of man, a good idea is not always given the recognition it deserves. The man who proposes something new may find himself as a voice crying in the wilderness,

Figure 17. The Jurassic ornithischian dinosaur *Camptosaurus*, from Como Bluff, as figured by Marsh. Note the ornithischian pelvis, the rather heavy hind limbs, the short front feet, and the lack of teeth in the front of the jaws

trying to make himself heard where there is no one to listen. He may find himself trying to overcome the inertia of established thought and custom. So it would seem to have been with Seeley's reclassification of the dinosaurs. He saw the dinosaurs for what they were—two evolutionary streams proceeding from a common source, but it was quite a while before this concept gained common acceptance.

Not that the matter bothered Seeley particularly. His paper on the classification of the "Animals Commonly Named Dinosauria" was but one of many paleontological problems with which he was concerned. He had said it—now it was up to others to accept it or not. He had other things to think about.

There was another man, however, who, in the early years of this century, did recognize the validity of Seeley's two new reptilian orders, the Saurischian, or reptile-pelvis dinosaurs, and the Ornithischia, or bird-pelvis dinosaurs. This was a young German by the name of Friedrich von Huene, a man who was destined to reiterate time and again the dualism of the dinosaurs. Von Huene was wholeheartedly interested in the dinosaurs; during his lifetime he became one of the great authorities on these reptiles.

Friedrich Freiherr von Huene was born in 1875, in the ancient and picturesque university town of Tübingen, Germany, a city in which he was to spend most of his life. A year after his birth the family moved to Basel, Switzerland, where they spent ten years. From Basel the von Huene family moved to Estonia, where young Friedrich lived briefly on an estate of almost baronial dimensions. Here he could spend many happy afternoons, riding through the broad fields on his pony, accompanied by his dogs. But in 1888 Friedrich returned to Basel, to attend the gymnasium.

After his graduation from the gymnasium, he entered the University of Lausanne, where he was faced with the decision as to whether his life would be devoted to theology or to science. He chose science, a decision of considerable importance to the history of dinosaurian studies, but through his long life he has maintained a strong and most sincere religious view of the world—past, present, and future.

Having made the decision in favor of a scientific career, von Huene transferred to the University of Tübingen, a famous center for the study of rocks and fossils. Here he came under the influence of Professor Koken, who in the course of time suggested to von Huene, now his assistant, that a study of the Triassic dinosaurs of southern Germany would be a most fruitful field of paleontological research. Von Huene accepted the suggestion, and this decision, like the one he had previously made, was important to the future course of his life and of paleontology. It was the beginning of his long scientific career devoted to dinosaurs and to other extinct reptiles.

He has spent many decades in the study of fossil reptiles, with a singleness of purpose and a degree of industry that are truly amazing. The volume of his publications through the years is prodigious, and his contributions to our knowledge of fossil reptiles are numerous and significant. They include papers on reptilian relationships and classification, descriptions of dinosaurs from all over the world, investigations of various Mesozoic marine reptiles, especially ichthyosaurs, and other technical studies too numerous to mention.

It should not be thought that von Huene, who at the time of this writing is still very much a part of the Tübingen scene, throughout his life has been immured in his study. He has been noted for his activity in the field, traveling all over the world to study and collect fossil reptiles—not only in his native Germany but also in other parts of Europe, in North America, in Brazil, in Argentina, in Africa, and in Asia. Such wide travels are an index of von Huene's devotion to his subject, because they frequently necessitated his absence for many months at a time from his comfortable home in Tübingen, and his lively family. But go he must, to search for fossils in the far corners of the world, and to collect specimens that would in time make Tübingen an important center for the study of ancient amphibians and reptiles.

Von Huene in 1966 was still vigorously active in spite of his ninety-three years. A tall, spare man of distinguished appearance, von Huene throughout much of his life has displayed incredible energy. He is noted as a walker—until quite recently he could hike all day up and down hill at a pace that tired out any associates who tried to accompany him. Only a few years ago, when he was well advanced in his eighties, he hiked for three days, a hundred miles across southern Germany, to attend a scientific meeting. Such abilities have served him well in the field. Moreover, von Huene in his later years has represented a link with the past, for he once knew and worked with a generation of paleontologists who are now gone and who, to the younger generation of fossil hunters, are of almost legendary proportions. Indeed, von Huene is in his lifetime something of a legend for

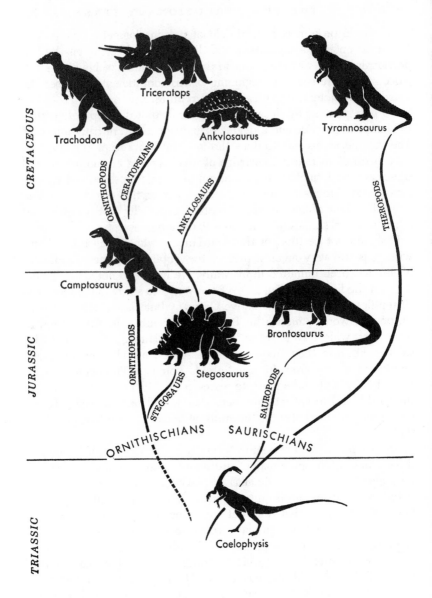

CRETACEOUS

Trachodon

Triceratops

Ankylosaurus

Tyrannosaurus

ORNITHOPODS

CERATOPSIANS

ANKYLOSAURS

THEROPODS

Camptosaurus

Brontosaurus

JURASSIC

ORNITHOPODS

Stegosaurus

STEGOSAURS

SAUROPODS

ORNITHISCHIANS

SAURISCHIANS

TRIASSIC

Coelophysis

his tremendous knowledge and experience in paleontology, as well as for his proverbial gentleness of spirit.

Before the First World War von Huene was in the early stages of a distinguished career, but even though a comparatively young man he had already established himself as an authority on fossil reptiles, especially those of Triassic age, and more particularly the dinosaurs. Thus he had the background of knowledge to appreciate fully the significance of Seeley's work. In 1914 he espoused the classification of the dinosaurs as two independent orders, the Saurischia and the Ornithischia, with vigor and with an array of evidence and arguments. He continued to hammer at this theme in later years.

As the result of his extended studies, von Huene had some ideas of his own as to the internal classification of the saurischian and ornithischian dinosaurs. The following diagram shows how he viewed them, as compared with the system of modern suborders that has been set forth on a preceding page:

ORDERS OF DINOSAURS	SUBORDERS OF DINOSAURS, AS PROPOSED BY VON HUENE	SUBORDERS OF DINOSAURS COMMONLY ACCEPTED IN RECENT CLASSIFICATIONS
Saurischia	⎰ Coelurosauria, small carnivores ⎱ Pachypodosauria, large carnivores ⎰ plus giant sauropods—	Theropoda Sauropoda
Ornithischia	⎧ Ornithopoda, duck-billed dinosaurs— ⎨ Ponderopoda, horned dinosaurs— ⎩ Thyreophora, plated and armored dinosaurs	Ornithopoda Ceratopsia ⎰ Stegosauria ⎱ Ankylosauria

Figure 18. A family tree, or phylogeny, of the dinosaurs, according to modern opinion. This shows the two orders of dinosaurs, one of which, the Saurischia, is subdivided into two suborders, the other, the Ornithischia, into four suborders. The theropods were carnivorous, or meat-eating, dinosaurs. The gigantic sauropods, the duck-billed ornithopods, the plated stegosaurs, the armored ankylosaurs, and the horned ceratopsians were herbivorous, or plant-eating, dinosaurs

The many papers that von Huene published about dinosaurs—about the relationships and the classification of these reptiles—greatly influenced another man, who at this time was actively engaged in the study of dinosaurian evolution.

He was von Huene's contemporary and Hungarian neighbor, Franz Baron Nopcsa von Felsö-Szilvás. Nopcsa (pronounced Nop'sha) perhaps von Huene's leading rival as a student of the dinosaurs, was very different from the rather unworldly Tübingen professor. For one thing, Nopcsa was strictly an "armchair" paleontologist, working in his study, in the laboratory, and in the library, whereas von Huene, even though an indefatigable research scientist, was at the same time an enthusiastic fossil hunter who spent many rigorous seasons in the field. But the differences go beyond this contrast in their professional lives.

Nopcsa was the scion of a noble Transylvanian family—for which reason he was commonly addressed as *Baron* Nopcsa. (Von Huene was a "Freiherr," more or less the equivalent of a baron, a fact that once gave him considerable distinction among his fellow Germans.) These are the resemblances—otherwise the lives of the two men diverge. Although Nopcsa came from a somewhat out-of-the-way corner of Europe, he was a thoroughly cosmopolitan person, even as a very young man. He had a broad and comprehensive education, and he spoke and wrote several languages with great fluency. Indeed, his scientific papers are in Hungarian, German, French, and English—accordingly signed Báró Nopcsa Ferenc, Franz Baron Nopcsa, Le Baron François Nopcsa, and Baron Francis Nopcsa. Moreover, his interests were as varied as his languages, for he wrote authoritatively not only upon dinosaurs and other fossil reptiles but also upon geology, archaeology, ethnology, and upon the geography of Albania. He had a very particular interest in Albania: this colorful, backward land and its primitive people cast a lifelong spell over Nopcsa.

Nopcsa has said that he became a paleontologist through mere chance; he certainly was not the first or the last student of ancient life to stumble into the profession. The mere chance was that during his last year of school before he entered the University of Vienna, his sister found some dinosaur bones on her estate. Nopcsa studied and wrote about the fossils in 1899 during his first year at the university, and so polished and well written is his paper describing the skull of a new genus, *Limnosaurus*, that there is no internal evidence in the publication that it represents the first paleontological effort of what in the United States might have been a college freshman. Perhaps Nopcsa was a bit dazzled by his own brilliance, for on a visit to Brussels, shortly after the publication of his paper on *Limnosaurus*, he said to Dollo, then a paleontologist with an international reputation, "Is it not marvellous that I, so young a man, have written such an excellent memoir?" (Edinger, 1955, page 36). From that time on, Dollo

---

Figure 19. A diagram to show the relationships of the various orders of reptiles

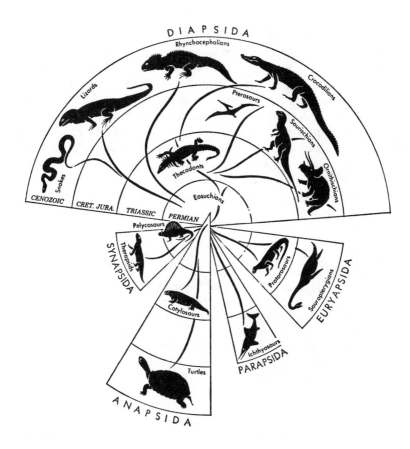

was not especially enthusiastic about Nopcsa, even though the young baron from Transylvania had a winning personality that charmed many of his acquaintances.

Because Transylvania is a region in which are found many Cretaceous dinosaurs, Nopcsa early became especially interested in these particular reptiles—so much so, in fact, that he published twenty papers on dinosaurs from the Cretaceous. Of course a man of Nopcsa's broad interests would hardly confine himself to purely descriptive accounts of ancient reptiles, and so it was that early in his career he turned his attention to the evolution and classification of extinct reptiles, publishing about a dozen papers in this field. The culmination of Nopcsa's concern with the broader aspects of reptilian history is expressed in his book published in 1923 on the families of reptiles, a work in which Nopcsa was much influenced by von Huene's ideas and publications on dinosaurs. Nopcsa accepted the evidence as to the dichotomy of the dinosaurs, particularly as shown by the structure of the pelvis, and now well established in paleontological circles, thanks to the efforts of von Huene. Thus in his classification of the reptiles he recognized two separate orders of dinosaurs, calling them the Saurischia and the Orthopoda (instead of Ornithischia) respectively. But Nopcsa could not quite give up the old idea of recognizing all dinosaurs as standing apart from all other reptiles, so he placed the two great orders of these reptiles within a higher categorical rank—a *superorder* of Dinosauria.

Consequently, his classification, which shows the von Huene influence, went like this:

DINOSAURIA
    Saurischia
        Pachypodosauria—Triassic dinosaurs
        Coelurosauria—Small carnivorous dinosaurs
        Megalosauria—Large carnivorous dinosaurs
        Sauropoda—Giant swamp-dwelling dinosaurs
    Orthopoda
        Poposauria—A group based upon a peculiar pelvis from Wyoming
        Ornithopoda—Iguanodonts and duck-billed dinosaurs
        Thyreophora—Stegosaurs, armored dinosaurs and horned dinosaurs

Although Nopcsa's ideas on dinosaurian relationships followed established and more or less conventional lines, some of his thoughts about the adaptations and ways of life among the dinosaurs as inferred from anatomical characters were less than conventional, even a bit unusual. For several years he was obsessed with the idea of sexual differences among the dinosaurs, as shown by their bony features. Thus he thought that the duck-billed dinosaurs with crests were males—those without crests were females. It was an intriguing idea; the great flaw in the theory was that these two types of hadrosaurian dinosaurs are found in different localities, and in beds of different ages. In other words, the crested hadrosaurs are several million years older than the ones without crests. This fact, when pointed out, was a fatal blow to Nopcsa's nice little theory, but it did not worry him especially. He went on to other things.

Nopcsa's views on the two streams of dinosaurian evolution, as well as his other ideas on dinosaurian relationships, were the result of his own detailed and comprehensive studies on the dinosaurs extending through a quarter of a century, and of course of the influence exerted upon his thinking by the immense volume of papers on these ancient reptiles pouring out of the mind and from the pen of von Huene. Nopcsa was indeed a foremost authority on dinosaurs.

Beyond his paleontological life Nopcsa simultaneously lived several other lives. Before the First World War, during those years when he was assiduously studying and describing Transylvanian and other dinosaurs, he was also living the life of a baronial lord, going from one Hungarian estate to another, with peasants bowing low before him as he drove by. His was on such occasions the life of a semiroyal person in a sort of dreamland out of an operetta. And this life seemed in part to be sufficient, for Nopcsa never married.

It was, however, much too ordered an existence for his adventurous spirit. As a young man Nopcsa became fascinated with the land and the people of Albania; that picturesque and backward corner of the Balkan world proved to be an irresistible lodestone to the youthful baron. For Nopcsa, Albania had the appeal of the exotic and the unusual, the lure of romance and adventure. He accumulated a large library on Albania; he learned the dialects of the country; and he came to identify himself with the people. He journeyed to and through Albania on various occasions, and his trips were anything but serene. In those days Albania was a part of the Turkish Empire in Europe; the rough Albanian mountaineers were restive; and the young traveler found himself involved in numerous exciting adventures.

Then in 1913, after the Balkan War, Albania was constituted an autonomous state. As such it was something of a political vacuum, and the Central Powers decided to provide the small country with a king. Nopcsa considered himself to be the man for the position. So in 1913 he wrote to the Chief of the General Staff of the Austro-Hungarian Army in Trieste, proposing a sort of filibustering expedition to Albania. Nopcsa would of course be the leader of this raid— for after all he knew the people, he knew the country, and he spoke the language and its various dialects. He suggested that in short order he could establish himself as the ruler of the country, riding down the streets of Tiranë on a white horse. All he needed was five hundred soldiers, who, however, would be clad in civilian garments, some artillery, and two small, fast steamships, which he proposed to purchase out of his own pocket. He would establish a beachhead, march into the country, and set up a regime friendly to Vienna. And once he was king he would marry the daughter of an American millionaire—any millionaire; they all had daughters eager to marry genuine kings and princes—thus providing himself and his kingdom with ample funds for the future. The scheme, attractive though it might seem to Nopcsa, did not impress the High Command. He was not chosen; instead Prince Wilhelm zu Wied was sent to Albania, and within six months was forced to flee for his life.

Before and during the First World War Nopcsa served as an officer in the Imperial Austro-Hungarian Army. But instead of wearing a handsome uniform and commanding troops, Nopcsa wore the rough garb of a Romanian peasant, let his hair grow long and shaggy, and lived the dangerous life of a spy along the border region between Hungary and Romania. With his command of several languages, and his knowledge of people, he was able to carry out his undercover duties in the best traditions of a fiction thriller.

Life became difficult for Nopcsa after the war, in part because he was a nobleman on the losing side. Some of his estates, originally in Hungary, were now in Romania; they were confiscated and he was not indemnified for them. The Hungarian government, aware of his abilities as a scientist, appointed him as president of the Hungarian Geological Survey. It was an office he held with indifferent success. He began sweeping reforms within the survey, and so antagonized his superiors and inferiors that finally, unable to stand the strain of constant quarreling, he left Hungary in a rage, and set off on a three-thousand-mile trip through Italy on a motorcycle, with his Albanian friend and secretary, Bajazid, on the seat behind him. They kept going until they ran out of money.

Nopcsa's differences with other people were frequent, and often sharp. On one occasion he almost met his end because of this. He had gone to Hungary after the war to visit one of his estates. Trouble was brewing among the peasants, for the times were hard, and the rules of law and order were in a confused state, to say the least. One day Nopcsa ventured out on a walk alone, was attacked by peasants wielding cudgels and pitchforks, and was beaten to the ground. He came out of the fray with a fractured skull, an injury that affected him for the rest of his life.

Figure 20. A caricature of Franz Nopcsa, by Jenö Teleki

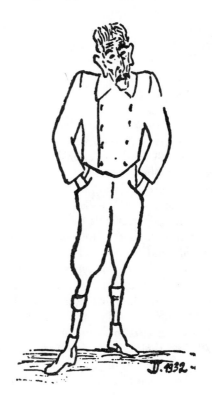

Bajazid, the secretary who lived with Nopcsa for many years, was more than a secretary; he was a lover. Indeed, Nopcsa maintained two Albanian homosexual boyfriends, who participated in his strange and unreal life. In his lucid periods he directed his brilliant mind to research on dinosaurs and other fossil reptiles, and to the study of the ethnology, archaeology, and geography of Albania. At other times his activities tended to run to bizarre extremes.

On the 25th of April, 1933, something cracked inside Nopcsa. He gave to his friend Bajazid a cup of tea heavily laced with a sleeping powder. He then murdered the sleeping Bajazid, shooting him in the head with a pistol. After that, he sat down and wrote the following note:

"The reason for my suicide is a complete breakdown of my nervous system. My old friend and secretary I shot in his sleep without his having the slightest idea of my deed. I did not want to leave him ill, miserable and poor, for further suffering in this world. My last wish is that my body be cremated."

Having written these final words, Nopcsa placed the muzzle of the pistol in his mouth, and pulled the trigger. His body was found, seated in a chair, his head drooped forward, the pistol fallen from his nerveless hand.

From the work of many men, but particularly of Marsh and Cope, Huxley, Seeley, von Huene, and Nopsca, the modern concepts as to the classification and the relationships of the dinosaurs have been established. It has been a process of growth, of the accretion of ideas based upon an ever-growing body of knowledge, this in turn derived from the influx of new fossils from field into laboratory, year after year. Of prime importance is the very basic idea concerning the dual nature of the dinosaurs, as to their division into two primary orders, the Saurischia and the Ornithischia. To the student of fossil reptiles this is one of the facts of life, a fact that has stood up during years of critical studies by many authorities throughout the world. These two great groups of reptiles that dominated the Mesozoic world evolved side by side through a hundred million years of earth history; they lived together, and their common presence on all of the earth's continents affected their separate courses of evolution; their long histories are paleontological records of interacting effect. It seems quite probable that if only one of these orders of dinosaurs had evolved, its history would have been very different, in either case, from what it actually was. It was the evolution of the two orders of Ornithischia and Saurischia together through the extent of the Mesozoic continents, constantly impinging upon each other, that determined the nature of these reptiles which dominated life on the land during the middle geologic era—the Age of Dinosaurs.

And it is possible to view the dinosaurs with this basis of understanding because of the insight of Harry Govier Seeley, based in part upon previous work by Marsh and Cope, and by Huxley, and given vigorous support by Friedrich von Huene, with additional confirmation from various paleontologists, among whom Baron Nopcsa was particularly prominent. The contributions of these men to our understanding of the dinosaurs has been of crucial importance—complementary to and fully as significant as the work of the many collectors who first brought the bones of these ancient reptiles to light.

CHAPTER 5

THE OLDEST DINOSAURS

TRIASSIC ROCKS AND FOSSILS

Where did the dinosaurs come from? What were the origins of the two lines of dinosaurian evolution as originally defined by Seeley? What were the first dinosaurs like, the earliest saurischian and ornithischian descendants of proto-dinosaurian ancestors? The answers to these questions have been sought by many men, and no man has pursued the quest more assiduously than Friedrich von Huene, whom we met in the preceding chapter.

It will be recalled that von Huene was the vigorous champion of Seeley's classification, placing the dinosaurs within two large groups or orders of reptiles; a concept the significance of which von Huene could appreciate, because the German paleontologist, even as a young man, was a close student of those extinct reptiles we call dinosaurs. And von Huene was interested in dinosaurs because he was at the University of Tübingen, in southern Germany, in a region where Upper Triassic rocks containing the fossil bones of some of the earliest and most primitive dinosaurs are exposed. Von Huene, an able paleontologist with a thorough training in the field of his specialty, might have studied the iguanodonts and other contemporaneous Cretaceous dinosaurs that had been of such interest to Mantell and to Dollo, or he might have studied the Jurassic dinosaurs found in Europe that had engaged the attentions of various authorities, but he didn't. He turned his expert eye on the earliest of the dinosaurs because these were the dinosaurs to be found near at hand—in the front yard of the university, so to speak.

It should not be thought that von Huene's interests were confined merely to the dinosaurs occurring within the Triassic beds of southern Germany—he was much too versatile a man, with much too broad an outlook upon the life of the past, to be so restricted. Von Huene was concerned with a larger paleontological theme—with all of the backboned animals that had lived during Triassic times, the fossilized remains of which were preserved in those rocks that once had been the beds of streams and rivers and lakes, when the earth was some 200 million years younger than it now is.

One can hardly imagine a lovelier land in which to search for fossils than southern Germany, especially the State of Württemberg, and particularly the region immediately surrounding Tübingen. Here, not far to the south of Stuttgart, the valley of the Neckar River, a land of rolling wooded hills and broad lowlands carpeted with productive fields of grain and dotted with numerous small country villages (the names of which all seem to end in "ingen"), is enclosed between the dark mountains of the Black Forest to the west and the long ridge of the Swabian Alps to the east. It is a land of its own, modern and yet ancient, a land enjoying the benefits of contemporary western European development, yet a land reflecting the long history of medieval occupation, and back of that the impress of the Roman conquerers, and back of that the wild days of the ancient Germanic tribes. To tramp through the Swabian countryside in search of rock exposures containing fossils, to sit on a grassy bank in the sun, munching on some good fresh bread and cheese, to look across the well-ordered landscape to a distant castle or chapel crowning a small hill, is to enjoy some of the pleasantest hours in the experience of any paleontologist. So it was a nearby land of paleontological opportunity, and of beautiful rustic surroundings, that beckoned to von Huene.

It was also a land famous in the development of the science of geology, for here and in contiguous parts of central Europe, the rocks and fossils that were to be designated as typical of the Triassic period of earth history were first studied and delineated. The early study and the definition of the Triassic system of rocks in central Europe is the result of one of those accidents of history that in the realm of science as well as of human affairs has determined the course of subsequent events. Triassic rocks and fossils might very well have been studied first and more appropriately in Africa or in Asia, but it so happened that they were not. They were defined and named in central Europe, specifically in southern Germany and Switzerland, because in the early and middle years of the last century these were the regions where there were not only good exposures of Triassic rocks but also where there were men with the requisite interest and knowledge to make such studies and definitions.

As long ago as 1780, pioneer geologists working in central Germany had recognized distinct groups of sedimentary rocks, in which were preserved characteristic fossils. They called these rocks the Buntsandstein and Muschelkalk beds. Not long afterward, in the early years of the nineteenth century, another group of rocks with definitive fossils, the Keuper beds, was delineated. At the same time it was seen that Keuper rocks, together with Buntsandstein and Muschelkalk rocks, were widely spread through southern Germany. Consequently, in 1834, a German geologist named Friedrich von Alberti brought these three groups of rocks together into what he named the Triassic system (because of its threefold nature), showing that in the system of Triassic rocks, the Buntsandstein rocks were the lowest and oldest, the Muschelkalk were of intermediate position and age, and the Keuper were the highest and youngest. The Buntsandstein and Keuper rocks are commonly reddish brown or gray in color, and consist of sandstones, shales, and clays deposited in streams and ponds or even as dunes on the ancient Triassic continent. The Muschelkalk generally consists of thick limestones that record the invasion of central Europe by an ancient mediterranean sea during Middle Triassic time.

As might be expected, the fossils reflect the environments in which these sedimentary rocks were accumulated. The Buntsandstein is not rich in fossils, but it does reveal rather numerous footprints that record the wanderings, to and fro, of various ancient land-living amphibians and reptiles. The Muschelkalk is very fossiliferous, containing the remains of numerous seashells and other invertebrate animals that in-

habited an ancient shallow-water sea, together with the bones of
fishes and of various marine reptiles. The Keuper is noted for its record of land life, especially the fossil bones of amphibians and reptiles
that inhabited Europe in late Triassic time.

So it was that by the middle of the nineteenth century certain paleontologists who enjoyed the pleasures of fieldwork in the picturesque
countryside of southern Germany, and who studied and described the
fossils found by them or by their associates, had named several dinosaurs from the Keuper beds. Some rather large, heavy bones were
called *Plateosaurus* by H. von Meyer, a famous paleontologist, in
1837. Other Keuper bones, almost equally large, were given the name
of *Teratosaurus* by this same author in 1861, while a few years earlier
in 1857, Ludwig Rütimeyer, a man prominent in the early annals of
European paleontology, had designated still other large bones from
the Keuper beds as *Gresslyosaurus*. During this same period two English students, Riley and Stutchbury, had described some rather small
dinosaurs from the Keuper beds of England, in 1836 naming these
fossils *Thecodontosaurus* and *Palaeosaurus*. These several genera of
dinosaurs, plus some others that came to light during this initial
phase of exploration and study, gave evidence of the fact that dinosaurs lived widely across Europe during late Triassic time.

The last few words of the preceding sentence are worth noting. The
oldest dinosaurs of Europe were found in Upper Triassic Keuper sediments, and not in any rocks of earlier age. Of course, one would
hardly expect under normal circumstances to find dinosaurs in the
marine Muschelkalk rocks, although it seems quite possible that occasional carcasses of these land-living reptiles might have been washed
out to sea, to be deposited in near-shore sediments. Yet the few
records of Middle Triassic Muschelkalk dinosaurs in Europe are very
equivocal, at best. No dinosaurs were or have been found in the
Lower Triassic Buntsandstein beds. All of which indicates that the
oldest dinosaurs were essentially animals of late Triassic age, although it is possible that they may have first appeared at some date
during Middle Triassic history.

THE PLATEOSAURS OF TROSSINGEN

It was against this background of discovery and research that Friedrich von Huene began his work in the valley of the Neckar, and in

other parts of southern Germany, at about the turn of the century. Von Huene was an indefatigable and prodigious worker, and before the first decade of the present century had run its course he had published two large monographs on Triassic dinosaurs—one on those of Europe, one on those found outside Europe. He thereby established himself as the authority on the earliest of the dinosaurs.

It should be said that these earliest dinosaurs, so fully elucidated by von Huene, were all saurischians, characterized, among other things, by the more primitive of the two types of dinosaurian pelves. They seemed to show features that might be expected in ancestral saurischians; many of them were small or of medium size; many of them were clearly meat-eating carnivores, as indicated by their sharp, blade-like teeth; and many of them were dominantly bipedal animals that walked around on strong hind legs, with the short front legs terminating in strongly clawed hands serving as aids to feeding, and possibly defense.

The ancestry of these primitive dinosaurs would clearly seem to be found in some other Triassic reptiles known as pseudosuchians, some of which approach very closely the form and structure of the Keuper saurischians. Thus, as a result of the work done by early German paleontologists, greatly supplemented and expanded by the explorations and studies of von Huene, the answers to some of the questions posed at the beginning of this chapter seemed to be forthcoming.

This picture of the early saurischian dinosaurs and their ancestors had become reasonably well limned in the mind of von Huene by 1908, the year that his massive monograph on the Triassic dinosaurs of Europe was published. But he continued his studies of early dinosaurs and of other Triassic reptiles in the years after 1908—studies that resulted, as we have seen, in his strong support for Seeley's concept of basic dinosaurian relationships, published by von Huene in 1914, a year fateful for mankind throughout the world. The explosion of the First World War, with all its violence and horror, caught von Huene in its dread course. At the end of the great conflict von Huene, in many respects a most unworldly scientist, returned to his Triassic reptiles and especially his Triassic dinosaurs.

With the advent of the twenties, von Huene reached the climax in his investigations on the oldest dinosaurs. His monograph of 1908 had been a very thorough study, it is true, but it was based to a considerable extent upon the discoveries made by other men, upon fossil remains that were anything but complete. Would it not be most desirable to have complete skeletons of some of these ancient Triassic dinosaurs—skeletons that would provide a wealth of anatomical detail, skeletons that would furnish the answers, surely and several times over, to various questions concerning the nature of the oldest dinosaurs? It would; and this desirable advance in our knowledge of Keuper dinosaurs was brought about, under von Huene's guidance, on a sloping hillside overlooking a farm and a mill, in a wooded valley near Trossingen, a little town some thirty miles to the south of Tübingen. Here, where the valley of the Neckar comes to its southerly point between the highlands of the Black Forest and the Swabian Alps, von Huene made his greatest dinosaurian discovery.

It was during the summer of 1921 that the quarry at Trossingen was opened—a quarry that was to reveal an unprecedented concentration of *Plateosaurus* bones, some of them isolated within the sediments, many of them articulated as partial or essentially complete skeletons. It was a large operation, and it took time and the combined efforts of many people. Students from the university joined forces with skilled technicians from the Museum of Geology to excavate the bones—all these people working under the constant and close supervision of von Huene. As the quarry inched its way back into the sloping hillside, following the essentially level strata in which the fossils were preserved, the amount of rock to be removed became ever greater. The dedicated bone diggers labored with picks and shovels —frequently a dozen or more of them at a time—to tear down the overburden above the bones. A mine dump car was procured for hauling away the excess rock, and a track was laid down, running out from the quarry face. Day after day the work progressed, as the quarry face grew higher and the dump opposite it grew larger. And as the men worked into the hillside, a platform was built—formed in its inner part by the quarry floor and in its outer part by the talus materials of the dump.

By the end of the summer it became apparent to von Huene that the deposit was far from exhausted, so plans were made to continue the work through the next summer. Through the next summer the work went on, and through the summer after that. As a result of all this digging, some two thousand cubic meters of rock were removed, and thousands of bones were collected—singly and in articulated series contained within blocks of rock. Of course, the most modern methods of fossil collecting known at the time were utilized for the recovery of the bones. They were carefully exposed and hardened with shellac. The fossils were then covered with a protective layer of thin paper, and subsequently encased in jackets of burlap and plaster of Paris, to immobilize them in order that they might be trucked back north to Tübingen.

The operation was complicated by the fact that the bones were not in a single layer, but rather in two distinct horizons, labeled by von Huene most reasonably as the "upper bone bed" and the "lower bone bed," these two bone beds being separated by about three meters of unfossiliferous sediments. With characteristic German thoroughness, the bones were mapped, horizontally and vertically, as they were exposed in both beds, and each bone or group of bones that were packaged in plaster bandages had numbers assigned to them.

At the laboratory the encasing bandages of burlap and plaster were removed, the bones were carefully cleaned and further hardened, and any new bones that were discovered during this process (and these were numerous, because not everything immediately comes to light in the quarry) were inserted into their proper places in the numbered sequence of bones. Of course, all this work at the university kept von Huene and his skilled assistants busy for some years beyond the termination of the work at the quarry.

The results were impressive. A series of *Plateosaurus* skeletons was obtained, and in addition many partial skeletons and miscellaneous bones. Several skeletons were set up for display in Tübingen, and one very fine skeleton plus additional materials was shipped to the American Museum of Natural History in return for financial aid during the quarrying operation, supplied by the New York museum. This was help given by friends to a friend, by the museum through Henry Fairfield Osborn, William Diller Matthew and Barnum Brown (all of whom we shall meet in the next chapter) to von Huene, whom they had known and worked with for years.

All this material was studied in detail by von Huene, and described in various publications, to make clear upon the basis of abundant evidence the nature of one of the earliest dinosaurs. In effect, von Huene did for *Plateosaurus* what Dollo, years before, had done for the much younger dinosaur *Iguanodon*.

It was von Huene's conclusion that the concentration of *Plateosaurus* bones at Trossingen was the result of numerous members of a

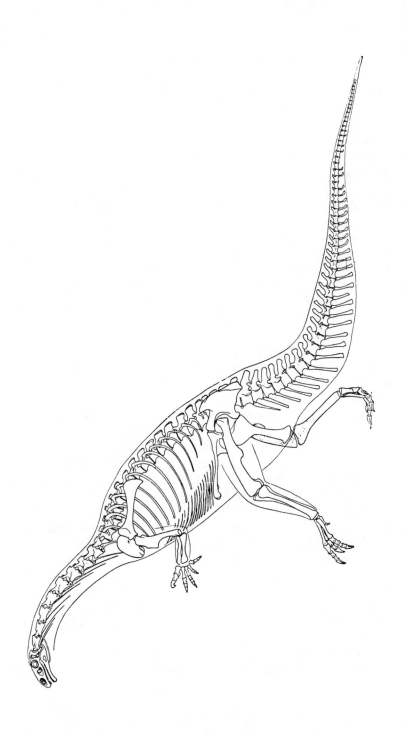

herd of these ancient dinosaurs having been overcome as they crossed a Triassic wasteland, during a migration from ancient highlands on the east, in what is now Bavaria, to the edge of the sea on the west, in what is now the borderland between Germany and France. This is one hypothesis that might account for the singular deposit of dinosaur bones near Trossingen, but there might be other explanations for the rich discovery made by von Huene and his associates. Here one enters the field of paleontological speculation, and a very uncertain field it is.

However that may be, the results were most satisfactory. The labors of von Huene and the technicians at Tübingen on the plateo-saurs from Trossingen truly added an important new chapter to the ever-growing story of dinosaurian evolution, a chapter that dealt with one of the dinosaurs that lived in Europe during the time when dino-surs were still in the early stages of their long history. Moreover, the digging at Trossingen, with the resultant work and study at Tübingen, was to bring about an unexpected expansion in our knowl-edge of these early dinosaurs, as we shall see.

It is interesting how, in the search for fossils, discoveries in one place will often lead to similar discoveries elsewhere. Such finds are not always the result of coincidence, for an important and spectacular collection of fossils from one particular region certainly stimulates fossil hunters in other regions, where rocks of the same age and type are exposed, to look with renewed energy and knowing eyes for sim-ilar fossils. Sometimes these subsequent searches for fossil treasures pay off.

Of course, von Huene's great plateosaur quarry at Trossingen at-tracted worldwide attention among paleontologists, especially among those men interested in dinosaurs. So it was that not many years after the dinosaurs from Trossingen had emerged from their age-old inter-ment to be reborn on the printed page, a group of Chinese geologists discovered similar dinosaurs, in rocks of the same age, in western

Figure 21. Von Huene's reconstruction of the skeleton of *Plateosaurus,* from Trossingen, southern Germany. This is the basis for the life restoration seen in Plate 37

China. These fossiliferous deposits, the now famous Lufeng Series, were first recognized by M. N. Bien in the late thirties near the city of Lufeng, which is some forty miles to the northwest of Kunming, the capital city of Yunnan Province. Bien, a paleontologist of experience (it was he who found the first fossils of Peking Man some ten years before this discovery of dinosaurs at Lufeng), immediately got in touch with his colleague Dr. Chung Chien Young, the leading vertebrate paleontologist of China. Young and Bien examined the site together and made plans for systematically quarrying the area. Their quarrying operations, carried out on a large scale immediately preceding the Second World War, revealed a rich association of fossils. There were various reptiles, dominated by a large series of saurischian dinosaurs of different types. What was particularly exciting to the Chinese paleontologists was the presence here of some extraordinarily important mammal-like reptiles, those unreptilian reptiles that stand on the threshold leading to the earliest mammals. To students of mammalian evolution the Lufeng locality is famous for these mammal-like reptiles; to students of dinosaurs the locality is equally famous for its wealth of saurischian remains.

Among these dinosaurs were found bones and complete skeletons of a plateosaur, very close indeed to *Plateosaurus* from Trossingen. Dr. Young considered it sufficiently different, however, to warrant a separate name, so he christened it *Lufengosaurus huenei,* after the locality at which it was found, and in honor of Professor von Huene. This particular Chinese dinosaur in truth duplicates the German form, and shows that during late Triassic times the plateosaurs spread far and wide across the Northern Hemisphere.

But the extent of their distribution was even broader than this east-to-west range across the breadth of Eurasia, a distance of some six thousand miles. For in the Upper Triassic rocks of South Africa there have been found plateosaurs, thereby demonstrating that these dinosaurs extended as widely in a north-to-south direction as they did from east to west. Among these South African dinosaurs is one genus very closely related to the German dinosaur, and named *Plateosauravus*—by von Huene.

In the end von Huene's special interest in plateosaurs, the result of his remarkable excavations at Trossingen, had worldwide effects. He published a large monograph on *Plateosaurus;* one of the Trossingen skeletons went to New York; a plateosaur from western China was named in his honor; and he in turn gave a new name to a plateosaur from South Africa. Here is a nice example of the fact that dinosaurs and dinosaur hunters are internationally oriented.

RICHARD SWANN LULL AND
THE CONNECTICUT VALLEY DINOSAURS

During those years when von Huene was collecting and studying the fossil remains of Europe's oldest dinosaurs, his contemporary and friend, Richard Swann Lull, was similarly engaged in a roundup of North America's oldest dinosaurs, specifically those that are to be found in the Connecticut Valley of New England. Lull worked separately, but parallel to von Huene, as so often happens in the study of paleontology. Thus each man complemented the other, and together they revealed the nature of those early dinosaurs now found across the wide longitudes of the Northern Hemisphere, as well as something of the Triassic world in which those ancient dinosaurs lived.

Lull was born in 1867 at Annapolis, Maryland, where his father, Captain E. P. Lull, was at the time on the teaching staff of the United States Naval Academy. The elder Lull had graduated from the academy in the class of 1855; Lull's mother was the daughter of General Henry Burton. Young Richard Lull grew up in a family in which there was a strong tradition of military service, and thus from an early age it was his ambition to follow a career in the navy. Alas! The best laid plans will, according to the old saw, often go astray, and such was to be the case with Richard Lull's hopes for a naval career. As a result of an adolescent illness his hearing was permanently impaired, which made him ineligible as a candidate for the Naval Academy.

So, instead of going to Annapolis, he entered Rutgers University, where as an undergraduate he distinguished himself both as a scholar interested in zoology and as an athlete. He was tall, over six feet in height, and strong; a natural star on the football field and at track meets. He played football in the days when the participants in that rugged sport were truly men of iron, and he played on a team that was famous in the annals of the game. As a sophomore he won a gold medal for oratory, an event prophetic of his great ability as a lecturer in later years.

In 1896, after his graduation from Rutgers, Lull worked for some time as a government entomologist, and then went to Amherst, Massachusetts, to teach entomology at the Massachusetts Agricultural College (now the university). This determined his future career. At the neighboring institution in the same town, Amherst College, was the great collection of Triassic dinosaur footprints made in earlier years by Professor Hitchcock. The tracks, although some decades before the objects of so much attention, were at the time of Lull's arrival in Amherst sadly neglected. Lull became interested in them, began a new study of the collection, and as a result determined to become a paleontologist.

In 1899 he joined the American Museum party working at the Bone Cabin Quarry in Wyoming (a noted paleontological venture of which more will be told in the chapter to follow), and helped to excavate the great brontosaur skeleton collected by that expedition. He then entered Columbia University as a graduate student, working with the already extensive collections at the American Museum, and obtained his doctorate under the guidance of Professor Henry Fairfield Osborn.

This took place in 1903. He returned to Amherst, but three years later he moved to Yale University, where he spent the remainder of his long life. In due course he rose to a full professorship at that venerable institution, and, following in the footsteps of Marsh (whom he never met), in 1922 became Director of the Peabody Museum.

Lull was, above all, a great teacher. Tall and very distinguished in appearance (in which respect he may be compared with von Huene), he had a commanding presence on the lecture platform, a vast knowledge of his subject, and a facility with language that had been foreshadowed in his student days at Rutgers. His course on Organic Evolution was one of the most popular courses ever given at Yale, attended by hundreds of students, augmented on many occasions by visitors who filled the auditorium to overflowing. He was also a noted mentor of graduate students.

In addition to his career as a distinguished teacher, Lull established himself as a museum man with a particular flair for the development of outstanding exhibits. During his tenure the old Peabody Museum was demolished, and a new structure was erected, in the planning and development of which Lull had a guiding hand. He devised many novel exhibition techniques, and was especially concerned with the execution of the "Great Hall" of the museum, dominated by a huge brontosaur skeleton,

Thirdly—Lull was equally distinguished in three aspects of his career; in a sense he had three careers—there was his work on dinosaurs, especially on the Triassic dinosaurs of the Connecticut Valley. Von Huene became an authority on the oldest dinosaurs in part at least because he was at Tübingen, surrounded by rocks containing the remains of dinosaurs and other Triassic reptiles; Lull became an avid student of the oldest dinosaurs first of all because of his initial interest in these fossils, aroused by his work on the tracks at Amherst, and secondly because during a large part of his life he was at New Haven, at the bottom of the Connecticut Valley, where he could continue at length his detailed studies on the bones and the footprints that had been found up and down the extent of that beautiful New England depression. Like von Huene, Lull fell heir to a large background of knowledge based upon the work done by his predecessors, because in New England, as well as in Europe, the study of geology and of fossils was well established during the early days of the nineteenth century.

Mention of Lull's predecessors brings back to the scene that noted and eccentric paleontologist Othniel Charles Marsh. To date, just five species of dinosaurs have been described from the Triassic rocks of the Connecticut Valley on the basis of bony remains, which are remarkably scarce there, even though footprints occur by the thousands. Marsh was the author of three of these.

The prize among the skeletons or bony remains of Connecticut Valley dinosaurs is a fairly complete skeleton, perhaps six or seven feet in length, christened by Marsh *Anchisaurus colurus.* It came to light in a stone quarry near Manchester, Connecticut, a discovery that epitomizes most of the finds of reptile bones that have been made in the Triassic rocks of New England. In short, they generally have turned up during the course of commercial quarrying. And why have not fossil quarries been developed, similar to von Huene's productive dig at Trossingen? The answer is simple; fossil bones are not common enough in Connecticut Valley rocks to justify such a procedure. Since they are quite rare and scattered in occurrence, about the only hope of finding them is to keep an eye on large rock-moving operations, like the development of a quarry or the digging of a road cut, in the hope that something may turn up. Usually it doesn't, but once in the proverbial blue moon a fossil does appear. In the expansive days of the late nineteenth century, when "brownstone" (Triassic sandstone) buildings by the thousands were being erected in New York and other eastern cities, there was some slight chance of now and then finding a Connecticut Valley dinosaur. Today, alas, brownstone is not at all popular in the architectural world, and so the opportunities for ancient dinosaurs from this source have accordingly diminished. As for modern roadcuts, of which there are many and of great size, the work is all done by dynamite and huge machines. Consequently the forces of destruction are great, and the opportunities for a discerning eye to

Figure 22. The skeleton of *Anchisaurus,* a Triassic dinosaur from the Connecticut Valley, as reconstructed by Marsh

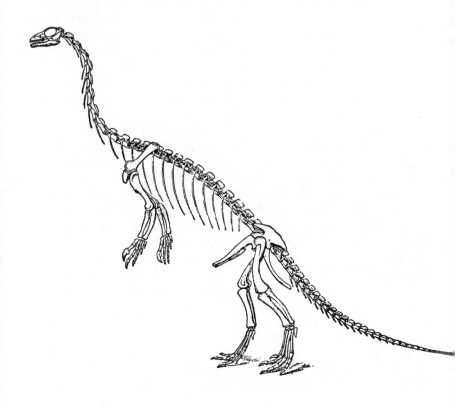

search out elusive fossils are almost nonexistent. It is to be noted that most of the dinosaur bones from the Connecticut Valley were discovered during the last half of the nineteenth century.

To get back to *Anchisaurus colurus,* this skeleton presents a very nice example of a primitive Triassic dinosaur. In effect it is very similiar to, although smaller than, the skeletons of *Plateosaurus* excavated by von Huene in Germany. It demonstrates the ubiquity of the primitive saurischian "basic patent"—the prototype for the earliest of these dinosaurs that was widely spread across the surface of the Triassic globe. As a footnote, it should be added that von Huene studied this skeleton many years after Marsh, and rechristened it *Yaleosaurus,* a name that may or may not be valid.

Of Marsh's other two species, both were found in the same quarry as *Anchisaurus* (or *Yaleosaurus*) *colurus.* Marsh named them *Anchisaurus solus* and *Ammosaurus major.* The story of the latter specimen has caused many a pang in the heart of many a bone digger. As mentioned, the fossil was discovered in the quarry at Manchester, Connecticut, operated at the time by Charles O. Wolcott. But it was discovered too late; when found it consisted only of the back part of the skeleton, the front part being in a block or some blocks that already had been removed from the quarry. As Lull has sadly noted, the front part of this skeleton "was built into the abutments of a bridge before the full value was realized. . . . Professor Marsh tried in vain to locate the block containing the specimen, but, when it became evident that little short of the total destruction of the abutments might be necessary, the search was given up and the bridge still has the unique distinction of being the mausoleum of a dinosaur" (Lull, 1953, page 125).

The circumstances of discovery of the other two known Connecticut Valley dinosaurs, the earliest and the latest to be described, are also interesting—they are as completely accidental as the discoveries made in Mr. Wolcott's quarry. The first of these dinosaurian bones were found at Springfield, Massachusetts, and came to the attention of none other than the elder Hitchcock, who had so assiduously searched for, excavated, and described the many dinosaur tracks that he thought were the evidence of ancient birds in the land. Says Hitchcock:

"The Springfield bones were discovered by William Smith, Esq., while engaged in superintending some improvements at the water shops of the United States Armory, which required blasting. He did not discover them till a large part had been taken away by the workmen. [This has a sad and very familiar ring.] General Whitney, superintendent of the armory, very kindly ordered a re-examination of the fragments, and Mr. Smith obligingly presented me with whatever pieces could be found. These I put into the hands of Professor Jeffries Wyman. . . ." (Hitchcock, quoted by Lull, 1953, page 99.)

So the bones, such of them as were left, to be described as *Anchisaurus polyzelus,* were made available for posterity.

As for the last of the Connecticut Valley dinosaurs to be described, this particular specimen, a partial skeleton of a very small dinosaur, came to the attention of Miss (Dr.) Mignon Talbot, Professor of Geology at Mount Holyoke College, in 1911.

"In a bowlder of Triassic sandstone which the glacier carried two or three miles, possibly, and deposited not far from the site of Mount Holyoke College, the writer recently found an excellently preserved skeleton of a small dinosaur. . . . The bowlder was split along the plane in which the fossil lies and part of the bones are in one half and part in the other. These bones are hollow and the whole framework is very light and delicate" (Talbot, quoted by Lull, 1953, page 131).

Miss Talbot made a study of the skeleton, and published a scientific description, naming it *Podokesaurus holyokensis.* But although this was a small and fragile fossil, coming to the attention of a distinguished lady with a delicately feminine name, it seems destined to have had a violent history. In the first place, it had been plucked from its original resting place by the fingers of a gigantic glacier, riding over the Connecticut landscape many thousands of years ago. Then the rock in which the fossil was entombed was split—a fortunate accident, since the specimen was thus exposed to view, but nevertheless an accident that did violence to the skeleton, breaking it into two halves. Finally, some years after Miss Talbot had studied the dinosaur, it was—alas!—completely destroyed in a fire that in 1916 rav-

---

Figure 23. A geologic map of the Connecticut Valley, showing the area of Triassic sediments (diagonal lines) and the exposures of Triassic volcanic rocks (solid black). This is the region worked so assiduously by Edward Hitchcock, and subsequently explored and studied by Marsh and by Lull. It is the region of untold thousands of dinosaur footprints, and a few skeletons

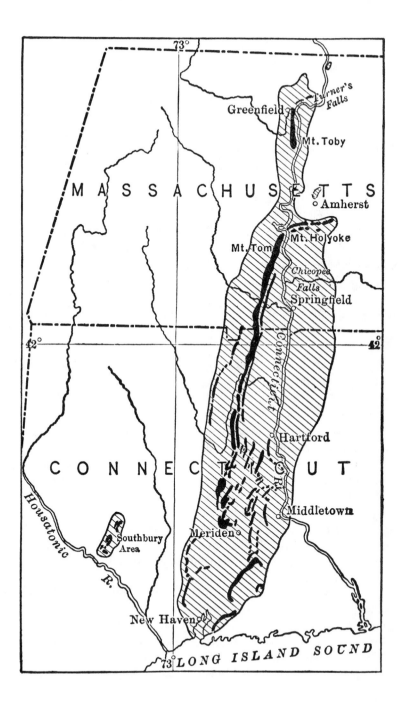

73°

Turner's Falls

Greenfield

Mt. Toby

MASSACHUSETTS

o Amherst

Mt. Tom

Mt. Holyoke

Chicopee Falls

Springfield

42°   42°

Connecticut

C O N N E C T I C U T

Hartford

C. R.

Middletown

Southbury Area

Meriden

Housatonic R.

New Haven

73° LONG ISLAND SOUND

aged Williston Hall, containing the geological museum of the college.

There is one moderately happy sequel to this story of misfortune. Luckily a cast of the skeleton had been made by the Yale Museum, and so a three dimensional record of the fossil is preserved, in addition to the description and the various figures that were made of it. Of course a cast is not as good as an original, but then something is better than nothing.

This story of the oldest dinosaurs of the Connecticut Valley has so far been largely a tale of Lull's predecessors, particularly Hitchcock and Marsh. But it has indicated something of the background on which Lull based his work. With these previously made collections and studies, to be used as a broad base on which to build a superstructure, Lull threw himself wholeheartedly and with much energy into the interpretation of ancient life of the Connecticut Valley. It was a labor that occupied him for years, and in the end resulted in the publication of his monograph on *Triassic Life of the Connecticut Valley.*

In this work, first published in 1915 and published again as a very much revised edition in 1953, Lull presented a full interpretation of the fossils—all the fossils—that had ever been found in the Triassic rocks of the Connecticut Valley. He drew a picture of an ancient world based upon plant remains, upon the indications of insects and other animals without backbones, upon the fishes, and upon the various reptiles, especially the dinosaurs. His interpretation of these oldest dinosaurs was concerned in part with the bones, scattered and few as they were, and in a very large part with the thousands of footprints and trackways, to which he gave a great deal of attention. He completely revised Hitchcock's old study of the tracks upon the firm knowledge that most of them had been made by ancient dinosaurs that many millions of years ago inhabited what is now a beautiful New England valley.

Thus did Lull make his contribution to our knowledge of the oldest dinosaurs. His was a study done largely within the confines of the laboratory, by a man who spent many hours with the fossil bones at hand, and a very great many more hours poring over large slabs of sandstone in which were the imprints of strange feet. When we think of the oldest dinosaurs of North America, we think of Richard Swann

Lull, just as when we think of the oldest dinosaurs of Europe, we think of Friedrich von Huene.

THE LITTLE DINOSAURS OF NEW MEXICO

Furthermore, when we think of the oldest dinosaurs in North America, we must also give a thought once again to Edward Drinker Cope. Cope had nothing to do with the dinosaurs of the Connecticut Valley —his attention was turned in directions other than toward Marsh's front yard. One of these directions was New Mexico, where Cope was very active in the field.

In New Mexico, Cope had a trusted assistant—one David Baldwin. Baldwin was something of an original character, a local collector of great acumen, proud of his efforts in the field and more than a little interested in their results. He had originally collected for Marsh, but in time he became dissatisfied with his employer at New Haven, in part at least because he felt that Marsh did not recognize the importance of his finds. So he transferred his allegiance to Cope.

David Baldwin's field techniques were in some ways a bit unusual; he liked to work during the dead of winter. Of course it was cold, often bitterly cold. But there was snow on the ground, and this provided moisture wherever he went—oftentimes a rare necessity in the middle of the desert summer. So Baldwin would go out by himself, with only a burro as a companion, and dig for fossils. In northwestern New Mexico there is a little town, a rather ancient town for the New World, with the unusual name of Abiquiu—and this was headquarters for Baldwin's operations during several years. He generally worked to the north and west of Abiquiu, where colorful cliffs of Permian and Mesozoic rocks rise into the thin blue air, and where there are many miles of Triassic exposures to be explored.

It was in this region that Baldwin discovered some scraps of early dinosaurs, which he packed and shipped off to Cope in Philadelphia with the following notation:

"Label Sack 2 Box 1 Prof. E. D. Cope Contains Triassic or Jurassic bones all small and tender. Those marked little bones are many of them almost microscopic All in this sack found in same place about four hundred feet below gypsum stratum 'Arroyo Seco' Rio Arriba Co New Mexico February 1881. No feet—no head—only one tooth
D. Baldwin—Abiquiu."

The bones were certainly "small and tender," and there could be little doubt as to their Triassic age. Cope quickly recognized them for what they were—the bones of some very small, lightly built carnivorous dinosaurs. It was a miscellaneous assortment—leg bones, vertebrae, pelvic bones, bits of ribs, and the like—and Cope thought he could sort the lot into three species. He did—and named two of them in honor of Marsh assistants, whom he regarded highly. These were *Coelophysis bauri* (after George Baur) and *Coelophysis willistoni* (after Samuel Wendell Williston). The third species he named *Coelophysis longicollis* (in reference to the long neck).

For threescore years *Coelophysis* remained an enigmatic little dinosaur, sometimes noted (but that is about all) in the literature dealing with these ancient reptiles. Then, in 1947, an expedition from the American Museum of Natural History discovered a concentration of *Coelophysis* bones along the Arroyo Seco that David Baldwin had mentioned in his notes. (This section of the Arroyo Seco now lies within a delightful establishment known as Ghost Ranch.) The de-

---

Figure 24. David Baldwin's label, enclosed with the first bones to be discovered of *Coelophysis,* the Triassic dinosaur from New Mexico, described by Cope

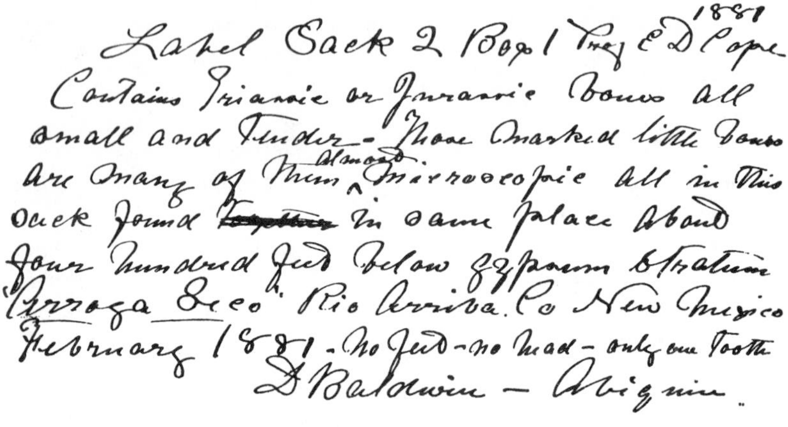

Figure 25. The Triassic dinosaur *Coelophysis*, as restored upon the basis of complete skeletons discovered by The American Museum of Natural History. Restoration by Lois Darling

posit was explored with scratchers and awls, as fossil bone deposits are often probed during the first preliminary investigations of a site, and the more the probing, the more it became apparent that here was a remarkably rich fossil bed, consisting not of single bones, but of articulated skeletons.

A large scallop consequently was cut into the hillside containing the almost horizontal bone bed, in order to expose the top of the layer. As the layer was exposed it revealed a most remarkable dinosaurian graveyard, in which there were literally scores of skeletons, one on top of another and interlaced with one another. It would appear that some local catastrophe had overtaken these dinosaurs, so that they all died together and were buried together.

Here were some of the most complete dinosaur skeletons ever discovered, constituting some of the best evidence ever obtained on early Triassic saurischian dinosaurs, and probably the most complete information presently available concerning one species of Triassic dinosaurs. In this agglomeration of mixed-up skeletons were individuals of all ages, from very young animals to full-grown adults. The little dinosaurs of Ghost Ranch show quite clearly that all of the *Coelophysis* from the Upper Triassic rocks of this region can be assigned to a single species, the proper name of which is *Coelophysis bauri*. The differences that Cope had seen in his materials, thought by him to represent differences between several species, were simply the variations within one species due to growth, the variations that one would expect between young and old individuals.

So it is that what we now know about the oldest dinosaurs of North America comes from the two sides of the continent, from the eastern seaboard and from the far Southwest. And this knowledge, the result of work by Hitchcock, Marsh, Cope, and later workers, adds much valued information to the interpretations of the oldest dinosaurs of Eurasia.

EARLY DINOSAURS IN THE SOUTHERN HEMISPHERE

Much more could be said about the oldest dinosaurs, and about the men who have found them and worked on them. The rest of the story will be limited, however, to two groups of discoveries in two regions—Argentina and South Africa. Both are especially significant in the early history of dinosaurian evolution.

Within recent years there have been found in northwestern Argentina the bones of what may be the oldest dinosaurs as yet discovered. These fossils represent primitive saurischians, similar in many respects to some of the earliest dinosaurs from Eurasia, Africa, and North America. The crux of the matter has to do with the age of the beds from which these fossils have been recovered. Some authorities think that they are of Middle Triassic age, which if true would certainly make the Argentinian dinosaurs the oldest on record. Other authorities believe that these particular Argentinian rocks, known as the Ischigualasto beds, are of late Triassic age, but probably represent the very beginning of late Triassic time. Even if this later dating is correct, the dinosaurs from Argentina probably still are the oldest of

Figure 26. Map of North America, showing localities of certain important and historic dinosaur localities. (1) Triassic of the Connecticut Valley. (2) Triassic of northern New Mexico. (3) Jurassic, Como Bluff. (4) Jurassic, Canyon City. (5) Jurassic, Dinosaur National Park. (6) Jurassic, Howe Quarry. (7) Cretaceous, Red Deer River, Alberta

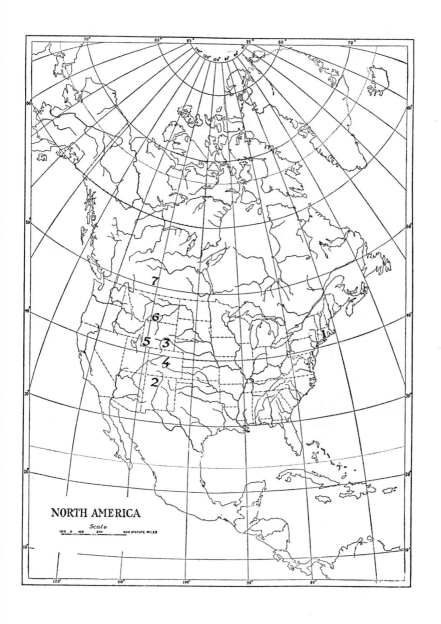

NORTH AMERICA

Scale

100   0   100   200   600 STATUTE MILES

known dinosaurs. Here, perhaps, is a record close to the beginning of saurischian history.

Also, within recent years, there have been found in the Upper Triassic rocks of South Africa the oldest known ornithischian dinosaurs. These discoveries, made by Dr. A. W. Crompton, formerly director of the South African Museum, now the successor of Marsh and Lull as director of the Yale Peabody Museum, and described by him in collaboration with Dr. Alan Charig of the British Museum, carry ornithischian history back to a point in geologic time as ancient as the beginnings of the saurischian dinosaurs. It is a great step forward in our knowledge of the ornithischians, the earliest ones of which heretofore have been from Lower Jurassic rocks. It reveals the ancient ornithischians as very like some of the ancient saurischians in some respects—they are small, bipedal reptiles. But they have the characteristic pelvis that sets them apart from the saurischians, and the chacteristic skull, with leaflike teeth that show them to be the true ancestors of the dominantly herbivorous ornithischians.

So it is that through the past century our concept of the oldest dinosaurs has taken form. It has been the work of many men—of the mid-nineteenth-century pioneer paleontologists, and after them of Marsh and Cope, of von Huene and Lull, and of the workers of this modern age. All these men have made their contributions to the fascinating opening chapter of dinosaurian evolutionary history, to the problem of what the oldest dinosaurs were like and where they came from. Of all these men, the one man who stands out with particular prominence as the most persistent hunter for the oldest dinosaurs, and the most voluminously productive student of these reptiles, is Friedrich von Huene of Tübingen.

CHAPTER 6

JURASSIC GIANTS OF THE WESTERN WORLD

OSBORN AND HIS ASSOCIATES

The explorations and studies by Marsh and by Cope in the plains and mountains of western North America, and the extended research by Dollo on the iguanodonts from Bernissart, had revealed to Victorian man a lost world of giant reptiles, known not from parts of dinosaurs, but from complete, articulated skeletons, often to be found in considerable abundance. The dinosaurs, hitherto known from the bones or the parts of skeletons that had been described by Buckland, Mantell, Owen, Leidy, and other pioneer students in this field of knowledge, were now emerging from the mists of obscurity as a full panoply of impressive skeletons—skeletons so nicely preserved, with the bones associated in their proper contiguities, that there were few doubts as to the osseous structure of these ancient animals. To a competent anatomist it was no great task to clothe the bones with reptilian muscles, and over the muscles to stretch a reptilian skin. Thus the form and appearance of the dinosaurs could be rather accurately realized—

perhaps the only question unanswered was that of their color. In truth the dinosaurs came alive during those last two decades of the nineteenth century.

The arrival of dinosaur skeletons of various and oftentimes weird aspect in the halls and laboratories at New Haven and Philadelphia and Brussels naturally stimulated intense interest among the men of science throughout Europe and North America. Reports on the fossil finds were published in scientific journals and presented at scientific meetings, and from such reports, especially of the latter kind, which were easily available to the gentlemen of the press, the excitement of the new discoveries was passed on to the public. Thus the English weekly *Punch* published in 1890 a cartoon showing Marsh as a circus ringmaster, bedecked in stars and stripes, presiding over a troupe of performing skeletons. He is seen standing on an enormous *Triceratops* skull, which is the platform from which he extends his authority over the extinct beasts. With interest in the dinosaurian giants continuing among men of science, it was inevitable that the fossil fields, especially those in North America explored with such spectacular results by Marsh and Cope, would receive further attention.

At this place the American Museum of Natural History in New York enters the story. This museum, today perhaps the largest natural-history museum in the world, was founded shortly after the Civil War by a group of public-spirited men in the City of New York who felt that the burgeoning metropolis deserved to have within its borders a great museum, devoted to the natural world that was so rapidly, even in those seemingly bucolic days, drawing ever farther away from the experience of the urban dweller. The museum accordingly was established and for some years it was housed in the old Arsenal within the southeast corner of Central Park, not far from the place where Waterhouse Hawkins' ill-fated Paleozoic Museum was to have been built. In due course of time it moved into the first wing of what was later to become an enormous complex of buildings on the west side of the park. The beginnings were relatively modest, which is in the nature of many beginnings, and for some years the only remains of extinct backboned animals to be seen in the museum were the skeleton of an Irish Elk, a large deer characterized by enormous antlers, that lived during the last ice age, and the skeleton of a Moa, a gigantic flightless bird that inhabited New Zealand within the past few thousand years.

And now Henry Fairfield Osborn, not only an outstanding paleontologist who devoted considerable attention to the dinosaurs, but also an administrator whose life was inextricably interwoven with the development of the museum, comes on the scene. But let us go back in time a bit.

Osborn was born in 1857 at Fairfield, Connecticut, into a family of considerable wealth—his father was a financier and an organizer of the Illinois Central Railroad. Consequently he grew up with certain advantages and requisites not available to the average lad. As a young man he was enrolled as a student at the College of New Jersey, now Princeton University, where he became the inseparable friend of another undergraduate, William Berryman Scott. Their friendship was destined to last through their lifetimes; both men were to become great paleontologists.

It all began on a warm June day in 1876, when Osborn, Scott, and a third crony, Francis Speir, were resting in the shade of a tree, after having been swimming in a canal near Princeton. It was examination time, and the three young men were relaxing from their arduous studies. Scott had recently read an article by O. C. Marsh, describing one of his collecting trips in the Far West, so the young undergraduate rather idly proposed to his fellows that they go out to collect fossils, in which they had recently developed an interest, the result of a course in geology at Princeton under Professor Guyot. To Scott's surprise the others took the suggestion seriously, and to make a long story short, preparations were begun and carried to completion during the ensuing academic year for an expedition to the Bridger Basin in Wyoming, in the summer of 1877. The three of them, accompanied by a coterie of other students whom they had interested in the project made their way west by rail, and then ventured into a land that was still largely uninhabited and untamed. It was a remarkably successful expedition, and was followed by others during the next two summers.

Osborn and Scott thus began their paleontological careers—in an atmosphere of considerable romance and a certain amount of high adventure. In his old age Scott liked to tell about those far-distant days and that far-distant land, almost neolithic it would seem in comparison with the middle-twentieth-century world into which he survived. They traveled by horseback and by wagon. They saw Indians. They even saw some of the old mountain men, survivors of the halcyon days of the fur trade, one of whom said to Osborn (who was blessed with a nose of generous proportions, at the moment burned to a fiery red by the intense western sun), "Young feller— either you had better pull out the brim of your hat or pull in your nose." [1] The two embryonic paleontologists had many exciting experiences, and they gained an appreciation for the field relationships of fossils that was important to their studies throughout their lives.

At this stage in their careers, Osborn and Scott became fervent disciples of Cope. Before setting forth on their first expedition to the Bridger Basin badlands, they had journeyed to Philadelphia, to get some advice from Cope. The first meeting was a rather cool one— Cope seemed to be a bit suspicious of the young men who were so avid to venture into territory that perhaps he thought of as his own, but subsequent meetings and the obvious goodwill of the young men prevailed, so that in short order the two young paleontologists were taken into the complete confidence of the Quaker naturalist, to establish a close friendship that prevailed until the day of his death—in 1897. Cope was in a very real sense the paleontological guiding light to Scott and to Osborn, and it was quite inevitable that they became involved to a considerable degree in the bitter and prolonged scientific feud that had developed between Cope and Marsh. They worshiped and respected Cope; they certainly did not respect Marsh. Needless to say the feeling was reciprocated by Marsh.

It has been told how once when Osborn and Scott went to Yale to look at some fossils, Marsh gave instructions to his assistants to see that all of the new and choice fossils were hidden away, where the two graduate students from Princeton could not see them. Then Marsh, donning a pair of soft carpet slippers, trailed Osborn and Scott around the museum, hiding himself behind storage cases, and peeking out to make sure that the visitors were confining themselves within those areas of the establishment to which they were supposed to be limited.

Even in his very old age, the mention of Marsh's name could inspire Scott to profanity.

After graduate school at Princeton, both Scott and Osborn went to Europe, where they studied under Huxley in London and under Francis Balfour, the famous embryologist, in Cambridge. Further

---

[1] As related to the author by Professor Scott.

studies were carried on in Germany. Both young men then returned to Princeton, to join the faculty of the university. Scott spent the rest of his life at Princeton, but in 1891 Osborn accepted an offer to join the staff of the American Museum of Natural History, as well as the faculty of Columbia University in New York. At the museum he founded the Department of Vertebrate Paleontology; at Columbia he was instrumental in founding the Department of Zoology and the Graduate School. He was for a quarter of a century the president of the museum, during which time, largely owing to his efforts, the institution grew into an immense organization, of worldwide fame. He enjoyed a long life of almost unprecedented scientific triumphs in New York; in fact, Osborn became quite a public figure in his mature years and old age. But that is a story in itself; here we are interested in Osborn, the museum, and dinosaurs.

Soon after he was established at the museum in New York, Osborn brought to his new department a group of men who were to become famous in the history of North American paleontology. One was Dr. Jacob Wortman, formerly an assistant to Cope, a man trained in medicine who had turned his attention to fossil vertebrates. Wortman, a taciturn man of rather saturnine appearance, was a complex individual who never remained long with any one institution. His was a peripatetic scientific career; finally he seemed to have become fed up with fossils (a most unusual reaction among paleontologists), and in 1908 he quit, went to Brownsville, Texas, where he established a drugstore, and remained there until the day of his death, almost twenty years later. Another was Dr. William Diller Matthew, who had just completed his graduate studies at Columbia University, and who was to be for many years the mainstay of the museum department. Still another was Walter Granger, a lanky youth from Vermont. And still another was Barnum Brown, a young man just graduated from the University of Kansas.

BONE CABIN

One of the first large field projects by the Department of Vertebrate Paleontology at the museum, working under the close guidance of Osborn, was a new exploration of the Jurassic Morrison beds at Como Bluff, Wyoming, among the sediments from which Marsh had reaped such a rich harvest. Osborn had at least three reasons for venturing

into the Como Bluff locality. In the first place he was intensely interested in Mesozoic mammals, and it was at Quarry 9, Como Bluff, that
Marsh's men had collected the only Mesozoic mammals then known
from North America. In the second place Osborn wanted to get some
big dinosaurs for the museum. The astute Osborn realized that while
the collecting of some Mesozoic mammals would be of great scientific
importance, directly in line with his own interests, the capture of
some big dinosaurs would be extraordinarily helpful in promoting the
welfare of the department and of the museum. Nothing succeeds like
success. A museum with a display of large dinosaurs would attract an
immense amount of public attention; this in turn would engender
support—both of the moral and of the substantial financial kind. Finally and thirdly, Osborn, a keen student of fossil reptiles, was gen-
uinely interested in dinosaurs.

Thus plans were made for a collecting program at Como Bluff, to
begin with the summer of 1897. The story of the work of the American Museum of Natural History in the Morrison beds of Wyoming
makes an interesting chapter in North American paleontological history. Moreover, it makes a nice example of how a campaign for the
acquisition of fossils is planned, how it develops, and how it finally
terminates—sometimes not quite in the way that was originally foreseen. In short, here is a case history of fossil hunting, and what is
especially pertinent at this place, of dinosaur hunting.

The first expedition, of 1897, composed of Dr. Wortman, Brown,
Granger, and H. W. Menke, an assistant, went to Como Bluff with
two objectives in mind. In the first place it was planned to reopen the
famous Jurassic mammal quarry, Quarry 9; second, an exploration of
the Morrison beds along the bluff would be carried out, in an attempt
to locate some dinosaur skeletons. Opening and working the mammal
quarry turned into quite a project. Marsh's parties had, as it were,
skimmed the cream from this deposit, so it was necessary for the
American Museum workers to remove a vast amount of "overburden"
as they followed the fossil level back into the cliff. The overburden
was taken down through weeks of hard work; the entire fossiliferous
layer thus uncovered was removed, boxed, and shipped back to the
museum, where subsequent work proved it to be barren. That aspect
of the summer campaign proved to be a fruitless operation.

But while the party was in the field, Osborn came out for a visit.
He and Barnum Brown went exploring along the bluff one day, and

had the good fortune to locate a dinosaur skeleton. Shortly after, Wortman located a second skeleton nearby. Thus, after the hard work of removing the mammal layer, the rest of the season was spent in excavating the two dinosaur skeletons.

The next summer the American Museum was again at Como Bluff, the party again led by Dr. Wortman. This year he was assisted by Walter Granger, Menke, and a new helper, Albert Thomson (who was to become one of the museum's most valued paleontological collectors and technicians, spending his life in the service of the institution). Work was begun in high hopes, but as the days wore on it became increasingly apparent that Como Bluff was not so rich in dinosaur skeletons as once it had been. The large number of fossils that had been removed had depleted the immediately available supply. It would be advantageous to wait for some years, until the inexorable forces of erosion should expose new fossil bones.

Late during the previous summer some exploratory excursions had been made on the Medicine Bow anticline, a ridge containing Morrison sediments, some miles to the north of Como Bluff. So with pickings thin along the classic Marsh hunting ground, the party removed to the north, and there, on June 12, 1898, the famous Bone Cabin Quarry was located.[2] At this spot the fossil hunters found a hillside literally covered with large fragments of dinosaur bones that had weathered out of the sediments composing the ridge. So abundant were the big indurated pieces of fossil bone that a sheepherder, regarding them as so many convenient building blocks, had constructed for himself a cabin of them. Hence the name "Bone Cabin." The party went to work, digging down into the surface of the hill, and as they dug, more and more bones came to light. In short, it was a veritable mine of dinosaur bones, and the fossil hunters spent a long summer and autumn there, removing paleontological treasures for shipment back to New York. The shipment was impressive. There were some sixty thousand pounds of bones that filled two special freight cars, these supplied through the munificence of J. Pierpont Morgan, the famous financier whose name generally is associated with gems, rare books, and works of art, rather than with dinosaur bones.

Through 1898, and seven successive years, parties from The Amer-

[2] It is possible, although this cannot be verified, that the Bone Cabin site was discovered in 1880 by Frank Williston, a brother of Samuel Wendell Williston. (See Ostrom and McIntosh, 1966, p. 37.)

ican Museum of Natural History worked the Bone Cabin Quarry, amassing a magnificent collection of Morrison dinosaurs, a collection that provided the skeletons forming the central theme of one of the two large dinosaur halls at the museum.

The details of the work, year by year, need not concern us. The personnel of the parties kept changing, but the digging went on, with developments that had hardly been expected when the operations were commenced. Thus, during the course of work at the Bone Cabin Quarry a second fossil locality was discovered as a result of side explorations, carried on in part perhaps to relieve some of the tedium of constant digging in one quarry. This was at the so-called Nine Mile Crossing of Little Medicine Creek, some five miles to the south of the Bone Cabin Quarry. A second camp was established here, and this "Nine Mile Quarry" was worked with profit, yielding a brontosaur skeleton. In 1900 it was thought that the Bone Cabin Quarry was "petering out," as one of the workers put it, so it seemed possible that only one more season of work could be carried on at this locality. The museum returned in 1901, and to the delightful surprise of the bone diggers new fossils came to light—to such an extent, in fact, that in the words of Walter Granger, in his annual report of work at Bone Cabin, "Altogether, the collection of 1901 is probably the most valuable yet taken from this remarkable quarry, and expectations were greatly exceeded, especially in regard to the area of bone bearing layer left unexplored." This is just one more example of the fact that bone diggers must work with open minds, ever ready to take advanttage of opportunities as they arise.

And a new opportunity did arise during that productive year of 1901, for who should appear at Bone Cabin but Bill Reed, the worthy railroad man, who, it will be recalled, had first found dinosaur bones a quarter of a century earlier at Como Bluff and had brought them to the attention of O. C. Marsh. Reed knew of a fresh prospect, and now he approached Walter Granger, who was this year in charge of the American Museum party, with the proposition that the museum extend to him a proper financial settlement for the discovery of this new locality, and for the privilege of working it. Negotiations entered into were soon concluded, with the result that the last two weeks of 1901 were spent at "Quarry R," located northwest of Rock Creek, some fourteen miles from Bone Cabin. It proved to be a good quarry, and plans were made to return to it the following summer.

So it was that early in the summer of 1902, Quarry R was reopened, and work was continued there during the first part of the season. It had been decided to dig here in the early part of the summer, because later on the available water would become scarce and foul (a bone digger has to think of many contingencies), and then to finish up the season at the Bone Cabin Quarry. This plan was carried out with good results, the party remaining at Bone Cabin Quarry until the second of November. Although it was becoming evident that bones were ever more scarce at Bone Cabin, still the locality deserved further excavation.

And this it got, during the season of 1903. Again work was begun at Quarry R, and then later in the summer continued at Bone Cabin. But now it was quite obvious that the fossil deposit at Bone Cabin was playing out. That autumn, as the season's haul was loaded in a freight car, again provided as in previous years by J. P. Morgan, it seemed as though the program of quarrying for dinosaurs at Bone Cabin, and indeed in the Medicine Bow anticline in general, had about reached its conclusion.

A final season was spent in the Medicine Bow region in 1905 by workers from The American Museum of Natural History, but with the end of that summer the great campaign to collect Jurassic giants for New York had come to a very definite end.

In this connection it is interesting to summarize the results of work at Como Bluff and along the Medicine Bow anticline for the years from 1898 through 1903. This makes a nice example of the development and decline of one particular fossil locality, a field that yielded a world-famous collection of Jurassic dinosaurs, large and small.

	NUMBER OF SPECIMENS COLLECTED	NUMBER OF BOXES SHIPPED	WEIGHT OF COLLECTION
Season of 1898	141	100	60,000 pounds
Season of 1899	132	70	40,000 pounds
Season of 1900	87	27	21,000 pounds
Season of 1901	54	44	No figures
Season of 1902	48	23	15,000 pounds
Season of 1903	21	11	10,000 pounds

The digging up of dinosaurian treasures along Como Bluff and the Medicine Bow anticline by the men from New York was destined to attract a lot of attention, from paleontologists and from the general public, too. And inevitably the acquisition by the museum in New York of such excellent dinosaurs started men at other museums to thinking about the possibilities of getting some Morrison dinosaurs of their own. There were no invasions of the Wyoming dinosaur field by other museum parties during the time the American Museum was engaged in this region, as there had been in the earlier years, when Cope's men "horned in" on the Marsh preserves. The collecting and study of fossils had become more regularized, one might say more civilized, during the interval between the time of the pioneer explorations by Marsh and Cope and the end of the century, when museums were planning and carrying on integrated and purposeful programs of paleontological research. Wealthy, independent, ambitious men, such as Marsh and Cope, might indulge in scientific vendettas, but these patterns of behavior would hardly suffice for institutions. Museums have long since learned to work together and to cooperate; it is the only sensible way for them to carry out their individual programs and build up their collections. So they respect each other's regions of interest, and this extends to fossil fields. None the less, there was interest on the part of other institutions in the program that was being carried on by the American Museum at Bone Cabin and adjacent regions.

One of these other institutions was the Carnegie Museum of Pittsburgh, a relatively young museum founded by the man whose name it honors. Carnegie Museum collectors were in Wyoming during at least one season when the American Museum parties were busily engaged at Bone Cabin, and on one occasion when the parties from the two museums were in the same general vicinity they got together for a big Sunday picnic. Little did the celebrants realize, on that jolly occasion, that the Carnegie Museum was destined eventually to amass one of the greatest—perhaps the greatest—assemblage of Jurassic dinosaurs ever made.

EARL DOUGLASS AND HIS GREAT QUARRY

Now another famous dinosaur hunter becomes an actor in this drama of digging up Jurassic giants in North America. The man was Earl Douglass, for many years a shining light in the annals of the Carnegie Museum.

Earl Douglass was born in Minnesota in 1862, and grew up in that state. As a young man he studied at the University of South Dakota and at the South Dakota Agricultural College, obtaining his Bachelor's degree from his latter institution in 1893. After teaching school for some years in Montana, followed by study at the University of Montana and a year at the Missouri Botanical Garden in St. Louis, he went to Princeton University on a fellowship, where he studied under Professor Scott. In 1902 he joined the staff of the Carnegie Museum.

During his first years at the Carnegie Museum he was very much occupied in a program of collecting and research on the early fossil mammals of Montana and Utah. In September, 1908, in the course of his season's work in the Uinta Basin of Utah, he was visited by Dr. W. J. Holland, the director of the Carnegie Museum. Dr. Holland has recalled a memorable result of that visit:

"One evening my admiration was excited by a brilliant sunset in which the lofty peaks of the Uinta Range to the northwest loomed up grandly. I remarked to him [Douglass] that a study of Hayden's Survey [Dr. F. V. Hayden had been the leader of one of the famous Territorial Surveys, immediately after the Civil War] disclosed the fact that in those mountains there were extensive exposures of Jurassic strata, and I said to him that we ought to find the remains of dinosaurs in that region. We decided that we would set forth early the next day with our team of mules and visit the foot-hills, where Hayden had indicated the presence of Jurassic exposures. We started shortly after dawn and spent a long day on the cactus-covered ridge of Dead Man's Bench, in making our way through the gullies and ravines to the north. At nightfall we found ourselves after descending a wild declivity by the edge of a small brooklet, where we slept under our blankets, while the mules grazed upon the scanty pasturage which was found at that spot. The next day we went forward through the broken foot-hills which lie east and south of the great gorge through which the Green River emerges from the Uinta Mountains on its course toward the Grand Canyon of Arizona. As we slowly made our way through stunted groves of pine we realized that we were upon Jurassic beds. We tethered our mules in the forest. Douglass went to the right and I to the left, scrambling up and down through the gullies in search of Jurassic fossils, with the understanding, that, if he found anything he was to discharge the shot gun which he carried, and, if I found anything, I would fire the rifle, which I carried. His shotgun was presently heard and after a somewhat toilsome walk in the direction of the sound I heard him shout. I came up to him standing beside the weathered-out femur of a Diplodocus lying at the bottom of a very narrow ravine into which it was difficult to descend. Whence this perfectly preserved bone had fallen, from what stratum of the many above us it had been washed, we failed to ascertain. But there it was, as clean and perfect as if it had been worked out from the matrix in a laboratory. It was too heavy for us to shoulder and carry away, and possibly even too heavy for the light-wheeled vehicle, in which we were traveling. So we left it there, proof positive that in that general region search for dinosaurian remains would probably be successful" (Holland, 1931, pages 282–283).

The discovery of the *Diplodocus* femur inspired Douglass to return to this locality the next year, in order to find the particular rock stratum from which the bone was derived. If he could locate the place of origin for such an excellent dinosaur bone, it stood to reason that he should find other bones, very probably complete skeletons. This supposition, or prediction if you will, was reinforced by the records of previous explorations along the Green River, especially along that section where it emerges from the Split Mountain Gorge to meander across the broad valley east of Vernal, Utah. Here John Wesley Powell, the famous explorer of the Grand Canyon, had recorded the presence of fossil "reptilian remains" in 1871, during his second trip down the Green River. Here O. A. Peterson, during the course of a field trip to the Uinta Basin in 1893 for the American Museum of Natural History, had reported dinosaur bones of Morrison age. Douglass had some precedents to guide him.

But it is one thing to have a general idea that fossil bones may be found in a particular region, and quite another thing to locate a productive fossil-bearing stratum. Douglass's task was to locate the bone-bearing bed, and then to determine whether it would produce bones in abundance or, as is frequently the case, only an occasional specimen. In the spring of 1909 he began his search hopefully, accompanied on his dinosaur hunt by a local resident, a patriarchal Mormon elder with a long white beard, Mr. George Goodrich. Success did not come easily. Day after day, through the ever-increasing heat of the spring and early summer, Douglass and Goodrich walked out the Morrison formation. Incidentally, to "walk out" a formation is a geological euphemism if ever there was one; the "walking" generally consists of hours on end spent in scrambling, climbing, slipping, sometimes falling, over rugged, rocky terrain, covered with scrub growth and cactus. Up and down, in and out of gullies they went, looking for the telltale bone fragments. And fragments they found—many of them—but nothing to warrant more than passing notice. Then, on August 17th, their tiring search was crowned with success. Douglass and "Dad" Goodrich had separated, as was their usual practice, each to continue the long, tiring search for bones in the rocks. (It is a time-honored technique among bone hunters to explore the rocks singly, but at no great distance one from another; in this way much more ground can be covered than if the men were to prowl around side by side.) During the course of that day's search, Douglass's keen eye spotted the glint of fossil bone, high in an upturned stratum of the Morrison formation—a jagged, saw-toothed ridge running almost due east and west, at right angles to the Green River as it emerged from the gorge of Split Mountain not far away. Could this be the clue for which he had searched so long? He scrambled up to the exposed bones, and scratched around them, and as he dug and probed, it became evident to him that here indeed might be the beginning of something big. For here Douglass found the vertebrae of a big dinosaur *in articulation*. It was this joining together of the bones in their proper relationships that was important; this was the clue to a possible complete skeleton, something much more significant than the discovery of a single bone or of isolated, scattered bones. Douglass was elated; he unlimbered the gun that he always carried during his explorations and fired two shots—the agreed signal. And after a while Dad Goodrich came puffing across the terrain, his white whiskers shining in the brilliant summer sun. It was an occasion to be celebrated by the two persistent fossil hunters, and this they did in their quiet way.

That evening, Douglass triumphantly wrote in his diary: "At last in the top of the ledge where the softer overlying beds form a divide . . . I saw eight of the tail bones of a *Brontosaurus* in exact position" (Good, *et al.*, 1958, page 28).

Douglass wrote to Dr. Holland in Pittsburgh, and the director of the Carnegie Museum lost no time in making the trip from Pennsylvania to Utah. Together Holland and Douglass examined the discovery and made plans for future work at this site. And during this time Douglass made exploratory excavations along lines indicated by the position of the eight dinosaurian tail bones in the rock. His prob-ings became more promising day by day. He exposed a large part of the skeleton, a skeleton that Holland later was to describe and to name *Apatosaurus louisae*, in honor of Mrs. Carnegie. Everything pointed in the direction of a large-scale operation.

A large-scale operation, especially one destined to handle thousands of dinosaurian bones, would be expensive. This was no deterrent, for Andrew Carnegie, the patron saint of the museum, and a man who liked to do things in the grand manner, contributed funds to carry on the work. The prospects did indeed look bright.

This was the beginning of the famous "Carnegie Quarry" at what was later to become the even more famous Dinosaur National Monu-ment. It was the beginning of a dig of unprecedented proportions, an excavation that would continue through many years, to involve the energies and skills of many men, and produce a mass of dinosaur bones probably never equaled in the history of dinosaur collecting. Moreover, it was the beginning of a quarry developed rather differ-ently from any quarries excavated before or since.

Some of the difference in the development of the Carnegie Quarry was owing to Douglass; he was in many respects a man different from other men. When he realized the scope of the task that lay ahead of him, he made preparations that were nothing if not thorough. This was to be for him no seasonal operation, lasting from the soft days of early spring to the sharp autumnal frosts. This, rather, was to be a year-round campaign, a campaign that would occupy his full atten-tion through all the seasons.

So he decided not to return to Pittsburgh that winter, where his wife and a year-old baby were waiting for him; rather he would spend the winter in this wild and inhospitable land in order to get work under way at what he envisioned as a great and productive dinosaur quarry. He recruited men with their teams and farm equip-ment from ranches nearby, to construct a road through what was then an empty country to the location of his discovery. He purchased the necessary tools and other equipment for digging in the heavy sand-stones and the soft shales at the quarry location. He hired three local residents as his assistants.

But what about his family? It did seem hard not to return to the East, to be with them during the winter. Yet could a man ask his wife to brave the rigors of the winter in this climate, with a very small child? Douglass put the question to Pearl Douglass, and she immediately and enthusiastically chose to come west, to share the hardships and the excitements of the winter at the dinosaur locality. In September she arrived, bringing the baby with her, and the family made their preparations for the days to come.

Their home during that first bitter winter consisted of a sort of tent, stretched over a wooden frame and heated by an iron stove, to serve as the living and dining room, with another tent for sleeping. Douglass had acquired a sheepherder's wagon, to be used as a sort of office and general headquarters for the operation, and the three assistants slept in that. It was a primitive arrangement all around, but the little party survived in spite of weather that saw the temperature descend at times to a chill thirty degrees below zero, Fahrenheit. And during this time Douglass was always busy—supervising the work of removing rock from above the bone layer, making observations and photographs of the natural history of the region, and every evening writing at length in his notebooks. Douglass was in many ways a naturalist of the old school, a man fascinated and enthusiastic about the world in which he lived. So he continued to accumulate notes and photographs on every aspect of the wintry environment, and those voluminous files today form a valuable record of one part of the Great West, as it was more than a half-century ago. All during the winter he was, of course, concentrating the major part of his attention and efforts toward opening the quarry.

From this time on, Douglass turned his back on Pittsburgh. His life was now to be spent in Utah and his complete energy devoted to the dinosaur quarry. In the years prior to the discovery of the eight tail vertebrae in those upturned sediments not far from the Split Mountain Gorge, Douglass had devoted his winters in Pittsburgh largely to research on early mammals—mammals that had lived long after the dinosaurs had become extinct—collected by him in the Uinta Basin. He had published a series of valuable papers on these fossils. But subsequent to 1910 his scientific publications ceased; after the summer of that year, when it became fully evident that the dinosaur quarry was to be a bone deposit of unprecedented magnitude, this great quarry was to be his career.

It was of course plainly evident that if Utah was to be his home, some definite arrangements for living would have to be made. Douglass could not adjust himself to the idea of settling in the nearest town, Vernal, some twenty miles distant to the west. In those days, when travel along western roads was still largely by horse, Vernal was no mere half-hour commuting trip from the dinosaur quarry as it is today. Douglass chose to settle himself permanently near the quarry.

He homesteaded a tract of land where water was available, and built for himself a solid log house. He laid out fields and bought a cow. He began to raise chickens. But in some respects Douglass's hopes ran ahead of reality. His vision of a prosperous homestead near the quarry, a self-sufficient farm on which he and his family would live in a state of semi-independence, was, alas, never quite realized. He built a dam across a gully to impound the groundwater, but there was not enough water for irrigating his fields throughout a Utah summer. Consequently he was forced to limit his horticultural efforts to the confines of a garden, where he raised some very fine vegetables; and he had his cow and his chickens. The Douglass family was able to live in reasonable comfort—to such a degree, in fact, that the sister and father of Earl Douglass came to live there, too. Thus the home was established, and maintained for more than a decade, while Earl Douglass devoted himself to the development of the huge dinosaur quarry.

Douglass, as has been said, located the great dinosaur quarry east of Vernal, Utah, by his discovery of eight tail vertebrae, all in articulation, these being the visible evidence of an almost complete skeleton of the gigantic dinosaur *Apatosaurus.* And, as has also been mentioned, the bones were in upturned strata. These two facts—the presence of articulated skeletons and the upturned strata—determined the development of the Carnegie Quarry, and for that matter, the subsequent development of Dinosaur National Monument. Digging here was not to be a matter of removing overlying sediments and exposing the bones on a large, more or less horizontal floor, as was the case at the Bone Cabin Quarry; rather it was to be a matter of cutting a gigantic trench along the longitudinal expression of the rocks, what geologists call the *strike* of the sedimentary layers, with one side of this trench being the fossiliferous bed. To put it another way—imagine a thick book standing on a shelf, but leaning over a bit, say at about fifteen or twenty degrees from the vertical. Hidden in the middle of this book is a wonderful page of pictures. Of course, we can pick up the book and turn to the page, but if we were reduced to sub-Lilliputian size—say to the size of ants, we would have to accomplish our purpose in another fashion, perhaps by taking a position on top of the book, and removing pages, bit by bit, contiguous to the page of pictures. Such was the method of getting at the dinosaurs buried in the upended strata, the gigantic pages of the sedimentary record turned up to an angle of about seventy degrees by the great earth movements that created the Rocky Mountains.

Douglass's original uncovering of the *Apatosaurus* skeleton had revealed the position of the fossiliferous-bearing layer. From there on, it was a matter of digging away the layers of rock to the one side of the fossil-bearing bed, the layers that, in the original horizontal position of the rocks, had been *above* the bone layer. This was a gigantic task, carried out in that relatively unsophisticated age by the use of judiciously placed dynamite charges, manpower, and horse-drawn scrapers. A rather professional touch was added to the operation by the employment of a mine railroad to carry away the vast amount of debris removed from the trench. Rails were laid and relaid along the bottom of the trench as it was dug down and the dirt was loaded into mine dump cars, to be wheeled to a natural cliff in the upended Mesozoic strata, there to be dumped over the edge. In this way the trench grew through the years, until finally it was about six hundred feet in length and some eighty feet deep. And in the steeply slanting wall, along one side of this trench, enormous numbers of dinosaur bones, many of them articulated as skeletons or partial skeletons, were exposed and removed. The dinosaurs were of several kinds, but the bones and skeletons of the gigantic sauropod swamp-dwelling reptiles, *Brontosaurus* (more properly *Apatosaurus*) and *Diplodocus,* and of the bizarre plated dinosaur *Stegosaurus,* prevailed. In addition there were skeletons of the aggressive carnivore *Antrodemus* (often known as *Allosaurus*), as well as bones of the small vegetarian dinosaurs *Laosaurus* and *Camptosaurus.* Thus the quarry preserved the relics of a *fauna,* an assemblage of animals that once were living together in a common environment. This made the quarry particularly valuable as a record of past life; often fossil quarries show the result of selective preservation, so that the remains of only one or two kinds of animals are present.

This remarkable fauna of giants was very much on Douglass's mind. How did they get to this one place? Why were they all buried here in such profusion? Certainly there must be some answer to these questions, something to explain the largest concentration of Jurassic dinosaurs ever discovered, a concentration representing some twenty or more skeletons, with bones and articulated segments of skeletons representing perhaps three hundred additional individuals. After much thought, the result of intimate familiarity with the sedimentary rocks of the developing quarry and the attitudes in which the bones were found in the deposit, Douglass came to the conclusion that this dinosaurian graveyard was not necessarily the place where the huge reptiles died; rather it was probably originally a sandbar in a large river—a shallow place where the carcasses of animals that had died from various causes and had floated down the river would have lodged, to be covered with the river sediments. Perhaps some of the dinosaurs at this place had actually become mired in the sandbar while trying to ford the river, but very likely a large proportion of the skeletons were those of animals that had floated down from farther upstream. There are certain lines of evidence that would seem to support this conclusion.

For instance, the undersides of the skeletons are frequently composed of bones in place, of the bones that were buried first, and held together even during the processes of decomposition. In contrast the bones of the upper sides of the skeletons are often scattered, as if subject to stream action. Moreover, the long tails and necks of the big sauropod dinosaurs are frequently strung out, as though they had been positioned in line with the constant flow of the river. It all represents an ancient tale of death and tragedy, a train of sad events for the gigantic reptiles that inhabited Utah when it was a low tropical land, some 130 million years ago, but a train of events that eventually was to have happy results for Earl Douglass and the other men who have dug out the bones from that immense quarry now known as Dinosaur National Monument.

ANDREW CARNEGIE'S *DIPLODOCUS*

During the course of the great excavation by Douglass and his fellow workers, there was discovered a beautifully complete, articulated

---

Figure 27. The skeleton of *Diplodocus carnegiei,* one of the dinosaurs from the Carnegie Quarry, later Dinosaur National Monument, Utah

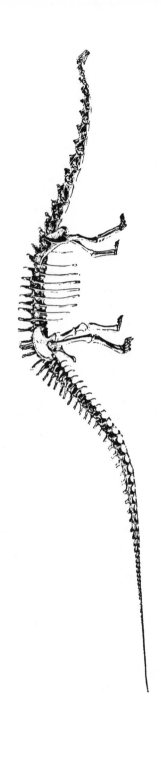

skeleton of the greatly elongated sauropod dinosaur *Diplodocus*. This skeleton was shipped back to Pittsburgh along with the rest of the materials from the quarry, and after it had been cleaned and prepared in the museum laboratory it was studied and described by Dr. Holland. He decided that it represented a new species, which he named *Diplodocus carnegiei*, in honor of the steel tycoon who had given so much support to the big excavation in Utah. This pleased Andrew Carnegie mightily, for it was said that he had always wanted something from the quarry "as big as a barn." Indeed, it pleased him so much that he decided that this beautiful skeleton, with his name attached to it, should be available to a wider audience than the one that visited the Carnegie Museum. Accordingly he gave funds for having the entire skeleton cast in plaster, bone by bone. This in itself was an enormous task, for it must be realized that the skeleton of *Diplodocus* is composed of nearly three hundred bones, many of them of great size and complexity. The casting, especially of the skull, was a task requiring the utmost technical skill and patience. Moreover, Carnegie wanted a large series of duplicates, with the result that in the end thousands of casts of bones had to be made. It was done.

When the casts were completed, Dr. Holland made a grand tour of various museums throughout the world, among which were the British Museum, the Musée d'Histoire Naturelle in Paris, the Senckenberg Museum in Frankfurt-am-Main, the Royal Museum in Vienna, the University Museum of Natural History in La Plata, Argentina, and the Museum in Mexico City. At each institution he presented a cast of the skeleton with the compliments of Mr. Carnegie. Furthermore, he usually remained at each museum to supervise the installation of the huge replica. And still furthermore, wherever he went with his enormous gift Dr. Holland was feted and honored and presented with honorary degrees and medals. So this particular *Diplodocus*, which gave up the ghost at such a distant time in the past, proved to be in the end a sort of dinosaurian benefactor to a number of people. Today a traveling museum visitor must not be surprised if, on his rounds, he encounters *Diplodocus carnegiei* time and again. He is not the victim of double vision; he is merely reaping the reward of the good paleontological fortunes of Earl Douglass and the self-esteem of Andrew Carnegie.

There is a happy epilogue to this little story. Some years ago Mr. G. E. Untermann, the director of the Utah Field House, a regional museum in Vernal, not so many miles distant from the Dinosaur National Monument, acquired from the Carnegie Museum the original molds for the *Diplodocus* skeleton. He then proceeded to make a new cast of the skeleton—this time in fiber glass, a replica that would be impervious to weather. Then he set the skeleton up on the grounds of the Utah Field House, so that today the unsuspecting tourist passing through Vernal on United States Highway Number 40 is to his surprise and delight suddenly confronted with a large sauropod dinosaur skeleton. In truth, the good works of *Diplodocus carnegiei* are still in effect.

THE WORK COMES TO AN END

Another dinosaur skeleton deserving mention was that of *Camarasaurus lentus,* recovered from the quarry in 1922, almost at the very end of the Carnegie Museum dinosaur campaign in Utah. (The museum worked here from 1909 until the spring of 1923.) This is one of the most perfect dinosaur skeletons ever found, for it is virtually complete and articulated, and what makes it especially interesting is the fact that it is a sauropod skeleton only about seventeen feet in length. In other words, it is the skeleton of a juvenile sauropod, a "teen-ager" so to speak, and as all dinosaur hunters will testify, skeletons of other than adults of these reptiles are very rare indeed. The skeleton of this young sauropod dinosaur gives us a picture of what such reptiles looked like during the process of growing up, what their proportions were in comparison with the proportions of the fully adult animals. As might be expected, the skull in this young dinosaur, one of the finest sauropod skulls ever found, is relatively larger than in the adult; the neck is relatively shorter. Moreover, the articulated limbs in this skeleton give some valuable information as to the pose in the sauropod dinosaurs; they show that these great reptiles walked with their limbs held more or less vertically beneath the body, as is confirmed by the trackways of huge sauropod dinosaurs found some years ago in Texas.

The work by Douglass and his assistants at the quarry, continuing year after year with ever-increasing and spectacular collections as proof of the richness of this deposit and the industry of the collectors, was not without its problems. And one of the biggest problems to confront the busy collectors arose in Washington, D.C. In short, the area in which the quarry was located, which was federal land, was thrown open for settlement. It was at once apparent that at any moment some wandering speculator might appear, to file a claim on the land where the dinosaur bones were being excavated. Therefore Douglass, acting on instructions from the museum, filed a mining claim on the land. But an official in Washington ruled that the fossils were not minerals, and the claim was rejected. It may be imagined that Douglass at this point would dearly have loved to transport the Washington lawyer to the wilds of Utah, to make him hoist and carry a brontosaur vertebra a few hundred yards across the rocky landscape. Especially under a July sun. Perhaps the legal mind would then have agreed that if fossil bones aren't minerals, they are none the less composed of something that makes them very heavy indeed.

Instead, Dr. Holland journeyed to Washington for a conference with Charles Doolittle Walcott, then the secretary of the Smithsonian Institution, and a paleontologist of great renown. A solution of the problem was seen. The matter was placed before President Woodrow Wilson, who in 1915 created eighty acres around the quarry site as the "Dinosaur National Monument." (The reserved land has since then been enlarged many times, so that now the Dinosaur National Monument embraces some of the most spectacular and geologically interesting scenery in western North America.) From that time until the end of the Carnegie Museum project in 1923, the museum worked the quarry under a special permit from the Department of the Interior.

By 1923 the museum had an immense collection of dinosaur bones and skeletons, three hundred tons of them, as a matter of fact. So it was decided to bring the project to a close, a decision brought about in part by the death of Andrew Carnegie, who during the years had enthusiastically supported the great dig. And so the Carnegie Museum withdrew from the field, its halls and laboratories and especially its storage rooms filled, almost literally, to overflowing with the bones of Jurassic giants.

The withdrawal of the Carnegie Museum saw the almost simultaneous entrance into the quarry of the United States National Museum. This government institution took up the work of excavation where the Carnegie Museum had left off. The University of Utah also did some work here under a government permit.

CHARLES WHITNEY GILMORE

Mention of the United States National Museum, a division of the famed Smithsonian Institution, brings up the name of Charles Whitney Gilmore, one of the great American students of dinosaurs, a quiet and a most modest man, a man of great generosity, truly beloved by his colleagues.

Gilmore was born in the small town of Pavilion, southwest of Rochester, New York, in 1874, and spent the first few years of his life on the family farm near this little town. As a small boy of six, Charles was taken by an aunt to Rochester, where they visited the famous Ward's Natural Science Establishment, a firm that through the years has supplied many museums and universities with materials for display and for teaching natural history. Incidentally Ward's was in those days a great training ground for museum men. Many years later Gilmore recalled the occasion when he saw "a number of men 'stuffing' all kinds of birds and mammals, for they did 'stuff' in those days. Among these were several who since have become very prominent . . . W. T. Hornaday [subsequently director of the New York Zoological Society], F. A. Lucas [subsequently director of the Brooklyn Museum and after that of the American Museum of Natural History], A. B. Baker, Nelson Ward, and others. Upon my return home, the 'museum bug' had been firmly implanted, for immediately collections of fossil shells, rocks, birds' eggs, and insects were started. Taxidermy, as a matter of course . . . I well remember a perfectly good cloth elephant stuffed with bran, which was slit open, re-stuffed, and sewed up again time after time until the poor thing lost all resemblance to its original form. . . . That was when the idea of following museum work as a life profession was implanted, an idea that never deserted me . . ." (Gilmore, quoted in Lewis, 1946, page 235).

When Charles was eight years old the family moved to Howell, Michigan, where he spent his boyhood, graduating from high school there. He then might have entered the University of Michigan nearby, but he was attracted to the West, so he journeyed to Laramie, to become a student at the University of Wyoming. According to his own account, written many years later: "Upon entering the University of Wyoming, the idea of preparing myself for some line of museum endeavor . . . was still fixed in my mind. . . . The collection of dinosaur specimens in the University soon attracted my attention, and from then until graduation all of my spare time was devoted to the study and collection of fossil specimens" (Lewis, 1946, page 236).

Charles Gilmore, after graduation, went on to become one of the outstanding authorities on the dinosaurs. The first few years of his professional career were spent with the Carnegie Museum, but in 1903 he moved to the United States National Museum, where he remained for the rest of his long and productive life, moving up successively through the several stages of advancement to become full curator, a position he held from 1923 until his retirement in 1945. He was in his middle and later years an outstanding member of the Smithsonian Institution scientific staff.

Although Gilmore gained great renown as a student of the dinosaurs, publishing forty-three scientific papers and monographs on these extinct reptiles, his work in the field was to a considerable degree devoted to other things. During his career at the National Museum he participated in sixteen expeditions, of which seven were directed completely or in part to the search for dinosaurs. Of these, only one was concerned with Jurassic giants, this being the expedition of 1923, the expedition that entered the quarry at Dinosaur National Monument after the cessation of work there by the Carnegie Museum.

But if Gilmore did not collect many Jurassic dinosaurs (he did collect a great many Cretaceous dinosaurs), he nevertheless studied them assiduously. Fifteen of his forty-three papers on dinosaurs are concerned with Morrison forms, and in his capacity as a student rather than as a field man, he had a great deal to do with the fossils collected by the Carnegie Museum. For he was invited by that institution to study and describe some of their specimens, and this he did during the later years of his life. Gilmore had the great virtue of being able to apply the seat of his pants to the seat of a chair, to get down on paper the knowledge that was in his head concerning dinosaurs and other fossil reptiles. Alas! It would seem that prolonged work in the field not infrequently develops a sort of restlessness in some paleontologists, so that during the winter months, when they must needs abandon cliff and quarry for the warmth of the laboratory, they spend much time planning and making preparations for the next season's field campaign instead of studying the fossils they have already collected. It was fortunate for the Carnegie Museum that Gilmore was available and that he was the sort of man he was. Thanks to his industry and ability, the results of some of the most important work at the Dinosaur National Monument were analyzed and recorded for the benefit of future students of dinosaurs and of fossil reptiles in general.

DINOSAUR NATIONAL MONUMENT

As early as 1915 Earl Douglass had set down in his diary the idea of developing the dinosaur quarry as an exhibit in place. The procedure would be to remove the "overlying" rock from that part of the wall of the trench that as yet had not been worked, and then to remove the matrix from around the bones so that they would stand out in relief. The tilt of the rock face—almost seventy degrees—would make such a treatment of its surface an almost perfect display for the visiting observer. But the idea remained hidden in Douglass's diary, or as a vague desideratum in his mind while the work went on for another eight years.

Then in 1923, with active excavation in the quarry at an end, Douglass again turned his thoughts to the idea of an exhibit in place, and this time he expressed them forcefully to Dr. Walcott, the secretary of the Smithsonian Institution.

"I hope that the Government, for the benefit of science and the people, will uncover a large area, leave the bones and skeletons in relief and house them in. It would make one of the most astounding and instructive sights imaginable" (Douglass, quoted in Good *et al.*, 1958, page 36).

It was an idea completely in line with the planning of the National Park Service, but thirty-five years would elapse before it would become a reality. There were various reasons for this. When it was first considered it perhaps had to germinate for some time in the minds of men, as is often the case with unusual and refreshing concepts. Then there was the perennial problem of funds—such a development of the quarry would not be cheap. Then came the depression, and after it the Second World War. So it was not until the 1950's that the program for developing the quarry as an in-place exhibit finally got under way.

In the meantime, in the thirties, there was a period of activity that helped to prepare for the future, permanent development of the quarry. With WPA funds (Works Progress Administration—a relief agency for putting unemployed men to work—is it still remembered, or even known to a younger generation?), the quarry was widened and deepened, and temporary buildings were constructed. A few bones were exposed. For quite a number of years this preliminary development of the site was all that was available to the curious sightseer who turned north from Highway 40 at Jensen, a small settlement east of Vernal, Utah, to drive several miles over a washboard road to the locality.

Then, beginning in 1953 and coming to its climax in 1958, the permanent development of the quarry was carried out by the National Park Service. A handsome building was constructed over the tilted fossiliferous bed, this upended layer serving as one wall of the building. The building was constructed with a large gallery along one side, so that visitors could see the bone layer from an upper as well as a lower level. Various explanatory exhibits were installed. And the work of reliefing the bones was commenced, and will continue for some years to come. It is a big job, one that requires time, and patient, skillful effort. It is a job that is being carefully supervised by a trained vertebrate paleontologist, Dr. Theodore White, one of the leading contemporary American students of fossil reptiles. Perhaps it may be said that Dr. White has a position unique in the annals of paleontology, certainly unique in the annals of dinosaurian studies. He is the permanent scientific custodian of a great dinosaur quarry, succeeding and carrying on the work and the desires of Earl Douglass. And in the words of Douglass, the quarry under White's guiding hand has become "one of the most astounding and instructive sights imaginable." Indeed, in many respects it is unique. Here, every year, hundreds of thousands of visitors come to view and to marvel at the display of dinosaur bones in the rock, gradually being exposed on an almost vertical surface some 190 feet in length and 30 feet in height, the bone-bearing layer being about 15 feet in thickness. Moreover, the development of the quarry at Dinosaur National Monument has resulted in scientific gains as well as in the preparation of a display of unequaled proportions, for as the work has proceeded new things have come to light. Some of them are skulls and bones or parts of skeletons superior to anything hitherto discovered; some of them are remains of animals hitherto unknown. These discoveries have been, of course, a source of delight to Dr. White and his paleontological colleagues.

The work at Dinosaur National Monument has pointed the way for the development of some future dinosaur sites. There has been increasing sentiment for fossil exhibits in place in North America, and other examples are now to be seen; in fact the National Parks Service maintains other displays of fossils (not dinosaurs) in place, generally on a rather small scale, in other parks and monuments. And as we shall see, the Province of Alberta has begun a somewhat similar development in a Provincial Dinosaur Park recently established along the Red Deer River, north of the border.

HOWE QUARRY

An epilogue may be added to this story of the search for the Jurassic giants of the Western world. It concerns Barnum Brown of the American Museum of Natural History. Brown, who, as we have seen, was a member of the first American Museum party working at Como Bluff and who had been actively engaged in the pursuit of dinosaurs since the turn of the century, became during the 1930's very much involved with Jurassic giants in western North America. He saw the possibilities of development of the Dinosaur National Monument quarry, and for some years was in the forefront of the movement for making an exhibit in place there, housed in a permanent building. He spent many hours in conference with government officials, and drew up suggestions for the project, which he envisioned as being carried out with the cooperation of the American Museum of Natural History. His particular plans never came to fruition; when the crucial time for the development of the quarry arrived, the work was carried out along other lines parallel to those proposed by Brown.

In the midst of his concern with Dinosaur Monument, Brown, who had been collecting Lower Cretaceous dinosaurs in Montana, learned of the presence of large bones on the ranch of one Barker Howe, at the foot of the Bighorn Mountains in Wyoming, to the east of Yellowstone Park. In 1934 Brown and his assistants went to the Howe Ranch, driving over primitive roads through magnificent scenery, and sure enough, they found large dinosaur bones quite obviously weathering out of a horizontal rock stratum hard by the ranch buildings.

Brown and his party began to dig, and the more they dug, the more they found. As the work progressed it became evident that they had a dinosaur quarry not unlike the one near Vernal, Utah, but on a

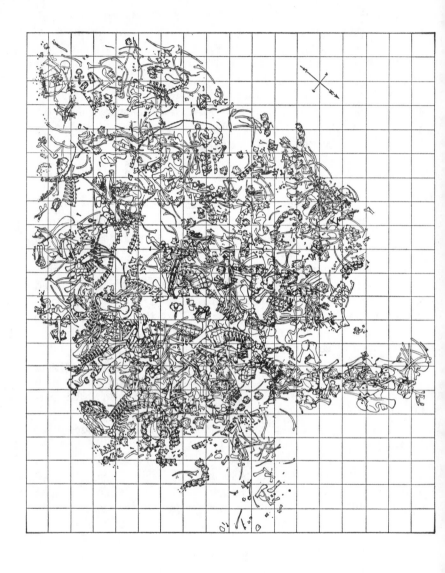

smaller scale, and horizontally placed instead of being almost vertical. This quarry was worked intensively, and a marvelous concentration of Jurassic dinosaur bones was exposed. It was primarily a deposit of sauropod remains, and the skeletons were disarticulated and mixed up to a much greater degree than was the case at Dinosaur National Monument. On the other hand, the concentration of the fossils was remarkable; they were piled in like logs in a jam. All of which made the removal of the fossils a tedious and difficult task.

The job was carried through to a successful conclusion, in part owing to an ingenious system for mapping the fossils. A large derrick was erected by the side of the quarry, and with this a member of the party could be hoisted in a large barrel thirty feet or so into the air for a near bird's-eye view of the diggings. From this vantage point photographs could be made of the quarry, which in the meantime had been marked off in three-foot squares, and in this way the position of the bones recorded. In addition, one member of the party, Roland T. Bird, for many years Brown's trusted assistant, made sketches of each and every bone in place. In this manner a most impressive quarry chart was developed in great detail. It is a permanent record of an unusual concentration of Jurassic dinosaurs, a concentration that probably records the entrapment of numerous dinosaurs in a diminishing pool, at a time when water was scarce. This may be compared with the bones at Dinosaur Monument, which as has been said appear to be the remains of skeletons washed down a river. The skeletons at the Howe Quarry certainly appear to have been disturbed and scattered, as if by trampling by many animals, and they are thicker in the center of the deposit than around the edges, as if they were concentrated in a restricted pool.

Brown made his collection and shipped it to the museum in New York, utilizing the capacity of a large railway boxcar, loaded literally to the brim, to transport the collection. Thus one of the big twentieth-

Figure 28. A map of the Howe Quarry, excavated by an expedition from The American Museum of Natural History under the leadership of Barnum Brown. Here is seen one of the most concentrated deposits of dinosaur bones ever found. The quadrants are three feet square

century collections of Jurassic giants was obtained. Other collections have since been made, notably a remarkable series of carnivorous dinosaurs from a quarry near Cleveland, Utah, worked by the University of Utah. But today perhaps much of the collecting of Jurassic giants is directed at individual skeletons. Dinosaurs are becoming very expensive objects, and it is indeed a sanguine institution that can contemplate without qualms the acquisition of a huge Jurassic brontosaur. Therefore it seems probable, as indicated by the activities of recent years, that the collecting of Jurassic giants in the future will be on a rather selective basis. This is in the nature of things, and to be expected.

Marsh and Cope with their pioneer efforts revealed the Jurassic treasures to be found in Wyoming and adjacent regions. The American Museum at Bone Cabin and more recently at the Howe Quarry, and especially the Carnegie Museum and the government institutions at Dinosaur National Monument, added immeasurable quantities of fossils to complement and complete the record of Jurassic dinosaurs in the Western world. Recent excavations and studies are supplementing this already vast accumulation of ancient dinosaurian remains.

So it would seem that our picture of dinosaurian life in North America during late Jurassic time should be very complete. In a sense it is. But there are still many new things to be discovered in the earth, and many new facts to be learned from the bones at hand, as well as the bones that are still to be found. Consequently, interest in the Jurassic giants of the Western world is bound to continue through the years to come, and new men will bend their efforts to the acquisition and the study of these ancient giants, adding to the work done by their predecessors—Cope and Marsh, Osborn and Brown and their associates, and Douglass and Gilmore.

Plate 62. George M. Dawson (standing in center), the first man to discover dinosaurs in western Canada, and his field party at Fort McLeod, British Columbia

Plate 63. Dawson's field party in southern Alberta, 1881. On this expedition dinosaur bones were found along the Belly or Oldman River—the first indication of the rich fossil field that was to be so extensively explored in the years to follow

Plate 64. Lawrence M. Lambe (right) and his assistant at their camp on the Red Deer River, 1901

Plate 65. Lawrence Lambe (left) and Charles H. Sternberg, collecting in the beautifully stratified Oldman Formation along the Red Deer River, 1912

Plate 66. Charles Hazelius Sternberg

BELOW LEFT. *Plate 67.* Levi Sternberg (left) and Professor W. A. Parks of the University of Toronto, an authority on Canadian dinosaurs. BELOW RIGHT. *Plate 68.* Personnel of four Canadian expeditions at the Sternberg camp on the Red Deer River, 1917. Charles M. Sternberg is third from the left in the back row; his father, Charles H. Sternberg, is second from the right in the back row

Plate 69. Barnum Brown excavating a skeleton of the duck-billed dinosaur *Corythosaurus*, in the Oldman Formation, Red Deer River, 1912

Plate 70. Brown's flatboat on the Red Deer River. Brown is the figure on the right

Plate 71. Alone on the still reaches of the Red Deer River. The Brown flatboat, with the tent down, is towed slowly past the thick exposures, its occupants viewing the cliffs with practiced eyes for telltale signs of dinosaur bones

Plate 72. Ready for a day in the field, searching for dinosaurs, and protected against the ravages of gnats and mosquitoes. Barnum Brown and his assistants on the Red Deer River, Alberta, 1912

Plate 73. Albert Johnson, Brown's assistant, with a partially excavated skeleton of the horned dinosaur *Styracosaurus,* near the Red Deer River, Alberta

Plate 74. Hoisting a bandaged dinosaur bone to be loaded on the wagon. The American Museum of Natural History expedition to Red Deer River, Alberta

Plate 75. Hauling dinosaur bones, collected by Barnum Brown and his assistants, out of the valley of the Red Deer River, Alberta. This picture shows an area now included in the Alberta Dinosaur Park. An automobile road descends into the valley, along the route of the old wagon trail

Plate 76. Charles H. Sternberg and George F. Sternberg setting out to explore Dead-lodge Canyon, along the Red Deer River. On this trip the elder Sternberg discovered the skull of the horned dinosaur *Styracosaurus*

Plate 77. Charles M. Sternberg (left) and his assistant, G. E. Lindblad, chiseling out a skull of a horned dinosaur, Oldman Formation, Red Deer River, Alberta, 1917

Plate 78. A Central Asiatic Expedition car at the northern gate of Kalgan, China, ready for the trip north into Mongolia. This was in 1923, before the days of jeeps. Henry Fairfield Osborn in the front seat

Plate 79. The automobile caravan of the Central Asiatic Expedition of The American Museum of Natural History entering the Gobi Desert of Mongolia

Plate 82. Members of the Central Asiatic Expedition of The American Museum of Natural History, 1923. Middle row, from left to right: Walter Granger, Henry Fairfield Osborn, Roy Chapman Andrews (leader), Frederick K. Morris (geologist), Peter Kaisen, experienced dinosaur hunter who had spent many years with Brown in western North America. Back row, third from left, Albert Johnson, who worked with Brown along the Red Deer River in Alberta; third from right, George Olsen, who had also collected dinosaurs on previous occasions in North America

Plate 83. George Olsen (left) and Roy Chapman Andrews (right) excavating a nest of dinosaur eggs at Shabarakh Usu, or Bain-Dzak, Mongolia

Plate 84. The camel caravan of the Central Asiatic Expedition at the Flaming Cliffs of Bain-Dzak, Mongolia

Plate 85. There is more to collecting dinosaurs than digging them out of the ground. Frederick Morris, geologist of the Central Asiatic Expedition, at the plane table making a map

Plate 86. Walter Granger, paleontologist and second in command of the Central Asiatic Expedition, in a less than formal pose. He is applying shellac and rice paper to a fossil bone

Plate 87. A partially exposed dinosaur skeleton at the "Tomb of the Dragons," Nemegetu Basin, Mongolia, with a member of the Russian Expedition happily seated on the hard sandstone ledge that protected the skeleton from erosion

Plate 88. Mongolian *yurts* (felt tents, supported by a lattice-like framework), the characteristic habitations of the Gobi nomads, with a truck of the Russian Expedition in the background

ABOVE. *Plate 89.* Paleontologists, all specialists in the study of fossil reptiles, on the Russian Expedition to Mongolia in 1948: I. A. Efremov, leader of the expedition, in the foreground; A. K. Rozhdestvensky, assistant leader, to the left; E. A. Maleev to the right. The desert is a rugged place; it can be very cold at times. BELOW. *Plate 90.* When the desert sun gets hot, the paleontologists retreat to the comparatively cool shade beneath a truck, to study their maps and make plans: Efremov on the left, Rozhdestvensky on the right, N. I. Novojilov, chief technician of the expedition, in the center

CHAPTER 7

CANADIAN DINOSAUR RUSH

THE RED DEER RIVER

The search for dinosaurs in the western reaches of North America advanced along many fronts and with great vigor during the last quarter of the nineteenth century. It was in truth the first great western dinosaur rush, fully as strenuous and exciting for the participants, and as filled with drama, as the famous gold rushes that loomed so large in the settlement of the western states. It was of course on a small scale, a rush that involved perhaps a few dozen people instead of the thousands that took part in the gold rushes, but for those chosen few it filled their lives as completely as the search for yellow dust and nuggets filled the lives of the armies of placer miners who worked the diggings of California and Colorado.

As we have seen, it began with Cope and Marsh in 1876 and 1877, and involved them and their various assistants and field men in a prolonged rivalry that at times became an out-and-out struggle to locate and excavate dinosaurian treasures. The final phases of this first dinosaur rush were seen in the excavations of the American Museum of Natural History groups at the Bone Cabin quarry, at the very end of the century, and in the work by Earl Douglass and parties from the Carnegie Museum of Pittsburgh at what is now Dinosaur Monument in the early years of the twentieth century. These diggings produced immense returns, as may be observed by anyone who visits the halls of those museums whose men were the principals in this late Victorian drama. Their work yielded dinosaur bones in prodigious numbers, with a very large proportion of these bones associated as articulated skeletons. Their efforts afforded abundant materials with which paleontologists might work and by means of which they might develop valid evidence as to the nature of species among the dinosaurs, as to the details of dinosaurian anatomy, and as to many other interesting problems, such as growth in these ancient reptiles. The fruits of this early rush to collect dinosaurs in western North America are still being enjoyed by scientists who continue to study the bones collected so many years ago, and by innumerable visitors to museums, who see many of these bones assembled as skeletons.

Then, beginning about 1910, there was a second notable dinosaur rush, this time taking place in western Canada, particularly along the cliff-like banks of the Red Deer River in Alberta, some two hundred miles south of Edmonton, and about one hundred miles to the east of Calgary. It was less far flung and more concentrated than the prolonged dinosaur rush that began with the excursions of Marsh and Cope into the Morrison beds of Colorado and Wyoming, and it was marked by friendly rivalry rather than by bitter feelings. But like the earlier dinosaur rush, it was notable because of the great mass of materials that it produced. Where the work of Marsh and Cope revealed unsuspected vistas of late Jurassic dinosaurian life, the work of various men in Alberta made known in marvelous profusion and detail those dinosaurs that had lived in this part of the world during late Cretaceous time.

The search for dinosaurs in the Cretaceous beds of Alberta may be compared after a fashion with the early explorations of the Jurassic Morrison Formation, in that for a number of years two principal parties were involved. But whereas Marsh and Cope and their men were the most antagonistic of rivals, and attempted to work in secrecy, hiding their efforts from each other, the two groups collecting in Alberta along the Red Deer River worked openly and in friendly competition.

These two parties consisted on the one hand of Barnum Brown usually assisted by Peter Kaisen, both of the American Museum of Natural History, as well as by other collectors from that institution in New York, and on the other of Charles H. Sternberg assisted at different times by some or all of his three sons, George, Charles, and Levi, working for several institutions, but especially for the Geological Survey and the National Museum of Canada, and the Royal Ontario Museum. The separate efforts of these two groups of men along the Red Deer River make one of the truly fascinating and happy chapters in the annals of dinosaur hunting. Indeed, the story deserves a book in itself. Here only a few of the more important details of their explorations can be recounted.

But first let us look at some of the background to this Alberta dinosaur rush. It should be said that neither Brown nor the Sternbergs went to the Red Deer River country by blind chance. Fossils had been found there previous to their collecting campaigns, so that they had the benefit of earlier experience, derived from the efforts of other men, on which to base their work. Which takes us back to the 1870's, to the days when Cope and Marsh were in the early throes of their long paleontological war.

The first dinosaur bones to be found in Canada were discovered in Saskatchewan by Dr. George Mercer Dawson, geologist and naturalist to Her Majesty's North American Boundary Commission, a government survey that worked with a similar group from the United States to establish the precise line of demarcation between the two countries. Dawson carried a name famous in the annals of Canadian geology and paleontology, for he was the son of Sir William Dawson, the first principal of McGill University, and one of the greatest of nineteenth-century Canadian geologists. George Dawson, who was born in Nova Scotia in 1849, received his undergraduate education at McGill University, after which he went to England for postgraduate studies. There he had the good fortune to study under some of the outstanding geologists and zoologists of the day. It was his particular good fortune to have as one of his professors none other than Thomas Henry Huxley. Thus George Dawson procured an excellent scholastic background for his chosen profession.

But in one respect he would seem to have been ill fitted for the strenuous life of a geologist working in the field, because he was a hunchback. Yet in spite of this handicap, plus the additional disadvantage of frequent ill health, he carried out his duties vigorously and with great skill, traveling with an assistant in a light wagon, camping out in wild country, making large collections of fossils as well as of modern animals and plants, and filling his field books with voluminous notes and observations. He worked with remarkable energy and application, and he expected equal efforts from his assistants.

It is indeed fortunate that the initial discovery of dinosaurs in Canada was made by a man of Dawson's training and capabilities, because he ensured the proper documentation of his find by working up a detailed study of its geological relationships. Dawson appreciated the fact that the worth of a fossil is determined to a large degree by the thoroughness with which its field relationships are recorded.

The materials first collected by Dawson were submitted by him to Cope for study, and the Quaker naturalist of Philadelphia identified the bones of a hadrosaurian dinosaur, some remains of turtles, and a gar pike. Later in this same year Dawson made another discovery of dinosaur bones, this time in what is now Alberta, where those sediments often referred to as the Belly River beds are exposed. These bones also were sent to Cope, who identified them as "portions of the sacrum and long-bone of a Dinosaurian." During subsequent years Dawson carried on further field investigations in southern Alberta, as a member of the Geological Survey of Canada, which he joined after the termination of the Boundary Survey in 1875, and in the course of his work made additional discoveries of Cretaceous dinosaur bones.

One of Dawson's assistants on the Survey was Joseph Burr Tyrrell, who began work with him in 1883. Tyrrell, a native of Ontario, was preparing himself at the University of Toronto for a legal career, when, because of threatened ill health, he decided on some kind of work that would take him out of doors. So he joined the Geological Survey, to devote the rest of his life to the study of field geology. Evidently the rugged life of a geologist was beneficial, for he managed to live to the ripe old age of ninety-nine.

In 1884 Tyrrell discovered fossil bones in the valley of the Red Deer River, in central Alberta. This first discovery of his, made during the course of explorations with a Survey field party, led in short order to other finds, and within a week he and his assistants brought to light the partial skull of a carnivorous dinosaur. This precious and unprecedented fossil was removed by Tyrrell and his helpers as best they could with the tools at hand, and was then packed by horseback out of the canyon where it had been discovered. Having thus been brought up to the rim of the prairie, the skull was hauled to Calgary in a wagon—a long and tedious journey across the plains, during which every effort was made to protect the precious specimen from the effects of a jarring, rough ride. From Calgary it was shipped to Ottawa for preparation and preservation. Like some of the previous Canadian discoveries, this skull was brought to the attention of Cope, who studied and described it. This is the skull now known as *Albertosaurus sarcophagus*.

Of course, the discovery of such an excellent specimen stimulated a great deal of interest within the Survey, with the result that in 1888 another geologist, Thomas Chesmer Weston, was sent to the Red Deer River for the specific purpose of collecting dinosaurs. It had been suggested to Weston that a practical way to carry on his exploration would be to float down the river in a boat, using it as his headquarters and base of supplies, and making from it daily excursions on foot along the cliffs and into the side canyons that bordered the river. This seemed like a good idea, so Weston had a boat constructed, and with some assistants began his voyage. The expedition was remarkably brief; the boat foundered within about eight miles of its starting point, for it was poorly made and Weston's assistants had no experience on the river. The bedraggled party scrambled to shore and made its way to a nearby farm, owned by a Mr. McKenzie, there to receive refreshment and to recount a sad tale of shipwreck and disaster. McKenzie, who had experience with boats and who knew the river, suggested that Weston return the following year, when he (McKenzie) would take Weston downstream successfully in a proper boat.

It was done. Weston came back the next year, and with McKenzie and his son made a successful, albeit at times an exciting, journey down the river. Dinosaur bones were found in abundance. The particular contribution made by these explorers was their discovery of the very rich fossil field that is located between Steveville, a small settlement that long since has become famous in the annals of dinosaur collecting, and Deadlodge Canyon. Moreover, Weston and McKenzie had demonstrated the feasibility of doing geological work along the Red Deer River by using a boat for their base of operations.

One more man became involved with the dinosaurs of the Red Deer River before the turn of the century. This was Lawrence M. Lambe, like his predecessors in the exploration of the Alberta fossil

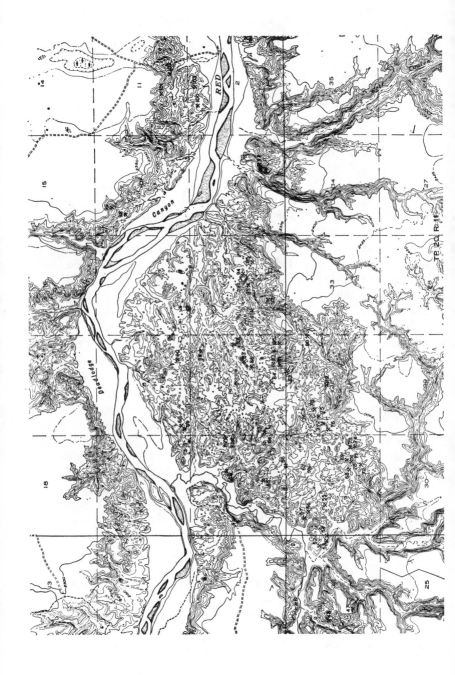

fields, a member of the Geological Survey of Canada. His connection with the Survey, like Tyrrell's, came about as the result of ill health. Lambe had prepared himself for a military career, but a bout with typhoid fever put an end to his ambition for the life of an army officer. He had some ability as an artist, and so he joined the Survey to draw illustrations of fossils.

In 1897 he was sent to Alberta on some routine work, and while there he arranged for a boat trip down the Red Deer River. What he saw impressed him, and the next year he returned with some assistants, to search for and excavate the fossil bones of dinosaurs. His efforts were moderately successful; Lambe was not well acquainted with the special collecting techniques that by then had been developed for the exhumation of fossil bones, so that the specimens he collected were for the most part rather fragmentary. Nevertheless his efforts marked an important milestone in the development of the rich dinosaur beds of Alberta, because Lambe not only collected the bones of dinosaurs but also studied, described, and interpreted them. Working in close conjunction with the American Museum of Natural History, and especially with Professor Henry Fairfield Osborn of that institution, he analyzed his materials upon the basis of comparisons with dinosaurs collected in other parts of North America, and demonstrated that the fossils from along the Red Deer River, which are found in two principal horizons, or geological levels, the Oldman Formation below and the Edmonton Formation above, were older than the late Cretaceous dinosaurs of the Lance formation, at that time the most completely known of Cretaceous dinosaurs.[1] He published his conclusions in a monograph written in collaboration with

---

[1] The dinosaur-bearing beds along the Red Deer River are more complex than is indicated by this simple statement. The Oldman and the underlying Foremost formations constitute what was formerly known as the Belly River Series, a name now generally going out of use. The higher Edmonton beds are, along the Red Deer River, separated from the Oldman Formation by the marine Bearpaw shale.

Figure 29. A portion of the Steveville, Alberta, Sheet, Geological Survey of Canada, along Deadlodge Canyon of the Red Deer River, showing the location of quarries from which dinosaur skulls and skeletons were excavated by the Sternbergs and by Barnum Brown

Osborn, to set the stage for those remarkable explorations by Brown and by the Sternbergs in the years to come. Lawrence Lambe truly opened the eyes of the paleontological world to the significance of the dinosaur-bearing sediments along the Red Deer River.

This brings us to the nub of our story, to the climax of the Canadian dinosaur rush, to what may be called the golden years of exploration along the Red Deer River from 1910 until 1917, during which Barnum Brown and the Sternbergs, father and sons, drifted down the river and explored and dug along the cliffs with phenomenal success. Let us first look briefly at the protagonists in this drama.

THE STERNBERGS—FATHER AND SONS

Charles Hazelius Sternberg, who has appeared earlier in this narrative as Cope's assistant during the explorations of the Judith River beds in 1876, was born in 1850, in Otsego County, New York. His father, a Lutheran minister, was the principal of a seminary, in which his grandfather was professor of theology. Sternberg thus grew up in a religious atmosphere, and this affected him throughout his years; he demonstrated in the writings of his mature years a devout attitude toward the world, ancient and modern, in which he lived such an interesting life. Growing up in a theological household did not, however, seem to inhibit young Sternberg. He was a very active boy, and with his twin brother and a cousin he spent many happy hours roaming through the woods of upper New York State. It was then that he developed the deep love for the out of doors and for the natural world that was to govern his life until the end of his days. As a boy he took note of fossil shells in the rocks around his home, and collected them —often wondering as to their origins and significance.

When he was fifteen years old the family moved to Iowa, and two years after that Sternberg and his twin brother, Edward, emigrated to Ellsworth County, Kansas, where an elder brother had a ranch. Here Sternberg spent several impressionable years on the frontier, where he had many adventures. He was the neighbor of untamed Indians, and he hunted buffalo under the great arching sky of the high plains. During his hunting forays across the plains young Sternberg inevitably found fossils, particularly the beautiful fossil leaves that are so remarkably preserved in the Dakota sandstone of Cretaceous age. Buffalo were soon forgotten, while Sternberg and his brother devoted their energies to making a collection of these Dakota sandstone leaves, a collection that in 1870 was sent to the United States National Museum.

The beauty of the fossil leaves, and the excitement and joy of collecting them, thrilled Charles Sternberg; so much so that "At the age of seventeen, therefore, I made up my mind what part I should play in life, and determined that whatever it might cost me in privation, danger, and solitude, I would make it my business to collect facts from the crust of the earth. . . ." (Sternberg, 1909, page 17.) Sternberg's "practical"-minded father could not quite see such a life as being suitable for his son, but Charles persisted in his ambition. So it was that in 1875 he enrolled as a student at the Kansas State Agricultural College in Manhattan, where he was able to study under the paleontologist Professor Benjamin Mudge (who has appeared previously in this book in his role as a collector for O. C. Marsh). In the spring of 1876 Sternberg had high hopes of accompanying Mudge into western Kansas, to collect for Marsh. But in this he was doomed to disappointment—the roster of Mudge's collecting party was filled.

Sternberg, being the young man that he was, could not be deterred by this setback. He immediately wrote to Cope for help. Sternberg's account of this fateful letter and its results are worth repeating:

"I put my soul into the letter I wrote him, for this was my last chance. I told him of my love for science, and of my earnest longing to enter the chalk of western Kansas and make a collection of its wonderful fossils, no matter what it might cost me in discomfort and danger. I said, however, that I was too poor to go at my own expense, and asked him to send me three hundred dollars to buy a team of ponies, a wagon, and a camp outfit, and to hire a cook and driver. I sent no recommendation from well-known men as to my honesty or executive ability, mentioning only my work in the Dakota Group.

"I was in a terrible state of suspense when I had despatched the letter, but, fortunately, the Professor responded promptly, and when I opened the envelope, a draft for three hundred dollars fell at my feet.

"That letter bound me to Cope for four long years. . . ." (Sternberg, 1909, page 33.)

And it in all probability determined the course of Sternberg's life, not to mention the fortunes of various museums throughout the world. For with the three hundred dollars Sternberg purchased his ponies and wagon, outfitted himself for camping and collecting in the lonely and truly dangerous country along the Smoky Hill River, a country still inhabited by unfriendly Indians, hired his cook, and went to work.

Here Sternberg spent many hot days of hard labor in the Kansas chalk, searching out the marine reptiles that had lived in a shallow Cretaceous sea, around the borders of which the land-living dinosaurs roamed in great variety and numbers. As a brief sidelight on the Cope-Marsh war, the subject of some attention in a previous chapter of this book, Sternberg had this to say:

"Here at Buffalo [Kansas] I had my headquarters for many years. A great windmill and a well of pure water, a hundred and twenty feet deep, made it a Mecca for us fossil hunters after two weeks of strong alkali water. At this well Professor Mudge's party [the party, it will be recalled, to which Sternberg had been denied membership earlier in the year] and my own used to meet in peace after our fierce rivalry in the field as collectors for our respective paleontologists, Marsh and Cope" (Sternberg, 1909, page 34).

Later in the summer Cope joined Sternberg for the collecting campaign in the Cretaceous Judith River beds of Montana, Cope's dinosaur hunt that immediately preceded his entrance into the Morrison beds of Colorado the following year. From these beginnings Sternberg continued his career as a collector of fossil vertebrates, especially fossil reptiles, and more especially dinosaurs, for the remainder of a long life. Although he generally worked on contract as an independent collector, he worked hard and conscientiously, and with the best interests of his clients at heart. The museums that purchased his fossils without doubt received full value and more for the specimens that were sent to them from the field by Charles Sternberg and his assistants.

His most trusted assistants as the years passed by came to be his sons, George, Charles, and Levi. And the three Sternberg brothers, all still living, in time graduated from their positions as assistants to their father, to become renowned fossil collectors and paleontologists in their own right. George, the eldest, became a collector with headquarters at Hays, Kansas, where for many years he has been associated with the State College there. Charles, the next, transferred his allegiance to Canada, the result of the years of work along the Red Deer River with his father, and became a valued paleontologist at the

Geological Survey in Ottawa. During his many years with that institution he has conducted numerous expeditions into the field, has discovered many new dinosaurs, and has described them in a valuable series of scientific papers. Levi, the youngest, also cast his lot north of the border, again after having worked with his father along the Red Deer River, and for many years before his retirement was paleontologist at the Royal Ontario Museum in Toronto.

Such is a brief summary of the background of the Sternbergs, who as we shall see explored the cliffs of the Red Deer River, conducting their own dinosaur rush, and digging out of the ground a grand array of skeletons, representing the gamut of these ancient reptiles that had inhabited western North America during late Cretaceous time.

BARNUM BROWN

Barnum Brown, whom we met in the preceding chapter, was, like the Sternbergs, a Kansan, and was born on Lincoln's birthday, 1873, at Carbondale, Kansas. His parents had emigrated to Kansas from Wisconsin before the Civil War, making their way westward by ox team and wagon. They had built a pioneer cabin on a hill, under which was a coal seam, and near which the town of Carbondale was to rise. At the time of Barnum's birth the Brown family, the father and mother, two daughters and an elder son, was enjoying a period of comparative prosperity, following a very trying and dangerous life during the Civil War, when eastern Kansas was overrun in turn by Federal and Confederate troops, as well as by renegades and outlaws. William Brown, the father, in addition to being a prosperous farmer, conducted a business of digging and selling coal, and he ran a freight line of ox-drawn wagons.

In 1889 Barnum accompanied his father on a four-month trip by horse and wagon from Kansas to Montana and back, a journey that covered about 3,000 miles. It was a memorable experience for the young lad, and afforded him an exciting introduction to the plains and mountains of western North America. In the autumn of that year young Brown went to Lawrence, Kansas, to attend high school, there being no high school in Carbondale at the time. Having completed his high-school studies he matriculated in the University of Kansas, where in due course he received his Bachelor's degree. At the university Brown, together with Elmer S. Riggs and Ermin C. Case, all three of whom were to make their names well known to students of paleontology, came under the influence of Marsh's former assistant, Professor Samuel Wendell Williston, by now one of the great authorities on fossil reptiles. At the end of his freshman year Brown, accompanied by Riggs and Case, as well as by other students, journeyed to Nebraska and South Dakota to collect fossils. In the following summer Brown worked in Wyoming, where he and his fellow workers found a skull of the Cretaceous horned dinosaur *Triceratops*. And during the summer after that, the summer of 1896, Brown met a field party from the American Museum of Natural History, led by Dr. J. L. Wortman. He worked with that party for a part of the summer, and obviously made such a good impression on Wortman that after his graduation in 1897 he was hired by the American Museum to participate in the expedition into the Morrison beds of Wyoming to collect dinosaurs.

This was the beginning of Brown's long association with the New York museum, lasting from that time until the day of his death, sixty-six years later. During his many years at the museum, Brown established himself as a collector, par excellence, of dinosaurs. He made many trips into the field all over the world, and he collected various types of fossil vertebrates, but the dinosaurs were throughout his life his first paleontological love. He seemed to have a particular affinity for dinosaurs, as though he were able to scent them from afar. Probably no other single individual has ever collected as many dinosaurs as did Barnum Brown; the small army of dinosaurian skulls and skeletons assembled by Brown through a half century or so of active fieldwork is indeed impressive. In fact, one of the dinosaur halls at the American Museum of Natural History in New York, the hall devoted to Cretaceous dinosaurs, is in effect a monument to Barnum Brown. Here, owing to his energy and skill in the field, can be seen the greatest display of Cretaceous dinosaurs in the world.

Such is a brief outline of the background of Barnum Brown, the rival of the Sternbergs in the dinosaur rush along the Red Deer River of Alberta.

In 1902, a few years after Barnum Brown had joined the staff of the American Museum of Natural History, he initiated a field campaign in the uppermost Cretaceous beds of eastern Montana, the sediments designated as the Hell Creek Formation. Here he worked for several years, during the course of which he excavated skeletons of the gigantic carnivorous dinosaur *Tyrannosaurus rex,* of which one, certainly among the finest dinosaur skeletons ever to be found, is exhibited in New York, and another in the Carnegie Museum in Pittsburgh. He also collected two very fine skeletons of the duck-billed dinosaur *Anatosaurus.* But by the end of the 1908 field season it was becoming apparent to Brown that he should turn to new regions, and therefore he began to think about the possibilities of work along the Red Deer River. He was, of course, familiar with the earlier work done there, through the publications of Lawrence Lambe.

FLOATING DOWNRIVER WITH BROWN

It so happened that in the spring of 1909 a rancher from the valley of the Red Deer River visited the American Museum in New York, where he immediately recognized the similarity between the fossils on display and bones that he had found on his ranch. This rancher's report so impressed Brown that he visited the Red Deer River valley during the summer, after having completed another field season in Montana. He saw bones, and his mind was made up. From now on, for the next few years, he would turn his face northward, from Montana to Alberta, to seek paleontological treasures along the Red Deer River.

Turn northward Brown did, the very next year. But it was with a heavy heart that he journeyed to the town of Red Deer in the early summer of 1910. On April 9th his wife of six years, Marion, had died after a short illness, leaving a bereaved husband and a baby daughter. The little girl was entrusted to the care of her grandparents, and Brown threw himself into the activities of the summer's expedition with great vigor. Perhaps hard work would help assuage the sorrow of his tragic loss.

At Red Deer Brown set to work, making preparations for the river trip. He was always something of an innovator in planning and prosecuting his fieldwork; now he inaugurated something new in the technique of fossil collecting in western North America. Perhaps it would be more correct to say that he developed a variation on the methods used by his predecessors, Weston and Lambe, for instead of going down the river by boat he proposed to float downstream in a large barge, a vessel of such capacity as to carry a fully established camp on its decks, with additional room and buoyancy for the transportation of large numbers of heavy fossils. Carpenters were hired, and a barge or flatboat was constructed, with a twelve-foot beam and a length of thirty feet. In the middle of this barge a large wall tent was set up, complete with a sheet-iron stove, the black chimney of which was poked through the tent roof. There was ample deck space fore and aft. The barge was steered by two large sweeps, each twenty-two feet in length and one at each end of the boat. In effect it was a flat-boat or scow very like the ones that a century earlier had floated down the Mississippi, carrying produce from the upper reaches of the Ohio to New Orleans.

The barge was successfully launched in the river at Red Deer, and soon Brown and his assistants were floating downstream toward the fossil fields. The first sixty miles of the river below Red Deer, locally known as "the Canyon," provided the voyagers with plenty of excitement. The current here flows at something more than four miles per hour, and there were intermittent rapids to add interest to the voyage. Consequently the fossil hunters were kept busy at the sweeps, holding the scow on its course. They managed it without coming to grief, and at the lower end of the canyon were swept through a narrow channel, where an immense landslide had formed a dam, almost blocking the river. Below this point they floated into more tranquil waters, which allowed them to devote at least a part of their attention to the cliffs along the river, searching with their eyes for likely collecting localities. Brown has given a short but graphic description of this part of the trip:

"In the long midsummer days, in latitude 52°, there are many hours of daylight, and constant floating would have carried us many miles per day; but frequent stops were made to prospect for fossils, and we rarely covered more than twenty miles per day. High up on the plateau buildings and haystacks proclaim a well-settled country, but habitations are rare along the river, and for miles we floated through picturesque solitude, the silence unbroken save by the noise of the rapids.

"During the day an occasional flock of ducks or geese would be disturbed by our approach, though few signs of life were seen along the shore; but among the trees, when the mystic hush of night had stilled the camp, all the underworld was alive, and many little feet rustled the leaves where daylight disclosed no sign of life.

"Then the muskrat and beaver would take courage to investigate

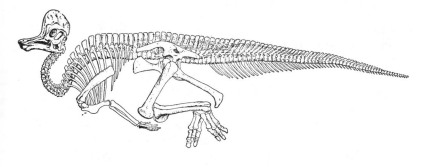

Figure 30. A skeleton of *Corythosaurus,* the Cretaceous duck-billed dinosaur from the Oldman Formation, Red Deer River, Alberta, discovered and excavated by Barnum Brown and his party. It is shown completely articulated—as it was preserved in the sediments

---

Figure 31. The Cretaceous duck-billed dinosaur *Corythosaurus.* Restoration by Lois Darling

the big intruder of their familiar haunts. From the distance some hungry coyote would send his plaintive cry echoing down the canyon, to be punctuated by the 'put-put-put, put, put' of a partridge drumming to his mate. . . ." (Brown, 1919, page 419.)

Brown's method for exploring and collecting along the Red Deer River proved to be an excellent one, and the results were gratifying in the extreme. By the time the summer was over, the flatboat was piled high with fossils, collected from the Edmonton Formation of late Cretaceous age, encased in their burlap and plaster jackets. The quantity of dinosaurs obtained by the Brown party was really impressive.

So much so, indeed, that he returned to the Red Deer River again in 1911, with equally gratifying results. This second summer he again worked in the Edmonton beds, as he did during the first part of the following field season. He then transferred his attention farther down the river, to the older Oldman Formation, from which level he collected dinosaurs during several successive summers. Thus, as a result of his fieldwork along the Red Deer River, Brown had representative collections of dinosaurs from two levels, collections that would, when prepared and studied, show evolutionary development among different lines of dinosaurs through an appreciable segment of geologic time. This, of course, greatly enhanced the importance and the significance of Brown's efforts. Commonly the sequence of fossil faunas, the assemblages of animals that have lived in past ages, is built up by a complex process of collecting from different localities, and then comparing and correlating the levels and the ages of the collections in various ways. But here, along the Red Deer River, it is possible to collect dinosaurs from the Oldman Formation of the Belly River sequence, and in contiguous localities to collect other dinosaurs from the higher Edmonton Formation, and by so doing to get some idea of the results of evolutionary development in one restricted region among these great extinct reptiles, through several million years of earth history. This Brown did.

To get back to the story. Brown had now been working along the Red Deer River for two field seasons, with the knowledge and complete approval of the Geological Survey of Canada, when cries began to be heard in protest against the invasion of western Canada by Yankee bone hunters, who were robbing the Dominion of its paleontological treasures. Of course, the fossils had been there all the time, waiting for the taking, but since the work of Lambe a decade earlier, no collecting efforts along the Red Deer River had been attempted by the Survey or by any Canadian museums. Brown's dinosaurs were too spectacular to ignore; the director of the Survey decided that it was high time for his organization to make some collections on its own behalf. Quite correctly he adopted the enlightened view that the proper procedure was to compete with Brown rather than to prohibit him from working, and plans were laid in accordance with this decision.

THE STERNBERG EXPLORATIONS

But who was there available to make the collections? Unfortunately, there was no one at the Survey, not even Lawrence Lambe, with the requisite skill and experience to compete with Brown and his fellow workers. Consequently the Survey called on the Sternbergs, who at this time happened to be available. As a matter of fact, Charles H. Sternberg and his son George spent part of the spring of 1912 in Ottawa, setting up some specimens that had previously been sold to the Geological Survey. With the elder Sternberg at hand, it was a simple administrative matter to appoint him as Chief Collector and Preparator for the Survey, to work under the direction of Lawrence Lambe. Plans for a summer field campaign were rapidly formulated, and Sternberg journeyed to Alberta, to begin, in July, his first season of work, assisted by his sons.

The Sternbergs decided to work during their first field season in Alberta with the combined facilities of a team and wagon, and a rowboat. Charles H. Sternberg had brought his field wagon from Kansas, and he proceeded to have a rowboat constructed in Calgary. With these items of equipment for operating by land and water, the campaign was launched, and a successful one it proved to be. Camp was set up near Drumheller, which is a hundred miles or so down the river from Red Deer, where Brown had first begun his voyage two years before, and from this camp the Sternbergs explored the cliffs and badlands exposures of the Oldman Formation. Their expedition that summer was highlighted by the discovery of some very fine skeletons of duck-billed dinosaurs.

In the meantime Brown had continued his explorations along the Red Deer River, moving downstream about seventy-five miles below Drumheller to the area between Steveville and Deadlodge Canyon, the rich fossiliferous region that had first been located back in 1889 by Weston and McKenzie. The collection that Brown made from the Oldman Formation in 1912 along this part of the river exceeded anything he had collected during the two previous years. Among other things he excavated a skeleton of the crested duck-billed dinosaur *Corythosaurus,* and a skeleton of the horned dinosaur *Monoclonius.* Indeed, this area proved to be so rich as to decide Brown to concentrate on it in future years, which he did.

So it was that 1913 found Brown back on the river, between Steveville and Deadlodge Canyon. And the Sternbergs were there, too. Brown's methods evidently had impressed Charles Sternberg and his sons, for this year they provided themselves with a large flatboat *à la* Brown, complete with two tents, set up end to end. Moreover, they enjoyed the luxury of a motorboat, with which to pull the scow back and forth along the river as well as to run errands. In addition they had their rowboat.

Figure 32. A skeleton of the Cretaceous horned dinosaur *Monoclonius,* excavated from the Oldman Formation, Red Deer River, Alberta, by Barnum Brown. This truly beautiful drawing by Erwin Christman is a classic example of the fine art of scientific restoration of a fossil skeleton

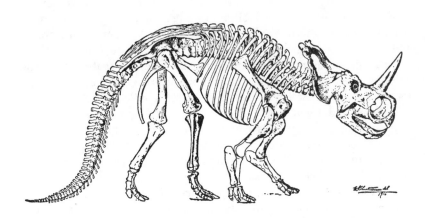

When all preparations were made, they set sail downstream toward Steveville with the motorboat towing the large scow. The trip was not without its adventures:

"We were early astir, and Charlie hauled us in mid-stream. A strong east wind blew in our faces, it was disagreeable, because we had to lower our tents to the deck, as they acted as sails, and the power of the wind on them was stronger than the current and the five horse power motor [and] would have driven us up stream. The choppy waves beat constantly against the front and sides of our scow curling over the deck itself. The wind howled in the few cottonwoods along the shore and on the islands, that we passed. . . . About nine o'clock we reached the fifth ferry below Drumheller. The ferry man had stretched a barbed wire across the river; Charlie saw it as he drove his motor under it and shouted to us, Jack [McGee, an assistant] rushed for the rear guiding oar and I for the front one, they were both stuck several feet up in the air, and if the wire had caught one, it would have swamped us. Jack had his back to the wire and when he released the oar and stood up, it caught his hat and threw it in the river. If the wire had been six inches lower, or the river six inches higher, it would have cut his head off as easily, and thrown it into the river" (Sternberg, 1917, pages 51–52).

It was a terrifyingly close call, but fortunately Jack did not lose his head, and the little convoy proceeded down river. Camp was set up about three miles below Steveville, not far from where Brown already had established his camp. And from these two almost contiguous camps, strategically located in one of the world's richest dinosaur-collecting grounds, the rivals explored and dug, always with their eyes directed toward each other's efforts. As has been said, their competition was of the friendly sort, but none the less the rivalry between the two parties must have stimulated all of the men to put forth their very best efforts. Fossil hunting is something of a fever, like the search for gold, and every individual in the field soon becomes infected with the desire to make the best and most spectacular discoveries. Indeed, such feelings of rivalry commonly obtain even within a single party of fossil hunters, so that on many an evening around the campfire A may be jubilant at the success of his day's explorations, while B is correspondingly glum at his lack of success. Of course, B reluctantly admits that he is more than pleased by A's success—are they not all working together and for the same institution?

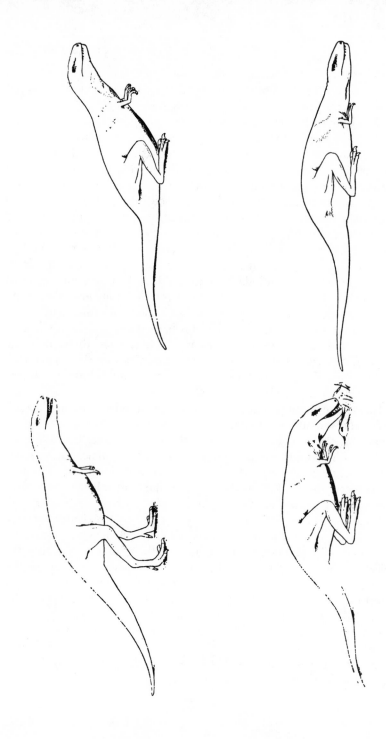

Will not A's discovery redound to the credit of the whole party? Yes; but none the less B wishes he might have been the lucky fellow who had made the discovery of the day. So it is not to be wondered at that the rivalry between Brown and the Sternbergs was keen.

Fortunately, they were working in a region where there were enough fossils for all. Their discoveries in that summer of 1913 were spectacular, and fossils continued to come to light through those years following, during which Brown and the Sternbergs collected in this region. In fact, a careful survey and map of the Red Deer River between Steveville and Deadlodge Canyon, about ten miles to the east, compiled by Charles M. Sternberg a few years ago, shows that more than a hundred dinosaurian skulls and skeletons have been collected from this area. These include some of the finest late Cretaceous dinosaurs ever to be excavated, many of which are to be seen on display in New York, Toronto, and Ottawa.

In 1913 the accumulation of these dinosaurian riches was still in its earlier phases, and the full extent of the collections being made by the two parties of collectors was yet to be realized. Even so the prolific occurrences of dinosaurs in this fossil field continued to astound the collectors. The Sternbergs in that season collected two skeletons of the crested duck-billed dinosaur, *Corythosaurus,* other duck-billed forms as well, armored dinosaurs, the carnivorous dinosaur *Gorgosaurus,* discovered almost immediately after they had made camp at Steveville, and some especially fine horned dinosaurs, including a skeleton (*Chasmosaurus*) with skin impressions, and the spectacular spiked-skulled form, *Styracosaurus.*

DINOSAURS WITH SKIN

The discovery of a dinosaur with the impression of the skin was important, but not new, either to the paleontological world or to the Sternbergs. Five years earlier they had discovered and excavated two

---

Figure 33. Reconstruction, by W. A. Parks, of the Cretaceous carnivorous dinosaur *Gorgosaurus,* from the Oldman Formation of the Red Deer River, Alberta. Parks has imagined *Gorgosaurus* in four poses: standing, sitting, feeding, resting

duck-billed dinosaurs with the fossilized skin preserved over great portions of the body. Dinosaurian skin was new at that time, and their discovery was something of a paleontological sensation. Perhaps it deserves a digression at this place.

The four Sternbergs had been working in southern Wyoming in 1908, about sixty miles from the town of Lusk. They had put in many hard and uncomfortable days in the field with indifferent success, for which reason none of them was feeling particularly happy about the results of their efforts. Food was running low, and it was decided that the elder Sternberg and his son Charles would drive into town for supplies, while George and Levi stayed in camp. Off went the two Charleses, father and son, leaving the two brothers to fend for themselves for several days.

George and Levi were not living very high during this interim— about all they had to eat was potatoes, an item of diet that they found tiresome when taken by itself three times a day. While they were waiting for the return of the relief expedition, they decided to dig out the remains of a duck-billed dinosaur George had found, a few bones of which could be seen protruding from a hard sandstone cliff. So they went to work with a will. At this point let us hear the story as it was told years later by George:

"Finally by the evening of the third day, I had traced the skeleton to the breast bone, for it lay on its back with the ends of the ribs sticking up. There was nothing unusual about that. But when I removed a rather large piece of sandstone rock from over the breast I found, much to my surprise, a perfect cast of the skin impression beautifully preserved. Imagine the feeling that crept over me when I realized that here for the first time a skeleton of a dinosaur had been discovered wrapped in its skin. That was a sleepless night for me. Had I missed my regular cup of coffee or eaten too many potatoes for supper?

"It was about dusk on the evening of the fifth day when we saw the wagon loaded with provisions roll into camp. 'What luck?' was my father's first question. And before he could leave his seat I had given him a vivid sketch of my find; for we had found every bone in place except the tail and hind feet which had protruded from the rock and had washed away. The head lay bent back under the body. Traces of the skin were to be seen everywhere. 'Let's go and see it,' he shouted as he jumped from his seat on the wagon. I grabbed some food from the boxes on the wagon and away the two of us went, leaving the others to prepare the meal for us. Darkness was nearly upon us when we reached the quarry and there laid out before us was the specimen. One glance was enough for my father to realize what I had found and what it meant to science. Will I ever forget his first remark as we stood there in the fast approaching twilight? It thrills me now as I repeat it. 'George, this is a finer fossil than I have ever found. And the only thing which would have given me greater pleasure would have been to have discovered it myself' " (Sternberg, G. F., 1930, pages 143–144).

This is the famous dinosaur mummy now at the American Museum of Natural History in New York. A second specimen with the skin was discovered by the Sternbergs at this same place; it is now in the Senckenberg Museum in Frankfurt-am-Main, Germany.

So it can be assumed that the Sternbergs were mentally prepared for the sight of dinosaur skin in their diggings along the Red Deer River. And indeed, this specimen of theirs proved not to be unique, for a number of the Red Deer River dinosaurs have been found with the skin preserved. One notable specimen is that of a crested duck-billed dinosaur, *Corythosaurus,* collected here by Barnum Brown, with large areas of skin present over the body. It should be added that Brown also found a partial skeleton of a horned dinosaur, *Monoclonius,* with the skin.

As the Sternbergs labored in their dinosaurian treasure trove, just down the river from Steveville, Brown decided to move to a new location. So he leapfrogged some four or five miles down the river, passing their camp on July 19th to establish a camp at Little Sandhill Creek, a tributary of the Red Deer River at the upper end of Deadlodge Canyon. Here, in the words of Charles H. Sternberg, Brown "never left that richest of all the camps in the Belly River Series in Dead Lodge Canyon for three seasons. . . ." The Sternbergs were subsequently to move into this area as well, where, as shown by Charles M. Sternberg's map, more than fifty specimens were collected through the years.

FINAL YEARS ON THE RIVER

To continue with a detailed account of the collecting carried on each year after 1913 by Brown and by the Sternbergs would make a story too long for this chapter. In summary, Brown continued his work through 1914 and 1915 in the cliffs and badlands to the south of the River in its Deadlodge Canyon portion, while the Sternbergs worked this region through these two summers and on through 1916 and 1917.

The close of the 1915 field season saw an end to Barnum Brown's six-year campaign of dinosaur collecting along the Red Deer River. It saw an end, too, to the concerted efforts of the Sternbergs working in this area as a family team. True enough, they continued their collecting along the Red Deer River for many years, but from 1916 on they worked in separate groups, and for much of the time singly and independently. This breaking up of the family party was completely amicable, and came about through various circumstances.

The elder Sternberg resigned from the Geological Survey in May of 1916 because of a disagreement he had with Lawrence Lambe over the plans for the summer fieldwork. Very probably this difference of opinion between the two men acted merely as a trigger, to release Sternberg from a situation that he found rather confining. He had always worked independently, and in this period of his late middle age it was probably difficult for him to adjust to the various limiting controls inherent in a large organization. However that may be, he left, and Levi went with him. George and Charles M. stayed with the Survey.

Once again Sternberg senior went into the fossil fields of the Red Deer River, accompanied by Levi. This summer the eldest and the youngest Sternberg were collecting on behalf of the British Museum. Their luck was good, and they excavated two excellent skeletons of duck-billed dinosaurs, together with some other materials. The dinosaurs were shipped east, to be placed on board a steamer, the *Mount Temple,* bound for Britain, and at this point the good fortunes that seemed to attend every effort connected with Red Deer River dinosaurs vanished. The *Mount Temple* was torpedoed, and the dinosaurs went to the bottom of the Atlantic. This was indeed a tragic loss—one of the few instances of fossils collected for museums failing to reach their destination.

Perhaps the venerable fossil collector was solaced for the negation of his 1916 efforts by the results of his work along the Red Deer River in 1917, the last year he was to collect fossils in this region. Again Levi was with him and again they worked in the Deadlodge Canyon region, where they collected three fine skeletons, one of a duck-billed dinosaur that went to the San Diego Museum, one a beautiful carnivorous dinosaur, *Gorgosaurus,* eventually named in honor of Sternberg, and one an armored dinosaur, both of the latter being acquired by the American Museum of Natural History. These specimens had been offered to the British Museum, but the trustees of that institution were so discouraged by the loss the year before of the skeletons destined for them that they were not interested in making another outlay of money for dinosaurs. The year 1917 was, one must admit, a very stringent time in Britain, a time of crisis during the First World War, when dinosaurs probably seemed items for very secondary consideration.

It is interesting that during the field season of 1917, while Charles H. and Levi Sternberg were collecting along the Red Deer River, a rival expedition was in the vicinity under the leadership of Charles M. Sternberg—working for the Geological Survey. This was the beginning of his long and distinguished career with the Geological Survey. During the course of the next three decades and more, until after the Second World War, he returned to the Red Deer River, to make additional collections of dinosaurs there, principally in the area of Deadlodge Canyon.

George Sternberg, the eldest of the brothers, likewise returned on various occasions to explore, operating in the tradition of his father as an independent collector. Levi, who joined the staff of the Royal Ontario Museum in 1919, also made frequent expeditions along the Red Deer River for many years after the end of his association with his father, during the course of which he was instrumental in building up the fine collection of dinosaurs now to be seen in Toronto.

So it was that the Sternberg brothers carried on the exploration of the Red Deer River badlands for several decades after the end of the family corporation, if so it may be called, that prior to 1915 had conducted so many successful dinosaur hunts in western North America. For George the work along the Red Deer River was more or less sporadic; he became increasingly interested and involved in the marine Cretaceous beds of Kansas that have yielded so many fine skeletons of mosasaurs, plesiosaurs, and other marine reptiles. But for Charles M. and for Levi, the Red Deer River became for each something of a life career. Charles, in addition to his collecting activities, became involved in research on his collections, and publication of the results, owing in part at least to the necessity of carrying on this phase of the work after the death of Lawrence Lambe in 1919.

With the close of the 1917 field season the big Canadian dinosaur rush was ended. The high excitement of those first half-dozen years was over—the excitement of going into a strange and unknown region to search for paleontological treasures new to science. Unfortunately, some of the romance had vanished, too. For with the passing of the years, there have been improvements in roads and in automobiles that have spelled the doom of the old flatboats and wagons. No longer do fossil hunters drift down the river, scanning the bluffs for likely collecting spots; no longer do they make camp on their paleontological arks, lulled to sleep at night by the lapping of little waves against the sides of the scow; no longer are they truly a part of the river. A new technological age has arrived, making the work of the fossil hunter perhaps more efficient, but certainly more prosaic.

Today the badlands exposures of Cretaceous beds between Steveville and Deadlodge Canyon have been made into a Provincial Park. The fossils are under the care and supervision of the Provincial Government, and the park region area is administered by a permanent superintendent. Several fossil skeletons have been exposed in place, and shelters have been constructed to protect them. Access roads have been built. So it is that this rich fossil field, certainly one of the most productive areas in the world for the remains of dinosaurs, can now be visited in ease and comfort, even by the casual tourist. And the visitor, if he is acquainted with some of the history of exploration that has been outlined in these pages, may gaze out across the sunlit cliffs and badlands, and think back, perhaps with some nostalgia, to the golden days of the great Canadian dinosaur rush.

CHAPTER 8

ASIATIC DINOSAUR RUSH

ROY ANDREWS LOOKS TO CENTRAL ASIA

The end of the great dinosaur rush along the banks of the Red Deer River in Alberta marked the close of a long and memorable chapter in the history of the search for dinosaurs. It was in effect a chapter covering four decades of exciting exploration in the western wilds of North America, beginning, as we have seen, with the intense rivalry between Marsh and Cope and their collectors in the Jurassic beds of Wyoming and Colorado, continuing with the turn-of-the-century diggings by the American Museum of Natural History at Como Bluff, continuing still with the massive quarry developed by Earl Douglass and his associates at what is now the Dinosaur National Monument, and culminating with the singularly romantic work by Barnum Brown and his rivals, the Sternbergs, who floated through the Cretaceous badlands of Alberta like hardy rivermen of a former age, in search of dinosaurian treasures. The discoveries made by the men who participated in the dinosaur hunts of western North America added new dimensions of unparalleled magnitude to our knowledge of the dinosaurs. They made North America in those days the center of the world for dinosaur hunters—the region where dinosaurs were to be found in the greatest abundance and studied with the greatest facility.

Then, in the early twenties of this century, the Asiatic dinosaur rush began, shifting the attention of dinosaur hunters (at least for the time being) from the Western to the Eastern Hemisphere. And it began by accident. For the initiation of this new phase of dinosaurian discovery and research was a side effect of other activities—something unexpected, something that came as a very pleasant surprise indeed, and something that led to later expeditions and studies, the ends of which are still in the future.

This beginning had nothing to do with dinosaurs—the opening of the Asiatic dinosaur rush began as a search for the origin of man. Around the turn of the century Professor Henry Fairfield Osborn of the American Museum of Natural History had suggested that central Asia, at that time a vast *terra incognita* in the world of natural science, was the center of origin for early man and for many of the various groups of mammals as well. This concept was elaborated a decade or so later by Dr. William Diller Matthew of the same institution in his classic work *Climate and Evolution,* in which he postulated that central Asia was the center of origin for most of the mammals, basing his thesis upon his profound knowledge of the relationships and distributions of mammals, fossil and recent, throughout the world. In brief, he saw central Asia as a sort of paleontological Garden of Eden for the ruling backboned, land-living animals of today. Therefore, said he, to get at the beginning of our modern world, let us look toward central Asia. This idea fired the imagination of Roy Chapman Andrews, a member of the scientific staff of the museum in New York, and soon after the First World War he began to dream of an expedition on a grand scale to central Asia, particularly to Mongolia, to that Asiatic grassland and desert known as the Gobi.

The guideposts for such a venture were indeed vague. An American geologist, Raphael Pumpelly, had traversed central Asia and the Gobi in 1865, as had the German scholar Ferdinand Freiherr von Richthofen, in 1873. In later years there were some occasional incursions into the Gobi by other naturalists, but all these trips were of a reconnaissance nature, and with but one exception, there were no reports of fossils. The exception was the discovery in 1892 of a single fossil rhinoceros tooth along the old caravan route from Kalgan, on the Chinese border, to Ulan Bator, the capital of Mongolia, by the Russian geologist and explorer Vladimir A. Obruchev. Andrews therefore necessarily envisaged an expedition into central Asia in search of early man with no more than the tooth of a long-extinct rhinoceros—a rhinoceros older by millions of years than the most ancient of men—to which he could point as evidence that there were *any* fossils in the Gobi.

It was a gamble, seemingly with the odds heavily against him, but he was not to be deterred, not even by the gloomy predictions of some geologists who could visualize central Asia only as a vast, unfossiliferous waste of sand. He had the enthusiastic support of Professor

---

Figure 34. A map showing the areas of Mongolia explored by the Central Asiatic Expeditions of The American Museum of Natural History. Cretaceous dinosaurs were found at (4) the Oshih Basin; (5) Shabarakh Usu, or Bain-Dzak; (9) Iren Dabasu; (12) On Gong. The capital city of Ulan Bator is designated on this map by its older name, Urga

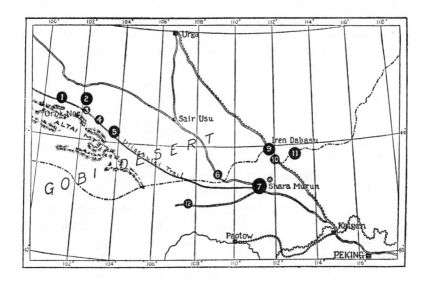

Osborn and other knowledgeable authorities, and this was encouragement enough for him to make the gamble. From just such shots in the dark have come many of the great discoveries in science.

So Andrews went ahead with his plans and his organization. These are some of his own remarks about the problem, and about how he proposed to deal with it:

"The main problem was to discover the geologic and palaeontologic history of Central Asia; to find whether or not it had been the nursery of many of the dominant groups of animals, including the human race; and to reconstruct its past climate, vegetation and general physical conditions, particularly in relation to the evolution of man. It was necessary that a group of highly trained specialists be taken *together* into Central Asia in order that the knowledge of each man might supplement that of his colleagues. This was indeed the first expedition of such magnitude to employ these methods. The fossil history of Central Asia was completely unknown. . . .

"Mongolia is isolated in the heart of a continent; and there is not a single mile of railway in the country [this was written in 1929], which is nearly half as large as western Europe. The climate is extremely severe; the temperature drops to —40° to —50° and the plateau is swept by bitter winds from the Arctic. Effective palaeontological work can be conducted only from the beginning of April to October. In the Gobi desert, which occupies a large part of Mongolia, food and water are scarce and the region is so inhospitable that there are but few inhabitants. The physical difficulties could only be overcome by some means of rapid transportation and that transportation the motor car successfully supplied. The automobiles could run into the desert, as soon as the heavy snows had disappeared, at the rate of one hundred miles a day, penetrate to the farthest reaches of Mongolia and return when cold made work impossible. Camels, which other explorers had used, average ten miles daily. Thus approximately ten years' work could be finished in one season" (Andrews, 1929, page 713).

Andrews had the audacity to think in big terms—at least in big terms for those unorganized days of the departed twenties, before government had rallied to the support of science with a capital S, as it now has on a large and at times a lavish scale. As Andrews remarked, it was a venture to be undertaken by a group of specialists, working together in the Gobi. But how was this group of men, the scientists and technicians, their helpers and the helpers of the helpers, to be carried into a trackless and strange desert, even with automobiles available, in such a way that they would be able to concentrate their efforts and attention on the job at hand, the job of searching for and collecting fossils, of gathering and recording geological data, of collecting specimens of living animals and plants, and of making meteorological observations, without spending all their time and energy at the mere task of traveling and keeping alive? The answer was to use not only newfangled automobiles but also time-tested camels —in other words, to rely upon fast-moving cars for exploration and the transportation of personnel, combined with slow-moving camels for the hauling of supplies. It was planned to send a large camel caravan across the Gobi along certain predetermined routes. These camels would carry food and supplies of all sorts, including numerous five-gallon cans of gasoline and oil. The scientists and technicians and their assistants would travel in a fleet of sufficiently rugged cars (this was before the days of jeeps), traversing the desert in zigzag paths, sometimes together, sometimes in separate small parties, looking and searching and collecting. At stated intervals the cars would meet the caravan at designated rendezvous points, there to transfer gasoline and oil and food from the backs of the camels to the cars, and fossils and other objects from the cars to the backs of the camels. The camels that had acquired loads of specimens in place of expendable supplies would return to a base, while the rest of the caravan would move on to the next rendezvous. And the cars would embark on new wandering courses across the rolling landscape. During one field season, for example, the expedition had a caravan of 125 camels that carried 4,000 gallons of gasoline, 100 gallons of oil, 3 tons of flour, 1½ tons of rice, and other food in proportion. This caravan left gasoline and food at two depots, and waited for the wandering cars at a well 800 miles out in the desert.

An interesting detail might be mentioned. The cars traveled across the undulating hills much as would ships across the long swells of a broad sea; consequently they were guided through the Gobi, back and forth, by the well-tested methods of navigation that have been used by ships' captains ever since the invention of the compass and the sextant.

It worked—beautifully. And the first year was so successful that there followed four other expeditions. There would have been even more, but for internal political troubles that racked China during

Party   1923

Roy Chapman Andrews
Walter Granger & F.K. Morris
George Olsen
: Peter C. Kaisen
Albert F. Johnson
: J. McK. Young
Chas. Vance Johnson

Kan Chuen Pao ("Buckshot")
Chih Hsiao Luen

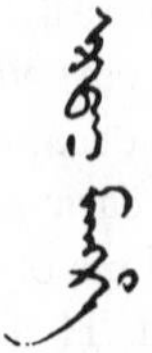

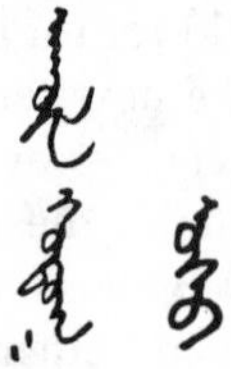

~~~~~~

Localities

Iren Dabasu	Irdin Manha	Ula Hotorh (Usu)
Artyn Obo	Shaburukh Usu	Oshih
		Gashato

ABOVE. *Plate 91*. Robert Broom, the great South African paleontologist, in his characteristic field dress—that is, in a regular business suit with jacket removed and shirt sleeves rolled up. Broom discovered fossil reptiles by the hundreds in South Africa, and described them in numerous scientific papers. LEFT. *Plate 92*. The Argentinian paleontologist Florentino Ameghino, who made paleontological history on the other side of the South Atlantic Ocean. He studied and described the first dinosaur bones that were discovered in Argentina

ABOVE LEFT. *Plate 93.* Collecting Triassic dinosaurs in the Red beds along the border between Lesotho and South Africa. A. W. Crompton, then director of the museum in Capetown, on the left; R. F. Ewer, then of Rhodes University, Grahamstown, on the right

BELOW LEFT. *Plate 94.* The site of a dinosaur excavation in Lesotho. A. W. Crompton, then director of the South African Museum, on the left. Numerous bones of Triassic dinosaurs were collected from this small quarry in a Basuto "backyard"

Plate 95. Tendaguru hill and village, in the days of German East Africa, before the First World War. This locality is now in Tanzania

Plate 98. A gigantic leg bone, exposed at Tendaguru

Plate 99. A dig at Tendaguru, with tons of earth removed and piled up around the borders of the excavation. Many gigantic dinosaur bones are thus exposed, ready to be catalogued, encased in protective plaster jackets, and removed from the ground

Plate 100. A restoration by one of the native workmen at Tendaguru, showing his idea of what a dinosaur skeleton might look like

Plate 101. A heavy bone, in its plaster jacket, is carried back to camp at Tendaguru

Plate 102. Here are being constructed a few of the hundreds of bamboo sheaths that were necessary for carrying the dinosaur bones from Tendaguru to Lindi, on the coast

Plate 103. Dinosaur bones on the way from Tendaguru to the seaport of Lindi

Plate 104. Manhandling boxes of dinosaur bones onto a dhow at Lindi, the next-to-last stage in the long trip from Tendaguru to Berlin

Plate 105. Digging out Triassic reptiles from the Santa Maria Formation, on the outskirts of the city of Santa Maria, Rio Grande do Sul, Brazil. The paleontologist is Llewellyn Price, an outstanding Brazilian student of fossil reptiles

Plate 106. Excavating Triassic reptiles from a *sanga*, or gully, in the Santa Maria Formation, Rio Grande do Sul, Brazil. This was the region in which von Huene worked in 1928

Plate 107. Dinosaurs from Down Under. Making casts of large dinosaur footprints along the shore at Broome, West Australia

Plate 108. The vertical cliffs at Festingsodden beacon, Spitzbergen, where the footprints of Lower Cretaceous dinosaurs were discovered. The prints can be seen above the person holding the measuring rod

Plate 109. Making a mold of a dinosaur footprint on the cliff at Festingsodden beacon, Spitzbergen — a locality only about 700 miles from the north pole. It was a frustrating experience, working against gravity and the effects of constant salt spray

Plate 110. The casts, successfully completed, are now ready for shipment from Spitzbergen to Oslo. From left to right: Lily Monsen, Arne Martinsen, Dr. Natascha Heintz and Erik Ståhl

Plate 111. Work in the field is but the prelude to much more work in the laboratory. Mounting the skeleton of *Brontosaurus,* from the Bone Cabin Quarry, at The American Museum of Natural History, New York

Plate 112. Dinosaur skeletons being assembled and put in place in a new exhibition hall at The American Museum of Natural History, New York

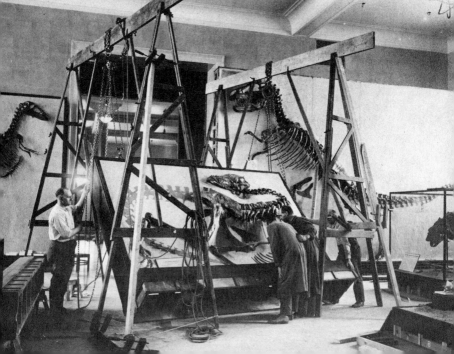

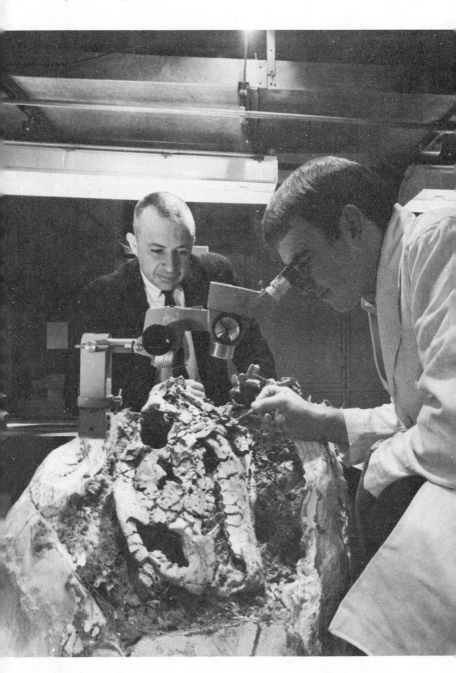

Plate 114. Reminiscences. Two of the "old-timers," William Berryman Scott, on the left, and Barnum Brown, exchange opinions based on their long years of work on fossils, in field and laboratory

Plate 115. A veteran returns to the field of his conquests. Charles M. Sternberg preparing a dinosaur skeleton for exhibition *in situ* at the Alberta Dinosaur Park

Plate 116. A magnificent result of great effort on the part of many men. Here we see the skeleton of a dinosaur—on public display, and available for research by pale-ontologists. This is the evidence of evolution that took place many millions of years ago. It is the testament from the earth as to past life on the earth. And to the appreciative eye this great skeleton is not only a source of much information and knowledge; it is an object of beauty in its own right. Perhaps this gives an indication as to why some men spend their lives in the search for dinosaurs

some of those years, and prevented the expedition from journeying into Mongolia.

So it was that on a spring morning in 1922 the first large-scale expedition of the Central Asiatic Expeditions of the American Museum of Natural History made its way out of Kalgan on the border, and entered Mongolia, to search for the birthplace of man in central Asia. The personnel of this expedition included, in addition to Andrews, the leader, Walter Granger, chief paleontologist and second in command, and Professor C. P. Berkey and Frederick K. Morris, two outstanding geologists, who unraveled many of the hitherto unknown geologic structures in this isolated land. Of particular importance to the success of the expedition was the representative for the Mongolian Government, T. Badmajapoff, without whose help the party would have been unable to reach the inner recesses of Mongolia. There were in addition technicians and a group of Chinese and Mongol assistants— in all, some twenty-six persons. The route for the motorcars was from Peking to Kalgan, the gateway to Mongolia, then northwest toward the capital of Mongolia, Ulan Bator (or Urga, the name then in frequent use), and from thence southwest into the desert.

WALTER GRANGER

The key person in the assemblage of scientific talent—if the expedition were to accomplish its avowed purpose of finding the remains of ancient man—was Walter Granger, the paleontologist. He was a good man to have along in every respect. He was a superb field paleontologist, an expert with many years' experience in the search for fossil vertebrates, and a man with an unusually fine personality, a man who could work well with other people because he was a man other people universally liked.

Walter Granger was born in Vermont in 1872, and grew up in that wooded and rocky state. As a boy he was intensely interested in the wildlife around him. Through various circumstances he appeared at

---

Figure 35. The first page of Walter Granger's field book for 1923, showing the names of the scientific and technical members of the Central Asiatic Expedition to Mongolia, and the localities explored with their Mongolian designations

the American Museum of Natural History in 1890, a long, gangling youth not quite eighteen years old, to begin his lifelong association, and what was to prove a very distinguished career, with that institution. His beginnings at the museum were indeed lowly—he was a sort of handyman in the custodial department, who lent a hand in the Taxidermy Department. As he recalled, many years later:

"In the taxidermy shop my task, aside from keeping the place clean, was to skin and preserve the birds, mammals and reptiles which died in the Central Park Zoo and elsewhere and I have never since been squeamish about odors!

"All this time I had visions of future field work. My chance came in 1894 when I was sent west to collect mammals, and used the fossil collectors' camps as a base. Two years later, on the advice of Dr. Chapman [Frank Chapman, the noted ornithologist] I changed from the Department of Birds and Mammals to that of Vertebrate Palaeontology, principally because of the opportunities it offered for field work in which I was getting more and more interested. During these 45 years I have been absent from the field but very few seasons" (Granger quoted by Simpson, "Memorial," 1942, page 160).

Young Granger quickly proved his worth as a paleontologist not only in the field but also in the laboratory, so that by 1897 he was playing a leading role in the American Museum excavations for Jurassic dinosaurs along Como Bluff. During six seasons he participated in the dinosaur project in Wyoming, devoting his energies to the diggings at the Bone Cabin Quarry, which he helped to locate. In 1899 Dr. Wortman, who had been in charge of the dinosaur quarrying, left the American Museum to go to the Carnegie Museum in Pittsburgh, and from that time on, Granger took charge of the work.

Granger's association with dinosaurs came to an end in 1902. From then until he embarked upon the first of the Central Asiatic Expeditions he was primarily concerned with those ancient mammals that became the rulers of the land after the extinction of the dinosaurs. Granger's contributions in this field of study were of enormous importance; in fact, it was his work, carried on in collaboration with Dr. William Diller Matthew, that virtually defined the nature of mammalian life during the Paleocene epoch, the time of the first great evolutionary radiation of mammals. During about two decades, beginning in 1903, Granger made a solid reputation as a collector and student of the most primitive mammals—a reputation for which his name will be remembered as long as men study the annals of paleontology.

Then in 1921 and 1922 Granger began a new scientific career—in Asia. On April 21, 1922, he, together with the other members of the Central Asiatic Expedition, left Kalgan on the first great journey into the unknown lands of Mongolia. It was a group of men who would share many experiences and even hardships before the end of the season. And long before the summer had run its course, every man of this historic group would be glad that Walter Granger was one of their party. A big, jovial person with a hearty laugh, Granger by his very presence, by the force of his remarkable personality, helped immeasurably to make the work of the expedition go smoothly. And Granger, by virtue of his expert knowledge of fossils and of how to look for fossils, contributed in a large degree to making the results of that first year in the Gobi most memorable indeed.

FIRST DISCOVERIES

Before the first Central Asiatic Expedition had reached Ulan Bator, at a locality known as Iren Dabasu, less than half the distance to the Mongolian capital, fossil bones were discovered. But they were not the bones of early man—they were the bones of ancient mammals, and at one place, the bones of Cretaceous dinosaurs that had inhabited the world perhaps a hundred million years before the first man made his appearance on the earth. Such are the fortunes of Science; the search for one thing almost as often as not leads to the discovery of something else quite unexpected, quite unrelated to the goal that is being pursued, and frequently as important as that which was originally sought. Which does not imply that ancient dinosaurs are more important than ancient men, but they *are* none the less important.

Some hasty collecting was carried out, and then the cars went on their way to Ulan Bator. Not much time could be spent at Iren Dabasu, for this was a summer for reconnaissance, for tentative probing, a summer during which much ground must be covered, a summer devoted to a general survey of the Mongolian scene.

From Ulan Bator, which was reached in due time, the motorcade turned toward the southwest and drove into the desert. Far out in Mongolia, at the end of many weeks of exploration to the west, the expedition finally turned eastward to begin the long journey back to the headquarters in Peking. The party had driven to the east along an old trail for several days, when unexpectedly one afternoon the trail led the procession of cars to the edge of a large, eroded basin formed in red sandstones. Within this basin and around its edges were weathered natural monuments and sculptured cliffs, of which one large line of cliffs was particularly impressive, especially when the setting sun illuminated the red rocks so that they seemed to catch fire and glow against the darkening sky of evening. These became the "Flaming Cliffs" of Shabarakh Usu, as the locality was designated by the expedition (it is now officially named Bain-Dzak), a locality destined to become famous in the annals of dinosaur collecting. At the foot of these cliffs the fossil hunters found bones that were then unfamiliar to Granger and his associates, and fossilized eggshells that at the time were supposed to be portions of the eggs of large birds. Again, as at Iren Dabasu, there was little time; the expedition was forced to push on—to get out of the Gobi before the bad weather of autumn settled upon the land. But as the cars drove over to the east and the south, the men were already making plans for the next year.

THE FLAMING CLIFFS

The next year arrived, as next years do, and again the expedition was in Mongolia. This time an adequate stop was made at Iren Dabasu, where bones and skeletons of Cretaceous dinosaurs were collected. The hurried work of the previous year had shown that the fossils of central Asia, if not the remains of ancient man, were none the less of great importance, for there were not only the bones of dinosaurs but also the bones of many other animals that were to add new and important facets to our knowledge of the history of life. Consequently the expedition this year included several trained paleontologists and collectors, men who were abundantly able to cope with any fossils that might be found, under any conditions in which they might be found. There was Walter Granger again, to continue the direction of the paleontological explorations, and with him were two of the American Museum's most able paleontological field men, Peter Kaisen and George Olsen. In addition there was another fossil collector, Albert Johnson, who had worked with Barnum Brown along the Red Deer River. With such men at hand the weeks spent at Iren Dabasu were almost certain to be productive. And they were. Several quarries were opened and developed, from which a considerable collection of bones and skeletons was removed. As Andrews said in his account of the expedition "bones of both flesh-eating and herbivorous dinosaurs, of several species and many individuals, were piled one upon the other in a heterogeneous mass." It was a profitable dig paleontologically speaking, but there were other things still to be done before the summer had run its course. The group was anxious to get back to Shabarakh Usu (or Bain-Dzak), to the Flaming Cliffs; it was an exciting spot, and it beckoned the men on to the west, into the heart of Mongolia.

To the west they journeyed, stopping for a rendezvous on the way with the camel caravan. On the afternoon of July 8, 1923, the expedition was again at the Flaming Cliffs, setting up camp and looking forward with eager anticipation to the pleasant task of searching for fossils in this remote and starkly beautiful corner of central Asia.

Figure 36. A page from the 1923 field book of Walter Granger, showing his map and diagram of the Shabarakh Usu, or Bain-Dzak, locality, where skeletons and eggs of the primitive horned dinosaur *Protoceratops* were excavated

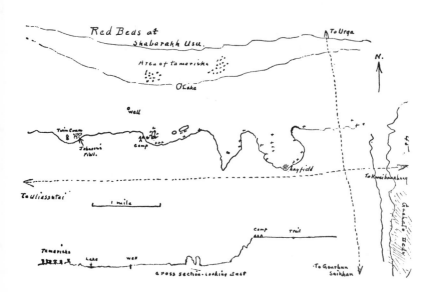

It did not take long for the enthusiastic fossil hunters to locate the treasures for which they were searching. This year they could prospect and dig with some degree of understanding, because in the interval since their preliminary discoveries of the previous season some studies had been made of the few fossils that then had been collected, so there were now available clues as to the nature of these fossils. In short, the bones at Shabarakh Usu were those of a very primitive horned dinosaur—one of the first of the horned dinosaurs—and this ancestor of what was to be during late Cretaceous time a flourishing line of dinosaurian evolution had been christened *Protoceratops andrewsi* by Drs. W. K. Gregory and C. C. Mook of the American Museum. The name was an apt one: *protos*—the first, and *ceros* plus *ops*—horn plus face. (This compound suffix is commonly applied to the horned dinosaurs.) The trivial name *andrewsi* was of course in honor of Roy Andrews, the leader of the expedition.

The work at the Flaming Cliffs was the first phase of a collecting program that extended through two seasons; the expedition returned to this locality again in 1925. And in the course of these two summers of work an unparalleled collection of *Protoceratops* was accumulated —skulls and bones and complete, articulated skeletons. All in all more than a hundred specimens of *Protoceratops* were collected, a series of dinosaurs that in numbers surpasses even the remarkable group of *Iguanodon* skeletons from Bernissart, described in Chapter 3.

There was more than mere quantity to make the skulls and skeletons of *Protoceratops* significant, even though the dinosaurs excavated at the Flaming Cliffs probably exceeded in numbers of individuals belonging to a single species any collection of dinosaurs that had ever been made before. For instance, in this collection there were individuals in all stages of growth, from those newly hatched to fully adult animals. For the first time in the history of the study of dinosaurs it was possible to get an idea as to how some of these ancient reptiles grew up. Strange as it may seem, there had been very few juvenile dinosaurs of any kind discovered before the collection was made at

Figure 37. Another page from the 1923 field book of Walter Granger, with notes concerning the occurrence of *Protoceratops*

for detailed notes on these
beds see Morris' record.

Red Beds (Djadochta)

Thickness is exposed along the face of the Flaming Cliffs — Shabarakh Usu about 150 feet.

Material almost entirely a fine sandstone (small rounded quartz grains) and colored by oxidization a pale brick red. A vertical cleavage in the prominent headlands and buttes. Concretions abundant and occurring usually in strata. Crossbedding frequent — a strong suggestion of wind deposition from great part of the sediment.

Fossils found more commonly in the concretions beds in the soft, loosely compacted material. The association of skeleton material and the many occurrences of egg clutches suggests a rapid deposition. Entire absence of aquatic forms suggests rather arid conditions. No turtles of any sort found.

Egg Clutch No. 867 and Dinosaur 868.

The eggs, some ten in number, were closely grouped occupying about eighteen inches square before weathering. The skeleton (No. 868) consisting of fore limb — foot and a series of vertebrae extending up to the skull lay above the eggs separated by about four inches of matrix. The fore-foot lay directly above the eggs with the claws reaching out.

weathering face

See photographs by Andrews and Granger.

Shabarakh Usu, and for that matter, very few have been discovered since. (We did encounter a juvenile sauropod dinosaur, it will be recalled, from the great quarry at Dinosaur National Monument.) Most dinosaurs are known from the adults; it is therefore a rare privilege to be able to visualize growth in one species of dinosaur, as is so nicely illustrated by the display of a dozen *Protoceratops* skulls in the American Museum of Natural History.

It will be remembered that on the first brief visit to the Flaming Cliffs in 1922 some fragments of eggshell, supposedly of extinct birds, had been found. Soon after the beginning of the work at this place in 1923, George Olsen found a group of three eggs. Were these birds' eggs, or might it be possible that they were the eggs of dinosaurs, specifically of *Protoceratops?* This question, which immediately came to the mind of Walter Granger, raised hopes and expectations, and plunged the whole group of fossil hunters into a fever of egg-hunting excitement. The basin was searched with avidity and in detail, and as the days went by fossil eggs came to light in great numbers—as fragments, as complete eggs, as clusters of eggs, and even as nests of eggs.

These obviously were not the eggs of birds. They were quite elongated, shaped very much like the eggs of certain modern lizards, and their surfaces were roughly corrugated. Some of the clusters were especially revealing, for these were composed of circles of eggs. In one instance there is an inner circle of five eggs, a circle surrounding it with eleven eggs, and beyond that two peripheral eggs indicating an outer circle that originally may have contained as many as twenty eggs. Here the record is plainly preserved in the rock. Quite obviously a female dinosaur dug a large pit in the sand of an ancient Cretaceous plain, just as today her reptilian cousins, the gigantic marine turtles, dig pits in the sand on beaches of oceanic islands. And in this pit she deposited her eggs, perhaps turning around and around during the process, so that the eggs were laid in concentric circles. Then she carefully covered the eggs with sand, trusting to the heat of the sun to hatch them, in the same way as do the marine turtles or many modern crocodiles and other reptiles.

Fortunately for the fossil hunters at the Flaming Cliffs, and for the science of paleontology, something happened so that the eggs never hatched. Perhaps there was a cool spell of weather, with the result that the sand never warmed up enough beneath the glowing rays of the sun to bring to completion the development of the embryos.

Whatever the cause of the failure, the eggs remained in the ground; subsequently they cracked, and their cavities were filled with sand. Eventually they were fossilized, to preserve in a dramatic way the story of a dinosaur and her nest as it took place almost a hundred million years ago.

Granger and his associates assumed that the numerous eggs at the Flaming Cliffs were those of *Protoceratops*, and it is a logical assumption. Here in the ground were untold numbers of a small ancestral horned dinosaur, the adults of which were about six or eight feet in length, and here were untold numbers of fossil eggs of the right size to have been laid by the dinosaur *Protoceratops*, eggs about eight inches in length. Why should not the fossil locality at Shabarakh Usu, or Bain-Dzak, be a burial ground for this particular dinosaur and for the eggs it laid, a paleontological cemetery preserving not only all stages of growth, as has been mentioned, but also the egg that preceded the growth? The association of *Protoceratops* skeletons with

---

Figure 38. The Cretaceous dinosaur *Protoceratops*. Restoration by Margaret Matthew Colbert

the eggs seems supremely reasonable, and has been accepted by most paleontologists, although some dissenters have denied that the eggs found at this locality belong to the dinosaur.

It should be added that in addition to the large quantities of eggs attributed to *Protoceratops* occurring at the Flaming Cliffs, several other types of fossil eggs also were found, though in quite limited numbers. Some of these eggs are round; others are elongated but rather small. How are they to be identified? If the most numerous eggs, the large elongated, rough-shelled eggs, are those of *Protoceratops*, then it follows that the other eggs may be associated with some of the other reptiles that were found at Shabarakh Usu. But how are any associations of eggs and bones to be made? It is a question as yet unanswered.

Perhaps a few words might be said about the animals that lived with *Protoceratops* so many million years ago. There were other dinosaurs, among them a large armored dinosaur that has been named *Pinacosaurus*. Then there were some small, lightly built meat-eating dinosaurs, *Saurornithoides* (birdlike dinosaur), *Velociraptor* (fast-running robber), and *Oviraptor* (egg stealer), as well as a large carnivore.

The discovery of *Oviraptor* provided a bit of unusual paleontological drama for the fossil hunters. Its skeleton was exposed in the rock amid a cluster of *Protoceratops* eggs. Did this small and rather elegant little dinosaur perish in the act of plundering a *Protoceratops* nest? Perhaps—perhaps not. Perhaps the occurrence of this skeleton is entirely fortuitous. But the vision of *Oviraptor* as a nest robber makes a pleasant bit of imaginative fancy and adds a certain touch of spice to the dinosaurian discoveries at the Flaming Cliffs; hence the name.

Some other reptiles were also found at the Flaming Cliffs: a crocodile and a pond turtle. This seems to indicate that the locality was a place of streams and perhaps small ponds, cutting through the sands across which *Protoceratops* wandered and congregated, to lay its eggs.

Our immediate interest is in the dinosaurs from Shabarakh Usu, but it should be mentioned that famous though this place may be for the dinosaurs and the dinosaur eggs found there, it is equally if not even more important, paleontologically speaking, by virtue of some tiny skulls of mammals, first collected at the Flaming Cliffs by the men of the Central Asiatic Expeditions. Here again a great step forward in our knowledge of the history of life was made through the working of chance. Andrews had organized his elaborate venture in central Asia to search for the beginnings of ancient man, but instead his expedition had found dinosaurs. Andrews and Granger and their co-workers had returned to Shabarakh Usu to collect dinosaurs—which they did on a grand scale. And to their surprise and delight they also found in these dinosaur beds the first placental mammals, small insect-eating animals related to modern shrews and hedgehogs. These ancient mammals are, in effect, representative of the ancestors of all of the dominant mammals that today rule the earth. There at the Flaming Cliffs, in rocks perhaps as much as a hundred million years in age, were the beginnings not only of shrews and hedgehogs but also in a sense of bats and lions, of rhinoceroses and cattle, of monkeys and apes and of ourselves. A few minute skulls and jaws were the "haul" from the Flaming Cliffs, a collection to be carried in a cigar box. Yet these few fossils, seemingly so insignificant, represented one of the greatest accomplishments of the expedition. Here was visible proof of the genesis of a new era in the long story of life history. Here were the ancestors of the animals that eventually, and at no great interval in terms of geologic time, were to replace the dinosaurs as the lords of the continents.

But let us get back to the dinosaurs. Certainly the discovery of dinosaur eggs at Shabarakh Usu caught the fancy of the public, and important though the Cretaceous mammals might be, it was the collection of *Protoceratops* bones and eggs that gained for the expedition into Mongolia its widest acclaim. Dinosaur eggs became objects of lively interest in the news columns, and dinosaurs, already widely appreciated by people in many lands, became increasingly well established in the public mind.

The Central Asiatic Expedition collected dinosaurs at several other localities in Mongolia—such places as Oshih, Ondai Sair, and On Gong, each of these localities located, as are Iren Dabasu and Shabarakh Usu, in an isolated basin, separate and disconnected from every other basin. But although important finds were made at the various dinosaur localities, none could measure up to the discoveries made at the Flaming Cliffs.

THE INTERIM YEARS—AND THEIR RESULTS

Such was the course of the Asiatic dinosaur rush—in its first phase. It is the story of three probing trips into Mongolia in 1922, 1923, and 1925. True enough, the Central Asiatic Expeditions ventured into the field again, in 1928 and in 1930, but after 1925 they never reached what was then called Outer Mongolia, where the dinosaurs are. Yet even though the men of the Central Asiatic Expedition were forced to limit their objectives and their activities in the later years of their work, they had already accomplished great things. In those three short summers, especially in 1923 and 1925, they had opened a new chapter in the buried record of the dinosaurs. They had established central Asia as a locale for the discovery of these extinct reptiles, comparable to western North America. They had made the first excavations in a paleontologically unknown land, just as Marsh and Cope had done, a half-century earlier, in another paleontologically unknown land.

The beginning of the Asiatic dinosaur rush was soon over; after 1925 there was a long lull in the search for dinosaurs in Mongolia. It was a lull occasioned by the militant march of world history, a procession of armies and battles across the face of Asia that crowded out the peaceful pursuits of fossil hunters and their ilk. This does not mean that the dinosaurs of central Asia were completely forgotten. In the practice of paleontology there is always a necessary time lag between discovery and collecting on the one hand, and study and description on the other. This is the interval during which the fossils are "prepared" in the laboratory, the long months during which they are chipped out of and freed from the encasing rock, and cleaned and hardened with various penetrating agents, to make of them significant objects suitable for study and interpretation. It is a tedious process—and it takes time.

Consequently the work on the dinosaurs from Mongolia continued for a number of years after the adventurous days of collecting had passed. After the fossils were prepared, there came the months and years of study and description, the end result being a series of technical publications by Granger and Matthew, Gregory, Mook, Gilmore, Brown, and Schlaikjer. This roster of names illustrates very nicely the change that had taken place since the days of Marsh and Cope; large projects were no longer the efforts of a single man and his subordinates. Many men were involved in bringing to light the dinosaurs of Mongolia—in the field, in the preparation laboratory, and at the study table. And the work at the study table, the hours of careful investigation from which flowed the stream of publications that are the ultimate goal of all serious research, revealed the nature and the significance of the dinosaurs that had been collected in Mongolia.

These scientific writings offered some clues as to the composition of dinosaurian life in central Asia during the Cretaceous period, when the gigantic reptilian rulers of the continents were at the climax of their evolutionary development. The clues to be read from the fossils indicated that in Cretaceous time this remote section of the world evidently had close connections with western North America, probably by way of a trans-Bering land bridge, so that dinosaurs and other land-living animals could wander back and forth from one region to the other. There would seem to have been connections with Europe, too, but the relationships with North America evidently were particularly strong.

Yet the evidence, satisfying though it might be, was still far from complete; indeed, it was, except for the abundantly recorded *Protoceratops,* based largely on scattered skeletons and skulls. Andrews, Granger, and their companions quite obviously had barely scratched the surface of the Mongolian dinosaur beds. This is not to be wondered at—they were the first paleontological explorers in an interior subcontinent, a country half the extent of the continental United States.

RUSSIAN EXPLORATIONS

Naturally, the work of the Central Asiatic Expeditions attracted the attention of paleontologists throughout the world. Consequently, when the turbulent days of the thirties and the cruel world conflict of the forties had run their successive courses eyes were again turned in the direction of Mongolia. But this time the view toward central Asia was not taken from America, but rather from a closer region.

Mongolia had come within the Russian sphere of influence as early as the mid-twenties; indeed, this was one reason why Andrews was unable to lead his party beyond the limits of Inner Mongolia after 1925. It was natural, therefore, that Russian paleontologists should turn toward the fossiliferous green pastures of central Asia soon after the guns ceased to roar in 1945. Mongolia was the place for them to explore, and there they went. So began the second phase of the Asiatic dinosaur rush.

It began in 1946 and continued through 1947 and 1949. It was, in effect, a modernized version of the Central Asiatic Expeditions of the twenties, with reliance placed upon heavy-duty trucks in place of camel caravans for the hauling of supplies, and upon jeep-like cars for scouting and exploration. It was a well-planned series of expeditions, based upon three years of preparations in Moscow, and crowned with success, the result of three summers of work in Mongolia.

This, being a Soviet effort, was strictly official. The expeditions were carried out under the auspices of the Academy of Sciences of the USSR, the central, controlling organization that is responsible for scientific research and technological development in Russia. The adviser for the expeditions was the late Academician I. Orlov, the dean

---

Figure 39. Map of Mongolia, showing the routes of the Russian expeditions of 1946, 1948, and 1949, and the fossil localities (in black) explored and excavated by those expeditions

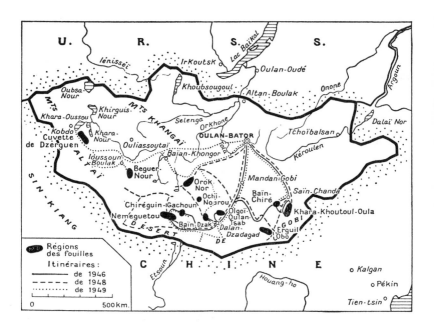

of Russian paleontologists, a gentle and charming man and an authority on fossil reptiles and mammals. (It should be said here that although the Academy of Sciences is a vast organization, employing thousands of people, it is ruled from the top by a small cadre of Academicians, in all, less than two hundred individuals. To be elected an Academician is perhaps the greatest honor that can come to a Russian scientist, an honor comparable to election in the United States to the National Academy of Sciences, in Britain to the Royal Society. Thus the expeditions to Mongolia had the personal attention from one of the élite in the scientific community of Russia.) The leader of the expeditions during the several field seasons was Dr. I. Efremov, renowned not only for the study of extinct animals, particularly reptiles, but also a very popular writer of fiction, a man with a large following of readers, most of whom are perhaps only slightly if at all aware of his reputation as a scientist. Efremov, a stocky individual with a keen mind and a restless temperament, was well fitted for leadership of such a large undertaking, and he led it with skill and vigor. Next in command to Efremov, also an outstanding authority on fossil reptiles, was A. Rozhdestvensky, who has written a lucid and fascinating account of the Muscovite campaign in Mongolia. Of course, there were other participating paleontologists, as well as a group of skilled technicians and assistants, together with the usual complement of truck

Figure 40. Twenty-five years later. The Russians follow trails first blazed by the Central Asiatic Expeditions of The American Museum of Natural History. Gone are the camel caravans; modern, powerful trucks now do the heavy hauling

drivers, mechanics, laborers, cooks, and other functionaries necessary to the success of the venture.

The second phase of the great Asiatic dinosaur rush began in 1946 with a preliminary reconnaissance journey through Mongolia during two summer months. The men on this first trip through the Gobi located various fossiliferous sites and made some preliminary excavations. Then, with the experience of the summer behind them, they were able to plan for a long and elaborate expedition during the next year, an expedition that began with the departure of some of its members from Moscow during the dead of winter, followed by two months or more of preparation at Ulan Bator before the caravan drove out of that city on March 18th. And the expedition remained in the field until the last possible moment, until the arctic winds from the north and the threat of impassable snows drove the group back to Ulan Bator. This extended exploration into the Gobi was followed, two years later, by another long expedition that not only retraced the tracks of the previous explorations but also probed far to the west, to the westernmost limits of Mongolia.

Of course, the Russians came into Mongolia from the north, entering Ulan Bator to find it metamorphosing into a modern city with shining new buildings, public squares and parks, a sizable university, and many other amenities, quite in contrast to the primitive Asiatic capital, hardly larger than a village, seen by Andrews and his companions in 1922. From Ulan Bator, Efremov and his caravan of five scout cars turned toward the south.

At a locality known as Bain-Chiré, in the direction of but several hundred kilometers to the northwest of Iren Dabasu, where the Central Asiatic Expeditions had worked so successfully, the Soviet expedition discovered dinosaur bones, including an interesting skeleton of an armored dinosaur. It was a significant discovery, but even greater things were to come.

The expedition then turned to the west—to Bain-Dzak (our familiar old locality of Shabarakh Usu), and there continued the work that had been carried on amid such scenes of excitement and anticipation by the Central Asiatic Expeditions, more than a score of years earlier. Naturally, the Soviet Expedition uncovered more *Protoceratops* and more eggs. Bain-Dzak proved to be as rich a hunting ground in the forties as it had been in the twenties, an illustration of the fact that as the land erodes, more fossils come into view. Indeed, if the proper trained persons are not at hand to discover and excavate fossils, the ancient remains soon weather away into fragments and are lost. One may only speculate as to the vast numbers of fossils that have disappeared as a result of erosion at a locality such as Bain-Dzak during the millennia before any men ever became paleontologists; such thoughts may lead one along various stray philosophical paths. Our concern is dinosaurs, of which the Soviet paleontologists discovered new as well as familiar forms at Bain-Dzak. Here was found an armored dinosaur, *Syrmosaurus*, that would appear to have been a connecting link between the plated dinosaurs so typical of Upper Jurassic deposits and the abundant armored dinosaurs that characterize the Upper Cretaceous beds of western North America. This was a most important new discovery, adding a link between two large groups of dinosaurs—one more building block in the evolutionary structure of these ancient reptiles.

THE GREAT NEMEGETU BASIN

The most important contributions of the Soviet expeditions perhaps were not so much in the work done at Baine-Chiré and at Bain-Dzak, as in the discovery and development of a series of fossil quarries in a great topographic basin some three hundred kilometers or more to the west of Bain-Dzak, an area of Cretaceous rocks known as Nemegetu. Much of the activity of these expeditions during three field seasons was centered in this fossiliferous region, and the efforts of the bone diggers were well repaid. It was an extraordinarily rich area, yielding many dinosaur skeletons, skulls, and bones. One of the main camps for the expeditions was at a spectacularly rich fossil locality, christened most appropriately "The Dragon's Tomb." For here were the bones of dragons—gigantic dragons that inhabited the earth in the distant past. There were other important dinosaurian graveyards scattered over a region more than a hundred kilometers in length within the Nemegetu Basin.

As a result of the digging here, at least ten complete skeletons of dinosaurs were recovered, not to mention numerous other fossils representative of these ancient reptiles. There was a gigantic carnivorous dinosaur, closely related to if not identical with the well-known giant predator from the Cretaceous beds of Montana, *Tyrannosaurus*. There was also found the gigantic duck-billed dinosaur *Saurolophus*, hitherto known from North America. These dinosaurs, as well as various other dinosaurian genera, including some of the small ostrich-like dinosaurs, indicate quite clearly the nature of the close connections that bound central Asia to western North America during Cretaceous times. As mentioned previously, the continental regions now separated by the Bering Straits were then one great tropical land, a broad lowland across which numerous dinosaurian giants and their lesser brethren wandered far and wide, from east to west, with great facility.

Thus the digs in southwestern Mongolia by Efremov, Rozhdestvensky, and their fellow workers revealed a new and a fabulous hunting ground for dinosaurian treasures. The Nemegetu Basin, in the heart of central Asia, now takes a position of first rank along with other classic dinosaur localities, especially those with which it is intimately related, such as the Red Deer River in Alberta and the Hell Creek area in northern Montana. Barnum Brown and the Sternbergs had revealed a chapter in Cretaceous history by floating down a northern river to dig in its bordering cliffs; Efremov and his party, like Andrews and the Central Asiatic Expeditions two decades earlier, added still another chapter to this history by driving in their scout cars and trucks through the outer reaches of Mongolia, to dig in the broad basins of that interior land. In the two continents prodigious quantities of new and significant dinosaur bones were discovered —partly by luck, partly by intuitive judgment, and very much by a vast amount of hard, backbreaking work.

The Soviet expeditions shipped back to Moscow some 120 tons of fossil bones, a considerable proportion of which was excavated from the Nemegetu Basin. Here is one measure of their success. And why should there have been such great numbers of dinosaur bones and skeletons deposited in the Nemegetu Basin? The answer to this question was given by Efremov and one of his associates, Novojilov, as a result of their study of the geology of Nemegetu. Here, they maintain,

Figure 41. The skeleton of the gigantic Cretaceous carnivorous dinosaur *Tyrannosaurus*, from Montana. Its counterpart was found by the Russian expeditions working in the Nemegetu Basin of Mongolia

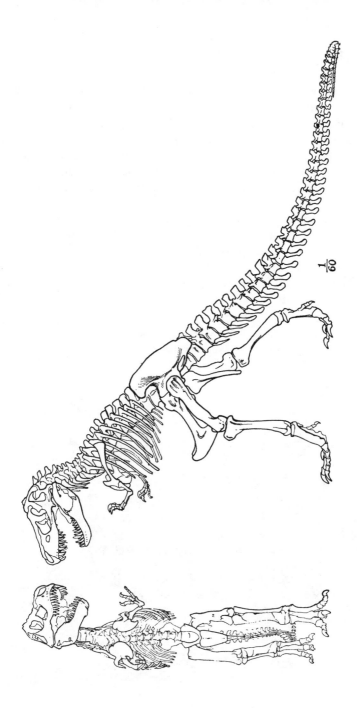

$\frac{1}{60}$

are sediments laid down in the delta of an enormous ancient river, sediments that represent not only deposition by the river itself but also accumulations of sands and muds on the bottom of ponds and lakes dotted about the broad delta. This delta, perhaps forty kilometers in width, and undoubtedly covered with lush vegetation, was the habitat of many dinosaurs—herbivorous dinosaurs that fed upon the abundant plant life at hand, and carnivorous dinosaurs that preyed upon the inoffensive plant-eaters. It was an ideal environment for the support of a large dinosaurian population; and where such a population existed there were bound to be deaths and burials. Some of these animals were preserved in the ever-accumulating flow of sands and muds, transported across the delta through numerous river channels or caught in the silt traps of small lakes and ponds. And so a record of the dinosaurian life of Mongolia was preserved, in the unlighted

Figure 42. Even as late as 1946, the heavy Russian trucks were strange and terrifying objects to inhabitants of the far reaches of Mongolia—and to their camels and their dogs

depths of sands and muds turned to rock; and so, as a result of long years of erosion, and of the efforts of some men in whom the bump of curiosity is strongly developed, this record was brought from its dark depths back to the light.

One interesting aspect of the Russian explorations in the Gobi, especially in the Nemegetu Basin, is the manner in which the discovery of late Cretaceous dinosaurs, especially the giant duck-billed dinosaur *Saurolophus,* fulfilled in part a prophecy made by Professor Osborn in 1930.

"There are still great unknown or unfossiliferous gaps to be filled in the prehistory of the ancient life of the Gobi Desert. Our explorations have as yet not revealed the closing periods of the Lower Cretaceous nor the closing period of the Upper Cretaceous in which large ceratopsians, like *Triceratops,* as well as large iguanodonts, like *Trachodon,* will doubtless be found" (Osborn, page 542, 1930).

Thus some of the gaps in the fossil record of Mongolia were filled, and the vision of central Asia as a great hunting ground in which would be found the fossilized remains of the last of the dinosaurs, as set forth by Osborn and Granger so many years ago, became a reality. It was the Nemegetu Basin within which Upper Cretaceous dinosaurs came to light in remarkable numbers, and it was to the Nemegetu Basin that the Russians returned, again and once again.

MONGOLS AND POLES

And it was the Nemegetu Basin that attracted other paleontologists to its fossiliferous slopes, a decade and a half after the Soviet expeditions had completed their explorations. In 1964 what may be called the third phase of the Asiatic dinosaur rush began—this time with Mongols and Poles as the dinosaur hunters. When Roy Andrews led the pioneering American Museum expeditions into central Asia in the twenties, the Mongols were by and large nomadic shepherds, with their attention centered upon mutton and wool and camels and horses. Dinosaur skeletons were to them esoteric and perhaps incomprehensible objects. When Efremov led the elaborate Soviet expeditions into central Asia in the forties, Mongolia was in the throes of an industrial and cultural revolution. Ulan Bator was becoming a modern city, and many Mongols were turning away from the primitive life of their forebears, to participate in a twentieth-century world of sophisticated art, technology, and science. The university in Ulan Bator was developing rapidly, and Mongolian scientists were making plans for the exploitation of their own scientific resources. Needless to say, one of the outstanding scientific resources of this nation is to be found in marvelous fossil beds of western Mongolia, with rich deposits of dinosaur skeletons. For the proper development of their plans, some outside help would be useful to the Mongolian paleontologists.

So an agreement was made with Polish paleontologists for joint work in Mongolia, and in 1964 the first Mongolian-Polish expedition entered the field. The Mongols and Poles concentrated a considerable amount of their efforts in the Nemegetu Basin, where they, like their Russian predecessors, collected late Cretaceous dinosaurs, including a tyrannosaur skeleton. They also gave a great deal of attention to the famous Bain-Dzak locality, the region of the Flaming Cliffs, which so long ago had been christened Shabarakh Usu by the American Museum expedition, and there they collected *Protoceratops* skeletons and eggs as might be expected, a complete skeleton of the armored dinosaur *Pinacosaurus,* and various other fossil reptiles. Of particular importance was their discovery at this locality of numerous Cretaceous mammals similar to the early mammals found here years before by Walter Granger and his associates, those little warm-blooded animals living with the dinosaurs, the ancestors of the many, varied mammals that became the rulers of the earth after the dinosaurs had become extinct. In addition to work at these two famous localities, the Mongolian-Polish expedition excavated excellent dinosaur skeletons and other remains at several other sites in Mongolia, adding to their collections still more tyrannosaur skeletons, as well as skeletons of armored and duck-billed dinosaurs. The results of their work were spectacular, not so much because of completely new and unexpected discoveries, as for the fine fossils of known and expected dinosaurs and other extinct animals. It is always a good thing to get abundant and complete fossils for study and display; the worth of such collections should never be underestimated.

This latest phase of the extended Asiatic dinosaur hunt is but one part of a search for dinosaurs that began in Mongolia almost a half-century ago. It shows us that in our modern world, so reduced in size by the development of twentieth-century technology and especially by the speed of jet communications, there are even now faraway places where the romance of hunting for dinosaurs in an empty land still awaits the fossil hunter. It carries on the search for dinosaurs that was begun initially by accident and then very much by design by Roy Andrews, Walter Granger, and their associates in 1922. It continues the tradition of great dinosaur expeditions and excavations, begun almost a century ago by Marsh and Cope in the wild and then uninhabited western territories of North America.

CHAPTER 9

BELOW THE EQUATOR

THE FIRST AFRICAN DINOSAURS

Through the years, from the days of Mantell and Buckland until modern times, the search for dinosaurs has been largely concentrated in the Northern Hemisphere. Although the lands below the equator have received the attentions of various dinosaur hunters, efforts in these southern regions have not been, generally speaking, so diverse or so widely applied as the work in the northern continents.

There are two good reasons why the story has been so largely a northern one. In the first place, the early history of the search for dinosaurs was as an accident of fate necessarily concentrated in northern Europe and in North America, because those are the regions in which the sciences of geology and paleontology had their origins and early-nineteenth-century development. Those are the regions in which the pioneer geologists and paleontologists, and certainly the pioneer students of dinosaurs, lived and worked. Those are the regions where Buckland and Mantell, Owen, Huxley, Hitchcock, Marsh and Cope, and other noted dinosaur men followed the stars of their separate destinies. It was that way because the history of the modern world was that way.

Aside from the vicissitudes of human history, especially the history of modern learning, there is another reason why any account of the search for dinosaurs must be a story largely centered north of the equator, and this is to be found in the distribution of modern land masses. Look at a map, or preferably a globe. The larger portions of the continental areas, by far, are located above the middle line of the sphere; only South America below the Amazon, the southward-pointing peninsula of Africa, Australia, and of course Antarctica represent large land masses in the Southern Hemisphere. This means that most of the geology of the world is in the north; most of the exposures are there; and consequently most of the opportunities for finding dinosaurs are there. It is that way because the configurations of the continents are that way.

Actually, the first records of dinosaurs in the Southern Hemisphere were made by men in Europe—and again the accidents of history are involved. During the nineteenth century the sun never set on the British Empire—its far-flung dominion circled the earth from east to west and from north to south, and everywhere where there was British rule there were Britons, always with their eyes turned toward the homeland. It was only natural, therefore, that when fossils and many other strange objects were found in lands across the seas they were sent home for identification and study—usually to that grand and curious old institution the British Museum. So it was that the Triassic dinosaur *Massospondylus,* from the Red Beds of South Africa, was described in 1854 by Sir Richard Owen. Which makes it one of the earliest of the dinosaurs to be described and named. Two other Triassic dinosaurs from South Africa, *Euskelosaurus* and *Orosaurus,* were named by Huxley in 1866 and 1867, respectively. And that is the last we hear of dinosaurs from South Africa until almost four decades later, until the year 1904, to be exact. Dinosaur bones might have come to the occasional attention of sharp-eyed people in the southernmost tip of the African continent during the years following the descriptions by Owen and Huxley, but so far as the published record is concerned there were no additions to our knowledge of these ancient reptiles in that part of the world throughout all the latter half of the nineteenth century or well into the 1900's. And why not? The answer probably lies in the fact that through all of those years there were no men, indeed there was no single man, in southern Africa with the training and the interest to search out, study, and describe any dinosaurs that might have then been eroding out of the earth. If dinosaurs were sooner or later to be found and recognized in South Africa, there had to be someone on the spot. That someone appeared; his name was Robert Broom.

ROBERT BROOM

There have been, as we have seen, more than the usual allotment of colorful characters among the men who have pursued dinosaurs in the field and laboratory. In this category Robert Broom stands well up toward the top. His was a long and exciting life—made so to a large degree by his vitality, by his insatiable curiosity, and especially by his unorthodox way of thinking and acting. Things were always happening when Broom was around.

Robert Broom was born in 1866, in Paisley, Scotland, where the shawls come from. In Scotland he spent his boyhood. As a young man he decided to go into medicine; he studied at the ancient University of Glasgow and there he obtained his medical degree. Then he took a giant step—and disappeared. Some years later a learned paper was sent to the editor of an anatomical journal in England by a well-known Australian professor on some details of marsupial anatomy. And quite coincidentally this editor received in the same mail a much better paper on the same general subject from an unknown medical doctor living in the backland of Australia. The author of this latter paper was, of course, Robert Broom. Broom had decided that his true professional interest was in the origin of mammals, so he had gone to Australia, where the most primitive mammals are living, the egg-laying monotremes such as the duck-billed platypus and spiny echidna, and the varied host of pouched marsupials—kangaroos, wombats, and their ilk. There, hanging out his shingle in the backwoods, he practiced medicine to earn a living, and studied the anatomy of any monotremes or marsupials on which he could lay his hands. To tell the truth, Broom, although trained as a medical practitioner, had the manner of thinking and the natural curiosity of a research scientist; he was much more interested in the natural world in which he lived than in human ills and the pills that cure them.

In 1896 Broom returned to Britain for a visit, and there he saw in the British Museum the Permian and Triassic mammal-like reptiles from South Africa that had been studied by Owen and by Seeley. And quickly he saw that these fossil remains of reptiles directly ancestral to the mammals were the things to which he should turn his attention in order to get at the problems of mammalian origins. So he then and there decided on a second giant step; instead of returning to Australia he went to South Africa, there to establish a medical practice and, more importantly, so far as he was concerned, to search for and study the mammal-like reptiles that occur in such abundance in the Great Karroo—that immense semidesert basin that occupies the tip of the Cape beyond the steep, folded mountains that guard Cape Town and the coastal fringe.

The almost horizontal geological strata of the Karroo are exposed in this great elliptical basin as a series of concentric rings, with the oldest ones of Permian age around its periphery, and the youngest ones, of late Triassic age, toward the eastern end of the ellipse, where the high mountains of Lesotho rise some ten thousand feet above the level of the sea. Throughout much of the Karroo, in rocks of late Permian and early Triassic age, are found the mammal-like reptiles that for so many years were the center of Broom's attention. But around the flanks of Lesotho are Upper Triassic beds containing the ancient dinosaurs of southern Africa. And these too, as we shall see, were objects for Broom's all-encompassing mind.

Broom's life in South Africa was unique—which is to say it was *Broomian.* During his earlier years he combined medicine and paleontology in a manner that harked back to the days of that very first student of the dinosaurs, also a man of medicine, Gideon Mantell. Broom sallied forth into the countryside on sick calls as frequently as possible—indeed, he was usually more than happy to have a patient summon him to some African farm out in the veldt so that on his way he could stop to look for fossils. He found them, too, because he had been careful to locate himself in the middle of one of the world's

Figure 43. A geologic map of the Great Karroo Basin of South Africa. In the center of the concentric rings of geologic formations are the Upper Triassic beds, in which are found the bones of early dinosaurs

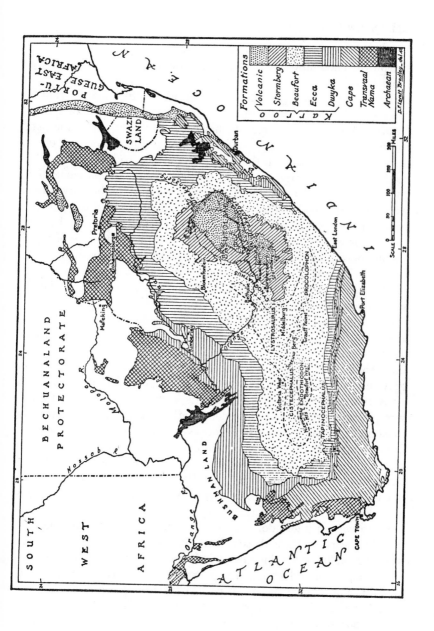

richest fossil fields and, what was especially helpful, he had a very sharp eye. Then he would take his fossils home, to clean and describe them.

Broom did not always bother to clean all the rock matrix from the surface of the fossil, because his discerning eye, so efficient at spotting fossils in the ground, seemed to have a remarkable power for penetrating the enclosing rock and interpreting the characters of the underlying bones beneath that rock. Broom was truly uncanny in his ability to "see" through stone, so that later workers who came along and laboriously cleaned the fossils originally described by Broom would find revealed to their amazed eyes the bones and the junctions between the bones, just about as Broom had said they would be. Of course this was a measure of Broom's remarkable knowledge of reptilian anatomy, a knowledge that was aided and abetted by the fact that he was possessed of a prodigious memory. In addition to these gifts, Broom had a facile pen for sketching, and most of the fossils he described were illustrated by him.

Broom spent long, hot days in the Karroo looking for fossils, and long, fruitful days in the laboratory studying and describing them, but wherever he might be, Broom presented the same appearance to the beholder. He was always dressed very formally—in a black or gray suit, with a white shirt, a stiff, wing collar and a black tie. Such a costume would have been appropriate, in Edwardian days, for a lecture platform or a formal office consultation, but so far as Broom was concerned it was appropriate for every occasion. The stories of Broom's expeditions into the rugged countryside of South Africa, toiling through the brush and across rough hillsides under a blistering sun in his black suit and stand-up collar, are legendary. He certainly did impress the Karroo farmers, who were inclined to be a rough-hewn lot.

There was an interlude, from 1903 to 1910, when Broom taught at the University of Stellenbosch. But the restrictions of academic life were too confining for this roving and restless man, so he resumed his life as a part-time doctor and a part-time paleontologist, with (it is probably fair to say) the major part of his attention given to the ancient bones in the ground rather than to the bones and other anatomical portions of his patients. For most of his life he thus worked on his own, but finally, in 1934, he retired from medicine to become a member of the scientific staff of the Transvaal Museum in Pretoria.

In this manner he worked year after year, and as his publications accumulated, for he was a prodigious writer, his fame grew; beyond the boundaries of South Africa, beyond the limits of the British Empire, to encompass the paleontological world.

Broom may be compared in some respects with his American predecessor, Edward Drinker Cope. Both men were individualists, if ever there were such. Both men were unorthodox characters, doing things in their own original ways, acting impulsively, making friends and enemies right and left, and leading fruitful and exciting lives. Both men published voluminously, and often hastily; Cope's bibliography runs to some 1,400 titles, Broom's to almost five hundred. Both men were theorizers, drawing large and far-reaching conclusions upon the basis of their fossils. Both men had interesting things to say. Both men made many mistakes, but they both made outstanding contributions to our knowledge of ancient life—and in particular to the extinct reptilian life of this planet.

Sooner or later Broom was destined to become involved with dinosaurs, and so he did in 1904 and again in 1911, when he published papers on the dinosaurs from the Cretaceous and Triassic beds of South Africa. These papers were in truth for him small dinosaurian interludes sandwiched between the outpouring from his pen on mammal-like reptiles. In fact, they were Broom's only contributions devoted to dinosaurs, and as such are works of rather small consequence when compared with his tremendous labors on the mammal-like reptiles, and his epochal work on the origins of man in South Africa. But they are of particular significance here because they mark the virtual beginning of sustained dinosaurian studies in South Africa. Before Broom there had been only the casual descriptions by Owen and by Huxley to indicate that there *were* any dinosaurs in this part of the continent. Then in 1904 and in 1911 Broom demonstrated that here was a region in which these animals had once flourished, a region that might yield many more dinosaurs to future bone hunters. It was because Broom was then and at that place the right man, the man with the necessary abilities and interests, that there came this fresh look at dinosaurs in South Africa. Perhaps it can be said that Broom, almost as an aside, began a renaissance in the search for South African dinosaurs.

THE SUCCESSORS OF BROOM

It was a beginning, and it was carried on by Sydney Haughton, an English paleontologist who followed Broom to South Africa and who devoted considerable attention to the dinosaurs of the Upper Triassic Stormberg beds. Also there was E. C. N. van Hoepen, for some years the director of the museum in Bloemfontein, and a man of many interests.

Since the early work by Broom, and the studies by Haughton and by van Hoepen, the search for South African dinosaurs has developed through the years until today it is being conducted with greater vigor and greater success than ever before. A. W. Crompton and Alan Charig (who, as we saw in a previous chapter, established the presence of ornithischian dinosaurs in the Upper Triassic beds of South Africa) and John Attridge of the University of London have been digging diligently in and around that mountainous core of the Karroo Basin contained within the new country of Lesotho. Their digging has been successful—with the result that a considerable array of new dinosaurs has come to light. Nor have they been alone—other paleontologists in South Africa also have taken up the pursuit of Triassic dinosaurs.

One of the most interesting of recent excavations in this part of the world was carried on at a locality known as Maphutseng, in Lesotho. Here, in the very backyard of an African house—a typical Basuto house with walls of mud and a thatched roof—a shallow quarry was developed by two French residents among the Basutos, the brothers Ellenberger, with Crompton and his associates participating in the dig. Many bones of large Triassic dinosaurs not unlike the bones excavated years earlier by von Huene at Trossingen in southern Germany were dug up from this reptilian graveyard, to the great interest of the native Africans of the region. And, like the excavations of the ancient dinosaurs of Trossingen, the excavation of equally ancient dinosaurs at Maphutseng will in time add new dimensions to our knowledge of these reptiles.

Yet the search for dinosaurs in Africa below the equator has not been by any means a hunt concentrated on the recovery of the earliest of dinosaurs, those of Triassic age. It has ranged higher in the geologic column, with, at one place, spectacular success. That place is Tendaguru, in eastern Africa, in the country now known as Tanzania.

Before the discovery was made of giant dinosaurs at Tendaguru—dinosaurs of late Jurassic age closely allied to the great dinosaurs of the Morrison beds that had been so assiduously collected by Cope and by Marsh in Wyoming and Colorado back in the days of the wild and woolly West—there came an inkling that later Mesozoic giants were to be found in subequatorial Africa. This indication of later dinosaurs in the African earth had been made known in 1904 by Robert Broom in his first paper on dinosaurs. He described the bones of a large marsh-dwelling dinosaur, a brontosaurian type that he called *Algoasaurus,* which had been found in Lower Cretaceous rocks at a locality near the coast of South Africa known as Uitenhage, a little to the east of Port Elizabeth. The bones of *Algoasaurus* had in a sense been waiting for Broom. He came to Africa, and soon after he came he was able to tell the world that here, in this portion of the Southern Hemisphere, dinosaurian giants were to be found.

And they were found in abundance a few years later at Tendaguru.

TENDAGURU

Tendaguru! It is a name that carries with it a sort of magic in the story of the search for dinosaurs. It is a name to be linked with two other names that epitomize the excitement and the romance of the hunt for giant dinosaurs—Como Bluff and Dinosaur Monument. For at Tendaguru there were found, in almost overwhelming abundance, the bones of gigantic Jurassic dinosaurs, some of them the same as the dinosaurs excavated at Como Bluff and Dinosaur Monument, some of them closely related to the great Jurassic giants that have made these North American localities so famous all over the world. Tendaguru is a record of an extension south of the equator of the same dinosaurian life that had dominated the Northern Hemisphere during the final years of Jurassic history.

Tendaguru is located on the eastern side of Africa, about forty miles inland on a line northwest from the seaport of Lindi, near the southern boundary of Tanzania, and exactly ten degrees below the equator. Today Tendaguru is not far removed from the outside world.

But sixty years ago Tendaguru was within a primitive world of its own—four days' march inland from Lindi. In 1907 there was no such

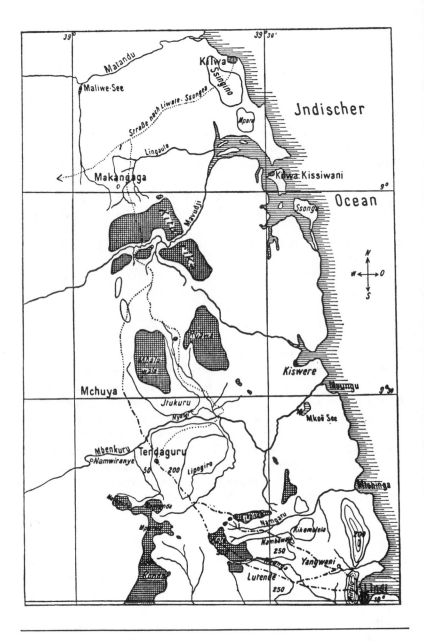

Figure 44. A map of a short section of the East-African coast, showing Lindi and the trail to Tendaguru

country as Tanzania; Lindi was a seaport of the colony of German East Africa, one of the many colonies of a largely colonial Africa.

Tendaguru was discovered one day in 1907 by Herr W. B. Sattler, an engineer working for the Lindi Prospecting Company, or, to give the Teutonic name, "Der Lindi-Schürfgesellschaft." Sattler found various pieces of gigantic fossil bones weathered out of the ground at Tendaguru, and he immediately appreciated the fact that these fossils were of real significance. He informed the director of the company. It happened that Professor Eberhard Fraas of Stuttgart, the noted German authority on fossil reptiles, was then in the colony, and he was requested to inspect the site at Tendaguru. When he had seen it and had probed into the possibilities for fossil collecting, his enthusiasm became almost boundless. It must have been an exciting sight—a veritable charnelhouse of immense, dense fossil bones, scattered through the tall grass beneath scrubby trees, gleaming in the hot African sunlight. Fraas collected some excellent bones to take back with him to Stuttgart, while at the same time he contracted a severe case of dysentery. As a consequence his work at the Tendaguru site was of limited extent.

It was enough, however, to give real paleontological meaning to the locality. Once back in Germany, Dr. Fraas expounded in forceful terms upon the wonderful dinosaurian graveyard at Tendaguru waiting to be dug up, nor did his words fall upon deaf ears. Dr. W. Branca, the director of the Berlin Museum, very quickly became interested in Tendaguru, and he began to do something about it, with much vigor and with characteristic German thoroughness.

Luckily, Branca realized through the information given him by Fraas that any worthwhile excavation at Tendaguru would have to be an operation on a large scale. Therefore he put himself to the task of organizing support sufficient to carry a large project to completion. A committee was formed to raise the money necessary for this undertaking, headed by no less a personage than the Duke of Mecklenburg, Regent of Brunswick. The committee went to work with a will, and support was obtained from a variety of sources—from the Akademie der Wissenschaften in Berlin, from the Gesellschaft Naturforschender Freunde, from the city of Berlin, from the Imperial Government, from certain other organizations, and from almost a hundred private citizens. Tendaguru caught the imagination of a large group of influential people, and as a result more than 200,000 marks were obtained.

In 1907 and 1908 such a sum, the equivalent of about $50,000, was a considerable amount of money—equal in purchasing power to several times that total at the present time. So it was that the Tendaguru Expedition was formed with a sound financial base with which to back its work. Time and the sequence of events were to prove that this large sum would be needed.

While the money was being raised, plans were going forward for the work of the expedition. It was decided that Dr. Werner Janensch, in charge of fossil reptiles at the Berlin Museum, should be the leader of the expedition, with Dr. Edwin Hennig as second in command. This arrangement was maintained during the three years, 1909–1911, for which the work of the expedition had been planned. In 1911 it was apparent that still another year of work at Tendaguru would be required, so a fourth season was spent in the field, with Dr. Hans Reck in charge of the work. During these years several other German paleontologists participated in the excavations at Tendaguru.

With all the plans made, and with a goodly sum of money at hand, Drs. Janensch and Hennig arrived in Lindi to begin their great adventure. It was in truth to be an adventure for which there were no real precedents, in spite of the large excavations of similar dinosaurs conducted by Marsh and by Cope and by the American Museum at Como Bluff, Wyoming. Everything about excavating dinosaurs in East Africa was to be different. The Germans were working in a tropical land, and allowances had to be made for the rigors of a torrid climate, quite unlike the rigors of a season in Wyoming where winds either cold or hot, blowing sand, and even snow had to be contended with. Moreover, the Germans had to work in a rolling country, where digging would be down among grass and tree roots, not into the side of rocky cliffs. And again, they would be working in a country where all effort in those years was based upon the availability of abundant hand labor.

It was the matter of hand labor, a matter that had been foreseen back in Berlin, that necessitated the employment of large sums of money by the expedition. During the first season at Tendaguru 170 native laborers were employed; during the second season there were 400 workers; during the third season there were 500 men at the task. Again, in the fourth year, 500 men were used. Added to these great numbers of workers—without much doubt the largest force of diggers ever used in the excavation of dinosaur bones—many of the workers had their families along. Consequently the dinosaur quarries at Tendaguru were the center of a populous village, often numbering between 700 and 900 individuals—large, small, and intermediate. The procurement of food and water for this concentration of people was truly a major problem in logistics, especially in those distant days when there were no roads and no motor trucks, when everything used in the camp must be carried in on the heads and the backs of porters. There was the purchasing of truly vast quantities of food and supplies, and that took money. Furthermore, all these people, at least all the men who worked in the quarries, had to be paid. Admittedly their wages were not very great, for those were colonial days when native labor was indeed very cheap, yet wages for four or five hundred men, even at a low figure in terms of European standards, none the less used up a great deal of money. Consequently the funds raised in Berlin disappeared in Africa at a remarkably rapid rate.

One must not picture the excavations at Tendaguru in the terms familiar to the Northern Hemisphere bone digger: of a large quarry in the side of a hill, or along a rocky bluff, an excavation in which there are a few people and quite a lot of equipment of various sorts. At Tendaguru there were numerous large pits dug in the ground over a distance north and south of two miles or more, over a somewhat lesser range east and west. These pits were centered around an eminence, Tendaguru Hill, at the foot of which was Tendaguru Village. The hill and the village formed the center of the operation, and work proceeded out from this center in different directions. In Tendaguru, as has been said, the work was carried on in the midst of rather dense growths of scrubby trees, an essay in digging that might look hopeless at first sight.

It succeeded by reason of the fact that there were many hands to do the digging. Janensch and Hennig were perforce supervisors of a large crew of diggers—or rather, a number of large crews. Of course, they had to train their assistants to do this work, a kind of labor that was new to the Africans engaged in this effort, and certainly a kind of work that must have seemed very strange to many of them. Fortunately, they had a most able lieutenant, their overseer, or *Oberaufseher*, Boheti bin Amrani, who, having quickly learned the requisites of successful bone digging, was able to direct the efforts and work of the hundreds of diggers. Fortunately, also, most of the bones being excavated were of large size, and fairly durable (even though as exposed they might be highly fractured), so it was possible to train sufficiently for the purpose many willing workers, men who heretofore had never seen a dinosaur bone, in the techniques of uncovering, hardening, plastering, and removing the fossils. The work at Tendaguru, different as it might seem in many respects, did employ the time-tested methods that had been developed through the years for the successful removal of large fossil bones from the ground.

The bones were taken up from the earth in which they had lain for so many millions of years by the thousands. Some of the statistics are most impressive, and reveal the large dimensions of the dinosaur dig at Tendaguru. Each bone or each articulated group of bones of the thousands that were excavated was necessarily exposed, mapped and recorded, hardened, encased in plaster and cloth bandages, and numbered. During the first three years of work at Tendaguru, 4,300

Figure 45. A reconstruction of the skeleton of the gigantic Jurassic sauropod *Brachiosaurus,* from Tendaguru, made by Janensch. In this skeleton, now assembled and on display, the skull is some forty feet above the level of the toes

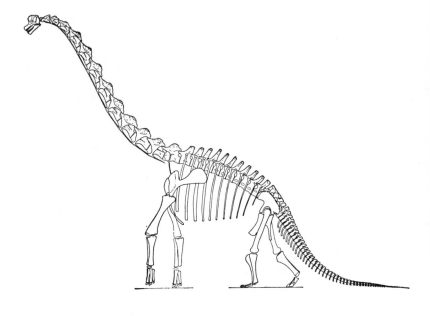

"loads" of fossil bones were packed out from Tendaguru to Lindi—four days away, on the heads and the backs of porters who made 5,400 trips to accomplish this work. These fossils were packed in 800 boxes for shipment to Germany, to a total weight on the order of 185,000 kilograms, or about 200 tons. During the fourth year, 1912, some 250 boxes, weighing 40,000 kilograms, or about 50 tons, were shipped from Lindi. All of which cost about 136 thousand marks—considerably more than half of the amount of money that had been collected for the project.

This left a considerable sum in the treasury, but the money was needed. There was a colossal task of preparation ahead—a task that required the best efforts of a corps of trained technicians for many years. For example, Dr. Branca in his report on the work of the Tendaguru Expedition points out that a single dinosaurian shoulder blade from the excavations, a bone about six feet in length, was fractured into 80 pieces, and required 160 hours of work to clean it, put it back together, strengthen it, and give it the final hardening treatment. One vertebra used up 450 hours of preparation time to put it in final shape. Of course, many of the bones did not require so much work, but many of them did, and even more. Multiply these examples by the thousands of bones from Tendaguru, and the enormous dimensions of the work involved on the collection become apparent. Is it any wonder that few museums feel sufficiently strong in funds, manpower, and skills to go after the giant dinosaurs?

The results of the Tendaguru Expedition were spectacular. Perhaps the most impressive skeleton from the Tendaguru pits was that of *Brachiosaurus,* the largest of the gigantic sauropod dinosaurs, an animal that in life weighed 80 or 90 tons. This huge skeleton as mounted in the Berlin Museum stands with its head some 40 feet above the floor, dwarfing all the other skeletons from Tendaguru, even though these are notable in their own rights. There were other sauropod dinosaurs, ancient swamp dwellers that fed upon soft plants. There was a most interesting plated dinosaur, *Kentrosaurus,* related to the North American *Stegosaurus* found in the Morrison Formation. There were carnivorous dinosaurs, too, as might be expected, and other reptiles as well. One interesting discovery at Tendaguru was the skeleton of a flying reptile, *Rhamphorhynchus,* the same that is found in Upper Jurassic rocks of Europe. Yet in spite of the variety of reptiles found at Tendaguru, this fauna, this association of ancient animals, was dominated by the overwhelming mass and numbers of gigantic swamp-dwelling sauropods, such as *Brachiosaurus* and its relatives.

All these facts, and many more besides, have been made known by the final and the truly crucial phase of the Tendaguru Expedition program—the study of the fossils and publication of the results of such study. Such seemingly prosaic activities as study and publication are often overshadowed in the popular view by the exciting and spectacular work of digging up the fossils in the field and preparing them in the laboratory. Nevertheless, of all the work of this expedition, of any fossil expedition for that matter, nothing is more important than the careful study of the fossils and their interpretation. Much of the work on the Tendaguru fossils was done by Dr. Janensch, the leader of the expedition, but of course various other paleontologists have published the results of their work on the fossils. As a result there are numerous large monographs and smaller papers describing in some detail the dinosaurs that were found at Tendaguru, as well as the conditions under which they lived and died and were buried.

There are, as might be expected, various views as to why such a concentration of great dinosaur skeletons and bones should be localized at Tendaguru. An interesting feature of the Tendaguru site is an alternation of freshwater sediments containing the bones of the giant dinosaurs with marine sediments containing seashells. Thus there are several levels at which bones are found, separated from one another by various thicknesses of marine sediments. It seems probable that the dinosaurs of Tendaguru were living along the mouth of a river that debouched into the sea. There must have been a great bar at the river's mouth, serving as a barrier to keep the marine waters from mixing with the water in the mouth of the river, because seashells are not found in the sediments containing the dinosaur bones. Dinosaurs frequented the riverbanks, where they lived and died, and some of those that died were washed into the river and buried. This would account for the occurrence of the bones in freshwater deposits. Then there would be periodic invasions by the sea, bringing in marine shells to be deposited *on top* of the bone-bearing strata. Then a retreat of the sea, with more freshwater deposits. Throughout this alternation of marine and freshwater sediments, there are two principal levels from which the bones of dinosaurs have been excavated—which together with the marine beds that separate them make up about 250 feet of sands and clays.

One man who worked at Tendaguru long after the Germans had been there, and was thus acquainted with the conditions at the site, pictured the scene as follows: ". . . the long lagoon, separated from the open water by a foam-edged bank of sand, was there, with a big river (concentration alone could have brought such masses of bones to one area) probably terminating in a delta, opening by various mouths, shifting, silting up, and changing behind its sand-banks, as does the Niger.

"At the entrance to the lagoon, pebbles and the larger grains of rock would settle downwards, but the rotting carcases, buoyed up by the gases of decomposition, float onwards to slow dismemberment . . . the sands in which the bones are found are invariably fine-grained, and for such weights to be transported by water having therefore necessarily a small velocity, argues that the whole was a mass of mud and sludge. . . .

"Doubtless many animals were caught and entombed in the lagoons themselves, many more swept seawards when the sandy barriers shutting out the sea were broken through, and mud, silt, and bones plastered out, fanwise, on to the shell-banks of the shore" (Parkinson, 1930, pages 127–129).

As was mentioned, the last German effort at Tendaguru was in 1912. Whether later attempts at further excavation at the locality would have been made is a moot question; in 1914 the world exploded, and there were other things than the digging of dinosaurs to think about. Then German East Africa ceased to exist; after the war it became British East Africa—divided into various territories, of which Tanganyika, in which was located Tendaguru, was one. The search for Tendaguru dinosaurs began again, this time under British auspices.

The British Expedition, beginning its work in 1924, was organized under the direction of W. E. Cutler of the University of Manitoba, a man with experience in collecting dinosaurs in western Canada. Also on this expedition was Dr. W. S. B. Leakey, born and raised in Kenya, educated at Cambridge University, a man long since famous for his work on early man in Africa. The expedition had its ups and downs. Cutler died in 1925 in Lindi, and his place was taken by F. W. H. Migeod, a traveler with many years of experience in Africa, assisted by Major T. Deacon. In 1927 Migeod was succeeded by John Parkinson, and the work went on.

There is no particular need to recount in detail the labors of the British ·workers at Tendaguru. In short, they continued where the Germans had left off, and of course they obtained more dinosaurs of the same kind that had been excavated by their predecessors. Fortunately, they too had available the services of Boheti bin Amrani, the skilled and knowledgeable overseer who had been a key figure in the successful operations of the Germans more than a decade earlier. As Parkinson has said: "Without Boheti, the·element of chance involved in the question, 'Where shall we dig next?' would have assumed almost overwhelming proportions. At first, at any rate, as far as we could see, bones might be anywhere, only they weren't" (Parkinson, 1930, page 31). Thanks to Boheti the British Expedition was able to dig profitably, and great quantities of bones were thus exposed, hardened, plastered, and removed from the ground. Moreover, the British extended their operations beyond the diggings around Tendaguru Hill, which had been so extensively explored by the Germans, to the locality of Kindope, some miles to the northwest, which had been only partially developed by the men from the Berlin Museum. This proved to be a very rich site, and from Kindope a harvest of many more bones was realized.

The work went on through 1929, by which time more than £ 10,000 (then the equivalent of about $50,000) had been expended. The search for dinosaurs at Tendaguru has thus occupied the energies of various people, and the expenditure of considerable sums of money, and the end is still not in sight. In short, the locality has much more to offer the dinosaur hunter. Once again, Parkinson may be quoted:

"Tendaguru is not finished yet, and it is clear that the investigation, while making a most excellent start under German auspices, is still with the greater part of its course to run: the more the amount of work done, the more does the astonishing number of bones, broken, weathered, or otherwise, around Tendaguru Hill become evident. Here and there it is a closely packed cemetery. . . . It is very noteworthy that an almost blank space of a few miles is passed through before we reach to the north of the district of Kindope, in German days astoundingly rich in bones.

"Surely Kindope cannot be the only one of these outstanding areas, surely there must be others awaiting discovery" (Parkinson, 1930, pages 64–65).

Surely there are. Not only at Tendaguru but in other parts of Africa below the equator. In Malawi, along the northwestern shore of Lake Nyasa, 350 miles from Tendaguru, and far to the southwest, in Bushmanland in South Africa, bones have been found that may be related to the discoveries at Tendaguru. And in Madagascar there are bones of dinosaurs both older and younger than the Tendaguru bones. Thus it can be said with much truth that surely there are still outstanding areas in this continent below the equator, where the giants of the Mesozoic are to be found. All that will be needed in the future are proper attitudes on the part of the peoples who govern and control the land, trained paleontologists with the interest to do the work, museums that are willing to support such projects, and—a lot of money.

THE DINOSAURS OF PATAGONIA

Across the South Atlantic, some six thousand miles to the southwest of Tendaguru, is the state of Rio Grande do Sul, Brazil, where the pampas reaches its northernmost limits. A thousand miles beyond that in about the same southwesterly direction are the states of Neuquén, Río Negro, Chubut, and Santa Cruz, Argentina, those states often known as Patagonia, where the pampas stretches mile after mile across vast distances of rolling plains and desert badlands toward the southern pole. Here are the locales for the discoveries of dinosaurs in South America.

The first discovery was made as long ago as 1882, when a certain official, Commandante Buratovich, found some very large fossil bones near the city of Neuquén, located at the point where the Neuquén River, flowing down from the northwest, from its headwaters in the Andes, and the Limay River, flowing from the southwest, also from Andean headwaters, come together to make the Río Negro, which continues on across the narrow, southwardly pointing peninsula of Argentina to reach the South Atlantic. These fossils were sent to Florentino Ameghino, the great Argentinian paleontologist, for identification. Not long after, another official at Neuquén, Captain G. Rhode, sent five boxes of fossil bones to Ameghino. With all of this material at hand Ameghino was able to determine that the bones were those of Upper Cretaceous dinosaurs. This was the beginning, and from then until fairly recent years dinosaur bones have been collected from southern Argentina, particularly from the several states that have been named above.

Some of the discoveries were of a casual nature—bones picked up by military officers in the vicinity of their posts or dug up by engineers during the construction of railroads and other public works. But not long after that first find in 1882, concerted efforts were made by various men and at various times to search out and systematically dig up the dinosaurs of Patagonia.

One of the early fossil hunters in the wide reaches of the pampas was Carlos Ameghino, the brother of Florentino. These two brothers had very interesting careers in paleontology. Florentino was the leader, a self-educated paleontologist who during the course of his lifetime virtually unlocked the chest containing the fossil history of backboned animals in Argentina, thus making for himself a worldwide reputation, and establishing himself as one of the immortals in the history of paleontology. Carlos was the field man; he collected the fossils that Florentino studied. The two brothers for many years performed these Herculean labors as independent workers, without benefit of a sponsoring institution. It was truly a remarkable achievement, of which one result is that the Ameghino brothers rightly take their place as pioneer dinosaur hunters and students in South America.

A contemporary of the Ameghinos was Santiago Roth. Soon after 1882 he was searching for dinosaurs in the vicinity of the city of Neuquén—and he found them. These bones were sent to England and described by Richard Lydekker, one of the great Victorian paleontologists of Britain. A few years later Roth extended his search to the south, into Chubut, and found more bones, and these were sent to Arthur Smith Woodward of the British Museum for description.

But the most important work on the dinosaurs of South America came a decade or so after the turn of the century. Dr. R. Wichman, working in the southern part of Río Negro, developed some large quarries, from which he obtained extensive and varied collections, including not only the bones of gigantic swamp-dwelling sauropod dinosaurs like those previously found in this part of Argentina, but also the remains of armored dinosaurs. His was the first large-scale digging for dinosaurs in Argentina, and it produced by far the most important collections that had been exhumed up to the year 1916, the year that Wichman published a short paper, briefly describing the work he had done.

Then, toward the close of the second twentieth-century decade, a museum entered the field with plans for an intensive dinosaur hunt in southern Argentina. The institution was the Museum of La Plata, for many years a leader in the study of Argentinian fossils. In 1918 a museum party established diggings to the east of the city of Neuquén and obtained some dinosaur skeletons. Then in 1921 and 1922 explorations were commenced farther south in Patagonia, under the direction of Santiago Roth, by now a man of considerable years, yet still vigorous enough to continue the search for dinosaurs that he had commenced back in the eighties, and Mr. W. Schiller. Their efforts were productive; more Cretaceous dinosaurs were dug up to be shipped to La Plata, there to augment the collections that had previously been brought into the museum.

So it was that by the end of 1922 the La Plata Museum had a large collection of Cretaceous dinosaurs from Neuquén and other regions in Patagonia, the collection being dominated by the bones of gigantic sauropods, the largest of the dinosaurs, but containing also the remains of predatory and armored dinosaurs. Here were the fossil remains to afford a good picture of dinosaurian life in late Cretaceous time—if there were only at hand a man who could interpret the fos-

---

Figure 46. The Cretaceous sauropod dinosaur *Titanosaurus,* from Argentina. Restoration by G. Biese, under the direction of F. von Huene

sils. Who could do this? There seemed to be no one at the time in Argentina (Florentino Ameghino was long since dead) with the necessary background and ability to make a proper study of the large bones that reposed in the storerooms of the La Plata Museum.

Who but Friedrich von Huene, the man who perhaps knew as much about dinosaurs as any man then living? Why not have the professor from Tübingen come to La Plata to work on the collection? It was arranged, and an invitation was sent to von Huene, who, needless to say, accepted with alacrity. He journeyed to Argentina, to begin what was truly a colossal task, but a task that did not faze him in the least, for the description of large collections of dinosaurs suited von Huene perfectly. He pitched into the work with verve, and of course with complete confidence. He knew what he was doing.

These Cretaceous dinosaurs had been gathered together from more than a dozen localities in Argentina. If von Huene were to understand the collection, it was necessary for him to visit at least some of the places where the dinosaur bones had been excavated, in order to get some comprehension of the relationships between fossils and rocks. So he made a trip into Patagonia to see the Cretaceous sediments in the field. And then back to La Plata he went, to continue his study of the great array of bones.

He worked hard, as was always von Huene's practice, and after his return to Tübingen he continued to work hard writing up the results of the notes he had made in Argentina. The result was a great monograph entitled *Los Saurisquios y Ornitisquios del Cretáceo Argentino,* published by the La Plata Museum in 1926. In this work von Huene was able to show that the great dinosaurs of late Cretaceous time roamed widely through what is now southern Argentina, living in a low tropical land bordering the sea, a land that also was inhabited by crocodilians, turtles and (in the ponds) lungfish. Moreover, the dinosaurs lived in Argentina through a considerable span of late Cretaceous time, extending their domination of the land, as in other parts of the world, to the very end of this period of geologic history. Thanks to von Huene, who summed up the work of the men who had preceded him, as well as adding much new information of his own, an adequate view of South America at the close of the Age of Dinosaurs was now to be had.

In recent years Llewellyn Price, of the Brazilian geological survey, has unearthed great dinosaurs of the same general age at Bauru, in the state of São Paulo.

VON HUENE IN BRAZIL

It would seem that this introduction to the dinosaurs of South America whetted von Huene's appetite for some fossil hunting in this southern land. So it was that in 1928 he again sailed across the South Atlantic, accompanied by a technician, Herr R. Stahlecker, this time making his way to southern Brazil to look for fossils in his favorite rocks, those of Triassic age. The locale for his fossil hunt was in the middle of the state of Rio Grande do Sul, in the vicinity of and to the west of the small city of Santa Maria.

Fossil bones were known from this region. They had been found by various people, and some of them had been described. So it had been established that the rocks were of Triassic age and that they were fossiliferous. To say that they are fossiliferous is to state the case mildly: the Santa Maria beds (for so they have been named) are in various places filled with the remains of ancient reptiles. This is particularly true around the city of Santa Maria, where on the outskirts of the town numerous gullies, in Brazil known as *sangas,* reveal in their eroded slopes the abundant remains of Triassic reptiles. These fossil-bearing sangas can be traced for many miles to the east and to the west of Santa Maria, indicating by their outcrops the presence of a long, east-to-west band of Triassic sediments crossing the middle of the state of Rio Grande do Sul. In these outcrops are found the bones of peculiar beaked reptiles known as rhynchosaurs, of various mammal-like reptiles, of pseudosuchians, among whose ranks were the immediate ancestors of the dinosaurs—and of at least one dinosaur.

The dinosaur, a small Triassic type, another of the oldest of the dinosaurs, was found and described by von Huene, who named it *Spondylosoma.* It was in a way a by-product of von Huene's digging around Santa Maria and in the country to the west of that city, for he, like Broom in the Karroo, was particularly concerned with the excavation of mammal-like reptiles. This one dinosaur, known from very fragmentary bones indeed, and the gigantic bones from Patagonia, all studied by von Huene, did indicate that dinosaurs had been in South

America from the beginning until the end of their long history. And von Huene's discovery of a Triassic dinosaur in southern Brazil has in recent years been corroborated by the discovery and description of various dinosaurs from the Triassic Ischigualasto beds of Argentina —perhaps the oldest of known dinosaurs. We had a brief look at these ancient Argentinian dinosaurs in Chapter 5.

There is not much more to say about von Huene's work in Rio Grande do Sul. He labored mightily, as usual, and under conditions that now forty years later would be considered as rather primitive, for in those days southern Brazil was a rather isolated place. Von Huene and Stahlecker plowed through the muddy roads on primitive carts, pulled by stolid oxen. They camped out or stayed at farms, known in that land as fazendas. They subsisted on very simple food when they were in the field. And they made a notable collection which they took back to Tübingen.

We see that the land below the equator in the Western Hemisphere contains the records of perhaps the earliest dinosaurs and certainly of some of the latest, which makes it evident, as has been remarked, that these reptiles inhabited South America through the extent of their tenure of the earth. Moreover, a little of what we know about the oldest dinosaurs, and much of our knowledge of the youngest dinosaurs in this part of the world, is owing to the energetic work of von Huene in the field and in the laboratory.

Early dinosaurs and late dinosaurs on both sides of the South Atlantic, in South and East Africa and in Argentina and Brazil. What does it mean? Does it mean that at one time these two continents were joined by a direct connection, so that the ancient land-living reptiles were able to wander back and forth and in a direct line, from one subequatorial region to the other, or does it mean that the dinosaurs of South Africa and South America migrated to and fro between their southern areas and the continents to the north of them—thus extending their ranges from Argentina to Africa the long way around? This is one of the liveliest questions debated by geologists today, a question that is argued back and forth and at interminable length, year after year. It will not be explored here—it is merely mentioned to show that there are still many problems about the days of the dinosaurs to be solved, problems that concern not only the dinosaurs themselves but also the distribution of the land masses on which they lived. There are indeed tasks remaining for future dinosaur hunters and future students of dinosaurs.

DINOSAURS DOWN UNDER

By whatever paths the dinosaurs may have moved back and forth between South Africa and South America, and between other continental areas, it is certain that at an early stage in their history they entered what is now the island continent of Australia, to occupy that segment of the Southern Hemisphere during the remainder of Mesozoic time. Beyond doubt Australia must have been connected to the rest of the world during the days of the dinosaurs—probably to southeastern Asia. The evidence is unequivocal, although there is not a great deal of it preserved.

Some of the evidence is in the form of fossilized footprints. In Queensland, for example, recent discoveries in the roof of a coal mine indicate the presence of rather large Triassic dinosaurs in this part of Australia, while very large footprints of carnivorous dinosaurs of early Cretaceous age on the other side of the island continent, on the northwest coast, provide good evidence for some of the later dinosaurs there. A few discoveries of bones may be mentioned—of a small Triassic dinosaur in Queensland, of a large sauropod of early Jurassic age, *Rhoetosaurus*, also in Queensland; of the claw of a Jurassic carnivorous dinosaur in Victoria, and rather recently, of the bones of a lower Cretaceous iguanodont, related to the *Iguanodon* described so long ago by Gideon Mantell, again from Queensland. Generally speaking this is the list—and it is far from being a big list. It is a sad fact that Mesozoic reptilian bones are very rare indeed in Australia, and thus our knowledge of the dinosaurs of that region is based at best on bits and pieces. It is not because of a lack of industry on the part of Australian paleontologists, either. Numerous well-trained men have worked in Australia, yet in spite of their efforts the record of dinosaurs is pitifully scanty. It would seem that for some reason dinosaurian remains have not been abundantly preserved Down Under.

Of course, there are many empty places in Australia, and it is very possible that in future years some good and abundant dinosaur bones will be discovered, to give us something more than a fleeting glimpse of the dinosaurian life of the continent. When such an event occurs, there will be a tale to tell about dinosaur hunting on the Island Continent; at present the story is one of isolated and accidental discoveries, none of the sort that have led to extensive quarrying as has been the case in Africa and South America.

Therefore the story of the search for dinosaurs below the equator is today largely a story of work in the two large continental areas on the two sides of the South Atlantic. It is largely a story of the present century, a story of expeditions that have worked in the hot bushland of East Africa, in the wonderfully beautiful, rugged terrain of South Africa and Lesotho, in the rolling pampas and desert badlands of Patagonia, and in the semitropical farm country of Brazil. Much has been revealed by the digging, and by the study that has resulted from this digging. There is much still to be learned of the dinosaurs that through millions of years inhabited this part of the earth in prodigious numbers, to the uttermost southern ends of the continents.

Will dinosaurs some day be found on the Island Continent of Antarctica? That is a question of great importance, a tantalizing question that is in the back of the minds of many dinosaur hunters today.

CHAPTER 10

CLOSING THE CIRCLE

THE ARCTIC *IGUANODON*

In the late afternoon of August 3, 1960, some geologists were climbing along the top of a sandstone cliff that rose sheer from the water
along the coast of West Spitzbergen (or Svalbard). It was a mixed
group of many nationalities, the members of a geological field excursion sent to Spitzbergen on the ship *Valkyrien* under the auspices of
the Twenty-first International Congress of Geology. The leader of the
group was Professor Anatol Heintz of the University of Oslo, a noted
authority on the earliest fishes, and he and his followers were spending the day tramping across the barren rocks, studying the geology of
this arctic island located just below the eightieth parallel of latitude,
east of the northern tip of Greenland and just halfway between the
northern edge of the Scandinavian peninsula and the north pole. It
was a characteristic geological field excursion of an international kind,
of which several are conducted every four years, in connection with
the meetings of the International Congress; its several members were

scrambling around over the rocks, pecking away with their hammers, talking in a babel of tongues, and plying the leader with questions or listening to his expositions concerning the geology of the landscape that they were visiting. It was the kind of trip that geologists love to participate in, an informal outdoor meeting between men of authority from countries all over the world, a meeting where ideas are exchanged and much is learned.

Late in the afternoon the group reached the Festingsodden beacon, a light perched on the crest of a vertical sandstone of early Cretaceous age, a sandstone that was once in a horizontal position but that long since had been tilted up to an attitude of 90 degrees as the result of great and powerful movements within the crust of the earth. As the geologists reached this place two members of the conference, Professor Albert F. de Lapparent of Paris, an outstanding authority on dinosaurs, and Robert Laffitte, climbed down to the shore, just to look around. From such casual curiosity are made many paleontological discoveries, and the divergent wanderings of these two men away from the rest of their fellows led to a most significant find.

As the curious pair looked up at the towering cliff, they saw, highlighted by the low slanting rays of the afternoon sun, a large group of huge footprints. These were three-toed prints, obviously made by ancient dinosaurs, and they formed a gigantic pattern of scattered trackways across the surface of the rock. Of course, De Lapparent and Laffitte called excitedly to the people on top of the cliff, who quickly scrambled down to view the footprints. There was much excited talk, accompanied by pointing fingers and speculative comments. Thirteen footprints could be counted, each about thirty inches in length. Seven of the prints formed a trackway, while the other footprints were scattered about in a rather haphazard arrangement; all were made by a large dinosaur walking on its hind legs.

It was a memorable and a frustrating sight. Here was evidence of dinosaurs far north of any previous northern records for these ancient reptiles. It was important evidence. But what could the little band of geologists do? The light was fading, and it was almost time to return to their base—the waiting ship *Valkyrien*. And they could not come back the next day because the schedule of the excursion had been set months in advance of the trip, the logistics were fitted to this schedule, and that was that.

Professor de Lapparent said: "As this discovery was entirely unexpected, we were unable to make castings. . . . We did not even have a piece of chalk, to show up the outlines of the prints. . . . After having measured the footmarks and made sketches, we were obliged to leave, as the *Valkyrien* was waiting to depart. . . ." (De Lapparent, 1962, page 15.)

However, the rough and rapid observations and sketches made by De Lapparent and his companions in the brief time available did give a few clues. At first the members of the party had thought that the prints might be those of a huge meat-eating dinosaur, but closer examination revealed that there were no claw marks at the ends of the toes. Rather the impressions were blunt and rounded, evidence that these prints were probably made by some kind of plant-eating dinosaur.

Such preliminary observations only whetted the scientific appetites of De Lapparent, Heintz, and other members of the group for more detailed knowledge of these very important footprints; consequently plans were made for an expedition to return to Spitzbergen during the following year to obtain a permanent record of some of the prints, and to map them. So it was that, just a year later, in August, 1961, a group of four persons journeyed from Oslo to Spitzbergen; two were from the Paleontological Museum in Oslo, one from the University of Oslo, and one, Dr. Natascha Heintz, the daughter of Professor Anatol Heintz, and herself a geologist, from the Norwegian Polar Institute.

The problems facing this expedition were unprecedented, to put it mildly. In the first place, it was out of the question to try to cut any of the tracks out of the rock; such an attempt, even if it were physically feasible, which it was not, would have required equipment and time that simply were not to be had in such an arctic, isolated place. The solution was to make casts. But how were the fossil hunters to make casts on this vertical, even overhanging, surface of rock? And how were they to handle plaster on a wet, vertical rock surface, in a cold climate, where wind-driven salt spray is in the air more often than not? The answer to these questions, it would seem, was not to use plaster, but rather one of the new casting compounds—in this case a latex emulsion. And to make sure that the answer was the right one, a considerable amount of experimenting was done in Oslo during the winter preceding the expedition. Various casting compounds were tested, and at last a suitable one was found. Equipped with an ample supply of this latex emulsion, as well as other accessory equipment, inclusing plaster of Paris, the expedition put to sea.

The job was accomplished, but not quite according to the original plans. The workers built a rough scaffold to raise themselves above high-tide level; they built wooden frames around the tracks to be cast, attaching these frames to the cliff, which in this place was actually overhanging to some extent, with strong adhesive tape and plaster, and then they applied the latex to the rock surface enclosed within the frames. Alas! Even the best-laid plans do not always work, and such was to be the case with this attempt. Try as they would, the fossil hunters could not get the latex to dry and set in that cold, wet climate. They even tried to heat the molds in place on the rock with primus stoves, to hasten the drying. Nothing would suffice; the latex emulsion on which they had set such great store simply would not set.

There was only one thing to do: fall back on the old-fashioned plaster of Paris, of which, luckily, they had, with excellent foresight, brought an ample supply. After some experimenting it was found that the rock, having first been washed thoroughly with fresh water to removed any traces of salt spray, could be coated thoroughly with soapy lather. Then very thin plaster was splashed over this as an undercoat, and after that, thicker plaster, reinforced with heavy sacking, was applied to form the bulk of the mold. And always great care was taken to prevent any salt spray from reaching the casts. By improvising, by solving problems as they went along, the members of the expedition succeeded in making casts of seven footprints to be shipped back to Norway.

CLOSING THE CIRCLE

These footprints were studied by Professor de Lapparent, who showed that they had been made by the lower Cretaceous dinosaur *Iguanodon*. Thus, 139 years after Mrs. Gideon Mantell saw those first teeth of *Iguanodon* shining in the rock by the side of an English country road, after 139 years during which many men working around the world had built up a complex reconstruction of the kingdom of dinosaurs, the search for these ancient reptiles had led back to one of the first known dinosaurs, *Iguanodon*. It might be said that work on these ancient reptiles in field and in laboratory had come through a full circle, from *Iguanodon* in southern Britain, the *Iguanodon* of Mantell, to *Iguanodon* in the arctic island of Spitzbergen, the *Iguanodon* of Natascha Heintz and her associates.

Discoveries within recent years show among other things that *Iguanodon* lived widely across the latitudinal extent of Europe—from the southern shores of the Mediterranean Sea, this dinosaur hav-

---

Figure 47. A map to show the distribution of *Iguanodon* and its very close relatives, north and south, east and west

ing been found in Tunisia, to a point within about ten degrees of the pole. Certainly Spitzbergen must have been connected to northern Europe in early Cretaceous time, to provide a path whereby *Iguanodon* could reach this now arctic isle. But what does the presence of *Iguanodon* in Spitzbergen imply with regard to the distributions of land masses and of climates in the remote age during which it lived?

There are some large questions, which are not easily answered. It can be assumed that the climate in which *Iguanodon* lived was necessarily of a tropical or subtropical type, because the gigantic dinosaurs, probably being ectothermic animals, as are all modern reptiles—that is, animals unable to manufacture internal body heat—were almost certainly confined to perpetually warm climates, as are large crocodiles and turtles today. The only way in which reptiles can survive in latitudes having severe winters is to hibernate deep underground, thus escaping the for them fatal effects of frost and snow. But the gigantic dinosaurs were much too large to retreat under the earth; consequently they must have been limited to benign climates. If, in early Cretaceous time, Spitzbergen was located in about its present position, and if the north pole were also in about its present position, then we must visualize *Iguanodon* inhabiting a land that was subjected to about four months each year of darkness, and, conversely, about four months of prolonged sunshine, day and night. This is assuming, of course, that, in spite of its high latitude, Spitzbergen then enjoyed a tropical climate.

What would happen to plants in a tropical land that had four months of each year devoid of sunlight? What would become of the food supply for the large herbivorous dinosaurs, such as *Iguanodon*, during this period of darkness? And what would happen to *Iguanodon*? These are indeed pertinent questions.

Perhaps *Iguanodon* was a beast of passage, like modern migrating birds, that wandered north into Spitzbergen during the summer months, and then back south, to some point below the Arctic Circle, and therefore a point at which the sun would shine, during the winter months. But to accomplish such a long migration twice each year probably would require at least two months in each direction on the part of such a large, ponderous, and slow moving reptile as *Iguanodon*. Moreover, it would require a great deal of reptilian energy. Such a supposition seems almost beyond the bounds of possibility. Furthermore, what would such a change of habitats between such

widely separated regions imply for the young iguanodonts that would
be hatched each year—wherever they might be hatched?

The alternative to these rather fantastic suppositions is to assume
that in early Cretaceous time Spitzbergen was considerably to the
south of its present position, or that the position of the north pole was
different from what it is now, or that both conditions prevailed. A
great deal of research is being done on this problem, and many leading geologists believe that in past geologic ages there were movements of the land masses and wanderings of the poles. Perhaps—but
this hypothesis is still very much in the realm of theory.

These several problems have been introduced here largely to illus-
trate the fact that discoveries raise problems as often as they solve
them. The discovery of abundant *Iguanodon* skeletons at Bernissart
solved many of the problems of the structure and anatomy of this ancient reptile. But the discovery of *Iguanodon* in Spitzbergen (as revealed by the footprints) has raised many new problems with regard
to the way in which this ancient and widely distributed dinosaur
lived. And the recent discovery of *Iguanodon,* or something very close
to it, in Australia raises still more problems—such as where was Australia in early Cretaceous time, and how did *Iguanodon* get there?

So in closing the circle in the search for *Iguanodon,* we see epito-
mized the larger circle of the search for knowledge about all the dinosaurs. No matter how much has been learned, there is still much to be
learned. No matter how completely we may think we understand any
particular dinosaur, some new discovery may raise new questions
about it that had never been dreamed of. Who would have thought
that *Iguanodon,* a dinosaur that lived in Europe when that was a
tropical land, would be discovered in arctic regions, thus bringing up
all manner of new questions concerning its habits, its distribution, and
the relationships of land masses at the time when it lived? Perhaps it
would be proper to say that the search for *Iguanodon,* as typifying
the large search for all the dinosaurs, has been on a spiral course
rather than a circle. The spiral continues, and leads to new and as yet
unforeseen possibilities.

One may be sure that the search will go on in the years to come.
One may wonder what this search will reveal in future years. Will
some paleontologist in the year 2106, the scientific descendant of Gideon Mantell, find still another *Iguanodon* in some far-off and unsuspected place?

Andrews, Roy Chapman, 1929. Mongolia—Explorations. New York, Ency-clopædia Britannica, 14th Edition, Vol. 15.

———, 1932. The New Conquest of Central Asia. The American Museum of Natural History: Natural History of Central Asia. Vol. 1, i + 678 pp., 129 plates.

Annual Reports of the Department of Vertebrate Paleontology, the American Museum of Natural History. 1897–1905.

Anonymous, 1966. Editorial. Antiquity, Vol. 40, No. 158, p. 85.

Board of Commissioners of the Central Park, 1868. Twelfth Annual Report, pp. 132–134.

———, 1869. Thirteenth Annual Report, p. 28.

Branca, W., 1914. Allgemeines über die Tendaguru-Expedition. Archive für Biontologie, Vol. 3, pp. 1–13.

Broom, Robert, 1904. On the Occurrence of an Opisthocoelian Dinosaur (*Algoasaurus bauri*) in the Cretaceous Beds of South Africa. Geological Magazine (5), Vol. 1, pp. 445–447.

Broom, Robert, 1911. On the Dinosaurs of the Stormberg, South Africa. Annals of the South African Museum, Vol. 7, pp. 291–308, plates 14–17.

Brown, Barnum, 1919. Hunting Big Game of Other Days. National Geographic Magazine, Vol. 35, pp. 407–429.

————, 1935. Sinclair Dinosaur Expedition, 1934. Natural History, Vol. 36, pp. 3–15.

————, 1935. Flying for Dinosaurs. Natural History, Vol. 36, pp. 95–116.

Buckland, William, 1824. Notice on the Megalosaurus or Great Fossil Lizard of Stonesfield. Transactions of the Geological Society of London, Vol. 21, pp. 390–397, plates 40–44.

————, 1829. On the Discovery of Fossil Bones of the Iguanodon, in the Iron Sand of the Wealden Formation in the Isle of Wight, and in the Isle of Purbeck. *Ibid.*, Second Series, Vol. 3, pp. 425–432, Plate 41.

————, 1841. The Bridgewater Treatises on the Power, Wisdom and Goodness of God as Manifested in the Creation. Treatise VI. Geology and Mineralogy Considered with Reference to Natural Theology. Philadelphia, Lea and Blanchard, two volumes, xv + 468 pp., vii + 131 pp., 69 plates.

Canada, Department of Mines, 1950. Map 969A. Steveville, Alberta.

Casier, E., 1960. Les Iguanodons de Bernissart. Brussels: Institut Royal des Sciences Naturelles de Belgique, 134 pp.

Colbert, Edwin H., 1947. The Little Dinosaurs of Ghost Ranch. Natural History, Vol. 61, pp. 392–399, 427–428.

————, 1957. Battle of the Bones. Cope and Marsh, the Paleontological Antagonists. GeoTimes, Vol. 2, No. 4, pp. 6–7, 14.

————, 1961. Dinosaurs, Their Discovery and Their World. New York, E. P. Dutton and Company, xiv + 300 pp.

————, 1964. Dinosaurs of the Arctic. Natural History, Vol. 73, pp. 20–23.

————, 1966. The Age of Reptiles. New York, The Norton Library, W. W. Norton and Company, Inc., x + 228 pp.

Colbert, Edwin H., and Katherine Beneker, 1959. The Paleozic Museum in Central Park, or the Museum That Never Was. Curator, Vol. 2, pp. 137–150.

Cope, Edward Drinker, 1866. On Anatomical Peculiarities in Some Dinosauria. Proceedings of the Academy of Natural Sciences, Philadelphia, Vol. 18, pp. 316–317 (publ. 1867).

————, 1867. Account of Extinct Reptiles Which Approach Birds. *Ibid.*, Vol. 19, pp. 234–235.

————, 1870. Synopsis of the Extinct Batrachia, Reptilia and Aves of North America. Transactions of the American Philosophical Society, Vol. 14, N.S., Part 1, Article 1, vii + 252 pp., 14 plates.

————, 1883. On the Characters of the Skull in the Hadrosauridae. Proceedings of the Academy of Natural Sciences of Philadelphia, 1883, pp. 97–107, plates 4–7.

Crompton, A. W., and A. J. Charig, 1962. A New Ornithischian from the Upper Triassic of South Africa. Nature, Vol. 196, pp. 1074–1077.

Cushman, Dan, 1962. Monsters of the Judith. Montana, Vol. 12, No. 4, pp. 18–36.

Dickens, Charles, 1852. Bleak House. First published, in installments, in *Household Words,* London, 1852–1853, beginning in March.

Dollo, Louis, 1882a. Première Note sur les Dinosauriens de Bernissart. Bulletin du Musée Royal d'Histoire Naturelle de Belgique, Vol. 1, pp. 161–180, Plate 9.

———, 1882b. Deuxième Note sur les Dinosauriens de Bernissart. *Ibid.,* Vol. 1, pp. 205–211, Plate 12.

———, 1883a. Troisième Note sur les Dinosauriens de Bernissart. *Ibid.,* Vol. 2, pp. 85–126, plates 3–5.

———, 1883b. Quatrième Note sur les Dinosauriens de Bernissart. *Ibid.,* Vol. 2, pp. 223–252, plates 9, 10.

———, 1883c. Les Iguanodons de Bernissart. Bulletin Scientifique et Pédagogique de Bruxelles, Vol. 3, pp. 25–34, plate.

———, 1884. Cinquième Note sur les Dinosauriens de Bernissart. Bulletin du Musée Royal d'Histoire Naturelle de Belgique, Vol. 3, pp. 120–140, plates 6, 7.

Dupont, E., 1878. Sur la Découverte d'Ossements d'Iguanodon, de Poissons et de Végétaux dans la Fosse Sainte-Barbe du Charbonnage de Bernissart. Bulletin l'Académie Royale des Sciences des Lettres et des Beaux-Arts de Belgique, Second Series, Vol. 46, pp. 387–408.

———, 1898. Bernissart and the Iguanodons. Royal Museum of Natural History of Belgium, Guide to the Collections. Brussels, Polleunis and Ceuterick, 52 pp.

Edinger, Tilly, 1955. Personalities in Paleontology—Nopcsa. Society of Vertebrate Paleontology News Bulletin, No. 43, p. 36.

Ellenberger, François, and Paul Ellenberger, 1956. Le Gisement de Dinosauriens de Maphutseng (Basutoland, Afrique du Sud). Société Géologique de France, 1956, No. 8, pp. 99–101.

Ellenberger, François, and Leonard Ginsburg, 1966. Le Gisement de Dinosauriens Triasiques de Maphutseng (Basutoland) et l'Origine des Sauropodes. Comptes Rendus Académie Sciences, Paris, Vol. 262, pp. 444–447.

Frazer, Persifor, 1900. The Life and Letters of Edward Drinker Cope. American Geologist, Vol. 26, pp. 67-132.

Gilmore, C. W., 1909. Osteology of the Jurassic Reptile *Camptosaurus,* with a Revision of the Species of the Genus, and Descriptions of Two New Species. United States National Museum, Proceedings, Vol. 36, pp. 197–332.

———, 1920. Osteology of the Carnivorous Dinosauria in the United States

National Museum, with Special Reference to the Genera *Antrodemus* (*Allosaurus*) and *Ceratosaurus*. United States National Museum, Bulletin 110, pp. 1–154.

———, 1936. Osteology of *Apatosaurus*, with Special Reference to Specimens in the Carnegie Museum. Carnegie Museum Memoirs, Vol. 11, pp. 175–300.

Good, John M., Theodore E. White, and Gilbert F. Stucker, 1958. The Dinosaur Quarry. Dinosaur National Monument. Washington, D.C., National Park Service, 1958, 47 pp.

Haughton, S. H., 1915. On Some Dinosaur Remains from Bushmanland. Transactions of the Royal Society of South Africa, Vol. 5, pp. 259–264.

———, 1918. A New Dinosaur from the Stormberg Beds of South Africa. Annals and Magazine of Natural History (9), Vol. 2, pp. 468–469.

———, 1924. The Fauna and Stratigraphy of the Stormberg Series. Annals of the South African Museum, Vol. 12, pp. 323–497.

Heintz, Natascha, 1962. Dinosaur-footprints and Polar Wandering. Norsk Polarinstitutt-Årbok, 1962, pp. 35–43.

———, 1963. Casting Dinosaur Footprints at Spitzbergen. Curator, Vol. 6, pp. 217–225.

Hennig, Edwin, 1912. Am Tendaguru. Stuttgart, E. Schweitzerbart'sche Verlagsbuchhandlung. 151 pp.

———, 1912. Die Deutsche Tendaguru-Expedition. Die Umschau, Vol. 16, pp. 413–418.

Hitchcock, Edward, 1848. An Attempt to Discriminate and Describe the Animals That Made the Fossil Footmarks of the United States, and Especially of New England. Memoir American Academy of Arts and Sciences, Vol. 7, pp. 129–256, plates 1–24.

———, 1858. Ichnology of New England. A Report on the Sandstone of the Connecticut Valley, Especially Its Fossil Footmarks, Made to the Government of the Commonwealth of Massachusetts. Boston, William White, xii + 220 pp., 60 plates.

———, 1865. Supplement to the Ichnology of New England. With an Appendix by C. H. Hitchcock. Boston, Wright and Potter, 89 pp., 20 plates.

Holland, W. J., 1931. Earl Douglass. A Sketch in Appreciation of His Life and Work. Annals of the Carnegie Museum, Vol. 20, pp. 279–292.

Huene, Friedrich von, 1914a. Das Natürliche System der Saurischia. Centralblatt für Mineralogie, Geologie und Paläontologie, Jahrgang 1914, No. 5, pp. 154–158.

———, 1914b. Über de Zweistammigkeit der Dinosaurier, mit Beiträgen zur Kenntnis einiger Schädel. Neuen Jahrbuch für Mineralogie, Geologie und Paläontologie, Vol. 37, pp. 577–589, plates 7–12.

———, 1928. Lebensbild des Saurischier-Vorkommens in obersten Keuper von Trossingen in Württemberg. Palaeobiologica, Vol. 1, pp. 103–116, Plate 10.

———, 1929a. Die Plateosaurier von Trossingen. Die Umschau, Vol. 44, pp. 1–3.

———, 1929b. Los Saurisquios y Ornitisquios del Cretáceo Argentino. Anales del Museo de La Plata, Second Series, Vol. 3, pp. 1–196, 44 plates.

Huxley, T. H., 1868. On the Animals Which Are Most Nearly Intermediate Between Birds and Reptiles. Geological Magazine, Vol. 5, pp. 357–365.

———, 1870a. Further Evidence of the Affinity Between the Dinosaurian Reptiles and Birds. Quarterly Journal of the Geological Society of London, Vol. 26, pp. 12–31.

———, 1870b. On the Classification of the Dinosauria with Observations on the Dinosauria of the Trias. Ibid., Vol. 26, pp. 32–50.

Lapparent, A. F. de, 1962. Footprints of Dinosaurs in the Lower Cretaceous of Vestspitsbergen-Svalbard. Norsk Polarinstitutt-Årbok, 1960, pp. 14–21.

Leidy, Joseph, 1858. Remarks Concerning Hadrosaurus. Proceedings Academy of Natural Sciences, Philadelphia, Dec. 14, 1858, pp. 215–218.

———, 1859a. Account of the Remains of a Fossil Extinct Reptile Recently Discovered at Haddonfield, New Jersey. Ibid., pp. 1–16.

———, 1859b. Extinct Vertebrata from the Judith River and Great Lignite Formations of Nebraska. Transactions of the American Philosophical Society, 1859, Article 13, pp. 139–154, plates 9–11.

———, 1865. Cretaceous Reptiles of the United States. Smithsonian Contributions to Knowledge, Vol. 14, iii + 135 pp., 20 plates.

Lewis, G. Edward, 1946. Memorial to Charles Whitney Gilmore. Proceedings Volume of the Geological Society of America for 1945, pp. 235–243.

———, 1964. Memorial to Barnum Brown. Geological Society of America Bulletin, Vol. 75, pp. P19–P28.

Lull, Richard Swann, 1953. Triassic Life of the Connecticut Valley (Revised Edition). State of Connecticut, State Geological and Natural History Survey, Bulletin No. 81, 366 pp.

McIntosh, John S., 1965. Marsh and the Dinosaurs. Discovery, Vol. 1, pp. 31–37.

McLeod, Roy M., 1965. Evolutionism and Richard Owen, 1830–1868: An Episode in Darwin's Century. Isis, Vol. 56, pp. 259–280.

Mantell, Gideon Algernon, 1825. Notice on the Iguanodon, a Newly Discovered Fossil Reptile, from the Sandstone of Tilgate Forest, in Sussex. Philosophical Transactions of the Royal Society, London, Vol. 115, pp. 179–186, Plate 14.

———, 1831. The Geological Age of Reptiles. Edinburgh New Philosophical Journal, Vol. 11, pp. 181–185.

———, 1834. Discovery of the Bones of the Iguanodon in a Quarry of the

Kentish Rag (a Limestone belonging to the Lower Greensand Formation) near Maidstone, Kent, *Ibid.*, Vol. 17, pp. 200–201.

———, 1839. The Wonders of Geology; or a Familiar Exposition of Geological Phenomena; Being the Substance of a Course of Lectures Delivered at Brighton. First American Edition. New Haven, Connecticut, A. H. Maltby, two vols., xvi + 821 pp.

———, 1844. Medals of Creation; or, First Lessons in Geology, and in the Study of Organic Remains. London, Henry G. Bohn, two vols., xvii + pp. 1–456, vii + pp. 457–1016.

———, 1848. On the Structure of the Jaws and Teeth of the *Iguanodon*. Philosophical Transactions of the Royal Society, London, Vol., 138, pp. 183–202, plates 16–19.

———, 1849. Additional Observations on the Osteology of the *Iguanodon* and *Hylaeosaurus. Ibid.*, Vol. 139, pp. 271–305, plates 26–32.

Marsh, O. C., 1884. On the Classification and Affinities of Dinosaurian Reptiles. Nature, Vol. 31, pp. 68–69.

———, 1896. The Dinosaurs of North America. Sixteenth Annual Report of the United States Geological Survey, pp. 133–244.

Nopcsa, Franz, 1900. Dinosaurierreste aus Siebenbürgen (Schädel von *Limnosaurus transsylvanicus* nov. gen. et spec.). Akademie der Wissenschaften, Vienna, Vol. 68, pp. 555–591, plates 1–6.

———, 1917. Über Dinosaurier. 1. Notizen über die Systematik der Dinosaurier. Centralblatt für Mineralogie, Geologie und Paläontologie, 1917, pp. 203–213.

———, 1922. Bemerkungen zur Systematik der Reptilien. Palaeontologische Zeitschrift, Vol. 5, pp. 107–118.

———, 1923. Die Familien der Reptilien. Fortschrift Geologie und Palaeontologie, Vol. 2, pp. 1–210.

Osborn, Henry Fairfield, 1913. Biographical Memoir of Joseph Leidy, 1823–1891. National Academy of Sciences, Biographical Memoirs, Vol. 7, pp. 339–396.

———, 1918. Samuel Wendell Williston, 1852–1918. Journal of Geology, Vol. 26, pp. 673–689.

———, 1919. Memorial of Samuel Wendell Williston. Bulletin of the Geological Society of America, Vol. 30, pp. 66–73.

———, 1926. J. L. Wortman—A Biographical Sketch. Natural History, Vol. 26, pp. 652–653.

———, 1930. Ancient Vertebrate Life of Central Asia. Discoveries of the Central Asiatic Expeditions of the Museum of Natural History in the Years 1921–1929. Livre Jubilaire, Centenaire de la Société Géologique de France, 1930, pp. 519–543.

———, 1931. Cope: Master Naturalist. Princeton, Princeton University Press, xvi + 740 pp.

Ostrom, John H., and John S. McIntosh, 1966. Marsh's Dinosaurs. The Collections from Como Bluff. New Haven and London, Yale University Press, xiv + 388 pp., 65 plates.

Owen, Richard, 1842. Report on British Fossil Reptiles. Part II. Report of the British Association for the Advancement of Science, Eleventh Meeting, Plymouth, July 1841, pp. 60–204.

———, 1854. Geology and Inhabitants of the Ancient World. London, Bradbury and Evans, Crystal Palace Library, 40 pp.

———, 1874. Monograph on the Fossil Reptilia of the Wealden and Purbeck Formations. Supplement No. V. *Iguanodon*. Palaeontographical Society Monograph, Vol. 27, pp. 1–18, plates 1, 2.

———, 1849–1884. A History of British Fossil Reptiles. London, Cassel and Co., Ltd.: Vol. 1 (text), xv + 657 pp.; Vol. 2, 85 plates; Vol. 3 (text), vii + 199 pp.; Vol. 4, 104 plates.

Owen, Richard Startin, 1894. The Life of Richard Owen. By His Grandson the Rev. Richard Owen, M.A. With the Scientific Portions Revised by C. D. Sherborn; also an Essay on Owen's Position in Anatomical Science by the Rt. Hon. T. H. Huxley. New York, D. Appleton and Company, two vols., xiv + 409 pp., viii + 393 pp.

Parkinson, John, 1930. The Dinosaur in East Africa. London, H. F. and G. Witherby, 188 pp.

Plate, Robert, 1964. The Dinosaur Hunters. Othniel C. Marsh and Edward D. Cope. New York, David McKay Company, vi + 281 pp.

Reig, Oswaldo, A., 1963. La Presencia de Dinosaurios Saurisquios en los "Estratos de Ischigualasto" (Mesotriásico Superior) de los Provincias de San Juan y La Rioja (República Argentina). Ameghiniana, Vol. 3, pp. 3–20.

Romer, Alfred Sherwood, 1951. Robert Broom (1866–1951). Society of Vertebrate Paleontology News Bulletin, No. 32, pp. 30–31.

———, 1966. Osteology of the Reptiles. Chicago, University of Chicago Press, xxi + 772 pp.

Rozhdestvensky, A., 1960. Chasse aux Dinosaures dans le Désert de Gobi. Paris, Librairie Arthème Fayard, 301 pp.

Russell, Loris S., 1967. Dinosaur Hunting in Western Canada. Royal Ontario Museum, Life Sciences, Contribution 70, 37 pp.

Schuchert, Charles, and Clara Mae LeVene, 1940. O. C. Marsh—Pioneer in Paleontology. New Haven, Yale University Press, xxi + 541 pp., 30 plates.

Seeley, H. G., 1887a. The Classification of the Dinosauria. Report of the British Association for the Advancement of Science, Manchester, LVII, pp. 698–699.

———, 1887b. On the Classification of the Fossil Animals Commonly Named Dinosauria. Proceedings of the Royal Society of London, Vol. 43, pp. 165-171.

Simpson, George Gaylord, 1942a. The Beginnings of Vertebrate Paleontology in North America. Proceedings of the American Philosophical Society, Vol. 86, pp. 130–188.

―――, 1942b. Memorial to Walter Granger. Proceedings of the Geological Society of America for 1941, pp. 159–172, Plate 4.

―――, 1958. Memorial to Richard Swann Lull. Proceedings Volume of the Geological Society of America, 1958, pp. 127–134, Plate 11.

Spokes, Sidney, 1927. Gideon Algernon Mantell: Surgeon and Geologist. London, J. Bale, Sons, and Danielson, Ltd., xv + 263 pp.

Stegner, Wallace, 1942. Mormon Country. New York; Duell, Sloan and Pearce, x + 362 pp.

Sternberg, Charles H., 1909. The Life of a Fossil Hunter. New York, Henry Holt and Company, xiii + 286 pp.

―――, 1917. Hunting Dinosaurs on Red Deer River, Alberta, Canada. Lawrence, Kansas; The World Company Press, xiii + 232 pp.

Sternberg, George F., 1930. Thrills in Fossil Hunting. Aerend, Vol. 1, pp. 139–153.

Straelen, Victor van, 1933. Louis Dollo (1857–1931). Bulletin Musée royal d'Histoire naturelle Belgique, Vol. 9, pp. 1–29.

Stucker, Gilbert F., 1963. Dinosaur Monument and the People: A Study in Interpretation. Curator, Vol. 6, pp. 131–142.

Swinton, W. E., 1950. On Dinosaurs. Journal Royal College of Science, Vol. 21, pp. 1–9.

―――, 1951. Gideon Mantell and the Maidstone Iguanodon. Notes and Records of the Royal Society of London, Vol. 8, pp. 261–276.

―――, 1952. The Prehistoric Animals of the Crystal Palace. Discovery, 1952, pp. 8–11.

―――, 1962. Harry Govier Seeley and the Karroo Reptiles. Bulletin of the British Museum (Natural History), Historical Series, Vol. 3, pp. 1–39.

Ward, Henry B., 1919. Samuel Wendell Williston. A Kansas Tribute. Sigma Xi Quarterly, Vol. 7, pp. 26–40.

Williston, Samuel Wendell, 1918. Recollections. Manuscript, 59 pp.

CREDITS FOR PLATES

The illustrations appearing as plates and figures in this book are derived from the sources listed below. The author is much indebted to certain individuals and institutions, as duly noted, for permission to use pictures under their jurisdiction.

Plate:

8, 19, 27, 42–47, 59–61, 69–75, 78–86, 93, 94, 105–107, 111–112, 116. With the express permission of the Director of The American Museum of Natural History, New York.

1. Permission of J. Bale, Sons, and Danielson, London.

10–16. Permission of M. le Président de la Commission administrative du Patrimonie, and Dr. Edgar Casier, Institut Royal des Sciences Naturelles de Belgique.

30. Permission of the Trustees of the British Museum (Natural History).

62, 63, 64. Permission of the Geological Survey of Canada, Ottawa.

36, 37. Permission of the Geologisches Museum und Institut, Tübingen University, Germany.

CREDITS FOR FIGURES

Figure:

1, 10, 26. Prepared especially for this book. World map by George M. Colbert.

2, 18, 19. From Edwin H. Colbert, 1955. *Evolution of the Vertebrates*. New York, John Wiley & Sons, Inc. By permission of the author and publishers.

3. Permission of the Trustees of the British Museum (Natural History).

4, 38. From Edwin H. Colbert, 1965. *The Age of Reptiles*. New York, W. W. Norton and Company, Inc. By permission of the author and publishers.

5. From W. E. Swinton, 1951. Notes and records of the Royal Society of London, Vol. 8.

7, 23. From Richard Swann Lull, 1915. *Triassic Life of the Connecticut Valley*. State of Connecticut Geological and Natural History Survey Bulletin No. 24.

8, 13, 14, 16, 17, 22. From O. C. Marsh, 1896. Sixteenth Annual Report of the United States Geological Survey.

11, 12. From Edgar Casier, 1961. *Les Iguanodons de Bernissart*. Institut

Royal des Sciences Naturelles de Belgique. By permission of the author and publishers.

15. From Louis Dollo, 1905. Bulletin Société Belge de Géologie, Vol. 19.

20. From András Tasnádi Kubacska, 1945. Verlag Ungarischen Naturwissenschaftlichen Museums.

26. From F. von Huene, 1926. Geologische und Palaeontologische Abhandlungen, Vol. 15, No. 2.

24, 25, 28, 35, 36, 37. From The American Museum of Natural History.

22. From W. J. Holland, 1905. Memoirs Carnegie Museum, Vol. 2, No. 6.

29. From the Geological Survey of Canada.

30. From Barnum Brown, 1916. Bulletin of The American Museum of Natural History, Vol. 35, Art. 38.

31. From Edwin H. Colbert and Margaret M. Colbert, 1958. *Millions of Years Ago*. New York, T. Y. Crowell Company. By permission of the authors and publishers.

32. From Barnum Brown, 1917. Bulletin of The American Museum of Natural History, Vol. 37, Art. 10.

33. From W. A. Parks, 1917. Geological Survey of Canada, Memoir 100.

34. From H. F. Osborn, 1930. Livre Jubilaire, Centenaire de la Société Géologique de France.

39. From A. Rozhdestvensky, 1960. *Chasse aux Dinosaures dans le Désert de Gobi*. Paris, Librairie Arthème Fayard. By permission of the author and publishers.

40, 42. From I. A. Efremov, 1956. *Road of the Wind* (in Russian). Moscow, All Union Scientific Pedagogical Publishers. By permission of the author and publishers.

41. From H. F. Osborn, 1916. Bulletin of The American Museum of Natural History, Vol. 35, Art. 43.

43. From W. K. Gregory, 1951. *Evolution Emerging*. New York, The Macmillan Company. By permission of the author and publishers.

44. From Edwin Hennig, 1912. *Am Tendaguru*. Stuttgart, E. Schweitzerbart'sche Verlagsbuchhandlung. By permission of the author and publishers.

45. From W. Janensch, 1950. Palaeontographica. Supplement 7, Series 1, Part 3.

46. From F. von Huene, 1929. Centralblatt für Mineralogie, etc., Section B, No. 10.

47. Modified from N. Heintz, 1963. Norsk Polarinstitutt, Oslo, 1963.

6, 9. From anonymous sources.

A CATALOG OF SELECTED
DOVER BOOKS
IN ALL FIELDS OF INTEREST

A CATALOG OF SELECTED DOVER
BOOKS IN ALL FIELDS OF INTEREST

CONCERNING THE SPIRITUAL IN ART, Wassily Kandinsky. Pioneering work by father of abstract art. Thoughts on color theory, nature of art. Analysis of earlier masters. 12 illustrations. 80pp. of text. 5⅜ x 8½. 23411-8 Pa. $3.95

ANIMALS: 1,419 Copyright-Free Illustrations of Mammals, Birds, Fish, Insects, etc., Jim Harter (ed.). Clear wood engravings present, in extremely lifelike poses, over 1,000 species of animals. One of the most extensive pictorial sourcebooks of its kind. Captions. Index. 284pp. 9 x 12. 23766-4 Pa. $12.95

CELTIC ART: The Methods of Construction, George Bain. Simple geometric techniques for making Celtic interlacements, spirals, Kells-type initials, animals, humans, etc. Over 500 illustrations. 160pp. 9 x 12. (USO) 22923-8 Pa. $9.95

AN ATLAS OF ANATOMY FOR ARTISTS, Fritz Schider. Most thorough reference work on art anatomy in the world. Hundreds of illustrations, including selections from works by Vesalius, Leonardo, Goya, Ingres, Michelangelo, others. 593 illustrations. 192pp. 7⅛ x 10¼. 20241-0 Pa. $9 95

CELTIC HAND STROKE-BY-STROKE (Irish Half-Uncial from "The Book of Kells"): An Arthur Baker Calligraphy Manual, Arthur Baker. Complete guide to creating each letter of the alphabet in distinctive Celtic manner. Covers hand position, strokes, pens, inks, paper, more. Illustrated. 48pp. 8¼ x 11. 24336-2 Pa. $3.95

EASY ORIGAMI, John Montroll. Charming collection of 32 projects (hat, cup, pelican, piano, swan, many more) specially designed for the novice origami hobbyist. Clearly illustrated easy-to-follow instructions insure that even beginning papercrafters will achieve successful results. 48pp. 8¼ x 11. 27298-2 Pa. $2.95

THE COMPLETE BOOK OF BIRDHOUSE CONSTRUCTION FOR WOODWORKERS, Scott D. Campbell. Detailed instructions, illustrations, tables. Also data on bird habitat and instinct patterns. Bibliography. 3 tables. 63 illustrations in 15 figures. 48pp. 5¼ x 8½. 24407-5 Pa. $2.50

BLOOMINGDALE'S ILLUSTRATED 1886 CATALOG: Fashions, Dry Goods and Housewares, Bloomingdale Brothers. Famed merchants' extremely rare catalog depicting about 1,700 products: clothing, housewares, firearms, dry goods, jewelry, more. Invaluable for dating, identifying vintage items. Also, copyright-free graphics for artists, designers. Co-published with Henry Ford Museum & Greenfield Village. 160pp. 8¼ x 11. 25780-0 Pa. $9.95

HISTORIC COSTUME IN PICTURES, Braun & Schneider. Over 1,450 costumed figures in clearly detailed engravings–from dawn of civilization to end of 19th century. Captions. Many folk costumes. 256pp. 8⅜ x 11¾. 23150-X Pa. $12.95

STICKLEY CRAFTSMAN FURNITURE CATALOGS, Gustav Stickley and L. & J. G. Stickley. Beautiful, functional furniture in two authentic catalogs from 1910. 594 illustrations, including 277 photos, show settles, rockers, armchairs, reclining chairs, bookcases, desks, tables. 183pp. 6½ x 9¼. 23838-5 Pa. $9.95

AMERICAN LOCOMOTIVES IN HISTORIC PHOTOGRAPHS: 1858 to 1949, Ron Ziel (ed.). A rare collection of 126 meticulously detailed official photographs, called "builder portraits," of American locomotives that majestically chronicle the rise of steam locomotive power in America. Introduction. Detailed captions. xi + 129pp. 9 x 12. 27393-8 Pa. $12.95

AMERICA'S LIGHTHOUSES: An Illustrated History, Francis Ross Holland, Jr. Delightfully written, profusely illustrated fact-filled survey of over 200 American lighthouses since 1716. History, anecdotes, technological advances, more. 240pp. 8 x 10¾. 25576-X Pa. $12.95

TOWARDS A NEW ARCHITECTURE, Le Corbusier. Pioneering manifesto by founder of "International School." Technical and aesthetic theories, views of industry, economics, relation of form to function, "mass-production split" and much more. Profusely illustrated.-320pp. 6⅛ x 9¼. (USO) 25023-7 Pa. $9.95

HOW THE OTHER HALF LIVES, Jacob Riis. Famous journalistic record, exposing poverty and degradation of New York slums around 1900, by major social reformer. 100 striking and influential photographs. 233pp. 10 x 7⅞.
22012-5 Pa. $10.95

FRUIT KEY AND TWIG KEY TO TREES AND SHRUBS, William M. Harlow. One of the handiest and most widely used identification aids. Fruit key covers 120 deciduous and evergreen species; twig key 160 deciduous species. Easily used. Over 300 photographs. 126pp. 5⅜ x 8½. 20511-8 Pa. $3.95

COMMON BIRD SONGS, Dr. Donald J. Borror. Songs of 60 most common U.S. birds: robins, sparrows, cardinals, bluejays, finches, more—arranged in order of increasing complexity. Up to 9 variations of songs of each species.
Cassette and manual 99911-4 $8.95

ORCHIDS AS HOUSE PLANTS, Rebecca Tyson Northen. Grow cattleyas and many other kinds of orchids—in a window, in a case, or under artificial light. 63 illustrations. 148pp. 5⅜ x 8½. 23261-1 Pa. $4.95

MONSTER MAZES, Dave Phillips. Masterful mazes at four levels of difficulty. Avoid deadly perils and evil creatures to find magical treasures. Solutions for all 32 exciting illustrated puzzles. 48pp. 8¼ x 11. 26005-4 Pa. $2.95

MOZART'S DON GIOVANNI (DOVER OPERA LIBRETTO SERIES), Wolfgang Amadeus Mozart. Introduced and translated by Ellen H. Bleiler. Standard Italian libretto, with complete English translation. Convenient and thoroughly portable—an ideal companion for reading along with a recording or the performance itself. Introduction. List of characters. Plot summary. 121pp. 5¼ x 8½.
24944-1 Pa. $2.95

TECHNICAL MANUAL AND DICTIONARY OF CLASSICAL BALLET, Gail Grant. Defines, explains, comments on steps, movements, poses and concepts. 15-page pictorial section. Basic book for student, viewer. 127pp. 5⅜ x 8½.
21843-0 Pa. $4.95

BRASS INSTRUMENTS: Their History and Development, Anthony Baines. Authoritative, updated survey of the evolution of trumpets, trombones, bugles, cornets, French horns, tubas and other brass wind instruments. Over 140 illustrations and 48 music examples. Corrected and updated by author. New preface. Bibliography. 320pp. 5⅜ x 8½. 27574-4 Pa. $9.95

HOLLYWOOD GLAMOR PORTRAITS, John Kobal (ed.). 145 photos from 1926-49. Harlow, Gable, Bogart, Bacall; 94 stars in all. Full background on photographers, technical aspects. 160pp. 8⅜ x 11¼. 23352-9 Pa. $11.95

MAX AND MORITZ, Wilhelm Busch. Great humor classic in both German and English. Also 10 other works: "Cat and Mouse," "Plisch and Plumm," etc. 216pp. 5⅜ x 8½. 20181-3 Pa. $6.95

THE RAVEN AND OTHER FAVORITE POEMS, Edgar Allan Poe. Over 40 of the author's most memorable poems: "The Bells," "Ulalume," "Israfel," "To Helen," "The Conqueror Worm," "Eldorado," "Annabel Lee," many more. Alphabetic lists of titles and first lines. 64pp. 5 3/16 x 8¼. 26685-0 Pa. $1.00

PERSONAL MEMOIRS OF U. S. GRANT, Ulysses Simpson Grant. Intelligent, deeply moving firsthand account of Civil War campaigns, considered by many the finest military memoirs ever written. Includes letters, historic photographs, maps and more. 528pp. 6⅛ x 9¼. 28587-1 Pa. $11.95

AMULETS AND SUPERSTITIONS, E. A. Wallis Budge. Comprehensive discourse on origin, powers of amulets in many ancient cultures: Arab, Persian Babylonian, Assyrian, Egyptian, Gnostic, Hebrew, Phoenician, Syriac, etc. Covers cross, swastika, crucifix, seals, rings, stones, etc. 584pp. 5⅜ x 8½. 23573-4 Pa. $12.95

RUSSIAN STORIES/PYCCKNE PACCKA3bl: A Dual-Language Book, edited by Gleb Struve. Twelve tales by such masters as Chekhov, Tolstoy, Dostoevsky, Pushkin, others. Excellent word-for-word English translations on facing pages, plus teaching and study aids, Russian/English vocabulary, biographical/critical introductions, more. 416pp. 5⅜ x 8½. 26244-8 Pa. $8.95

PHILADELPHIA THEN AND NOW: 60 Sites Photographed in the Past and Present, Kenneth Finkel and Susan Oyama. Rare photographs of City Hall, Logan Square, Independence Hall, Betsy Ross House, other landmarks juxtaposed with contemporary views. Captures changing face of historic city. Introduction. Captions. 128pp. 8¼ x 11. 25790-8 Pa. $9.95

AIA ARCHITECTURAL GUIDE TO NASSAU AND SUFFOLK COUNTIES, LONG ISLAND, The American Institute of Architects, Long Island Chapter, and the Society for the Preservation of Long Island Antiquities. Comprehensive, well-researched and generously illustrated volume brings to life over three centuries of Long Island's great architectural heritage. More than 240 photographs with authoritative, extensively detailed captions. 176pp. 8¼ x 11. 26946-9 Pa. $14.95

NORTH AMERICAN INDIAN LIFE: Customs and Traditions of 23 Tribes, Elsie Clews Parsons (ed.). 27 fictionalized essays by noted anthropologists examine religion, customs, government, additional facets of life among the Winnebago, Crow, Zuni, Eskimo, other tribes. 480pp. 6⅛ x 9¼. 27377-6 Pa. $10.95

FRANK LLOYD WRIGHT'S HOLLYHOCK HOUSE, Donald Hoffmann. Lavishly illustrated, carefully documented study of one of Wright's most controversial residential designs. Over 120 photographs, floor plans, elevations, etc. Detailed perceptive text by noted Wright scholar. Index. 128pp. 9¼ x 10¾. 27133-1 Pa. $11.95

THE MALE AND FEMALE FIGURE IN MOTION: 60 Classic Photographic Sequences, Eadweard Muybridge. 60 true-action photographs of men and women walking, running, climbing, bending, turning, etc., reproduced from rare 19th-century masterpiece. vi + 121pp. 9 x 12. 24745-7 Pa. $10.95

1001 QUESTIONS ANSWERED ABOUT THE SEASHORE, N. J. Berrill and Jacquelyn Berrill. Queries answered about dolphins, sea snails, sponges, starfish, fishes, shore birds, many others. Covers appearance, breeding, growth, feeding, much more. 305pp. 5¼ x 8¼. 23366-9 Pa. $8.95

GUIDE TO OWL WATCHING IN NORTH AMERICA, Donald S. Heintzelman. Superb guide offers complete data and descriptions of 19 species: barn owl, screech owl, snowy owl, many more. Expert coverage of owl-watching equipment, conservation, migrations and invasions, etc. Guide to observing sites. 84 illustrations. xiii + 193pp. 5⅜ x 8½. 27344-X Pa. $8.95

MEDICINAL AND OTHER USES OF NORTH AMERICAN PLANTS: A Historical Survey with Special Reference to the Eastern Indian Tribes, Charlotte Erichsen-Brown. Chronological historical citations document 500 years of usage of plants, trees, shrubs native to eastern Canada, northeastern U.S. Also complete identifying information. 343 illustrations. 544pp. 6½ x 9¼. 25951-X Pa. $12.95

STORYBOOK MAZES, Dave Phillips. 23 stories and mazes on two-page spreads: Wizard of Oz, Treasure Island, Robin Hood, etc. Solutions. 64pp. 8¼ x 11. 23628-5 Pa. $2.95

NEGRO FOLK MUSIC, U.S.A., Harold Courlander. Noted folklorist's scholarly yet readable analysis of rich and varied musical tradition. Includes authentic versions of over 40 folk songs. Valuable bibliography and discography. xi + 324pp. 5⅜ x 8½. 27350-4 Pa. $7.95

MOVIE-STAR PORTRAITS OF THE FORTIES, John Kobal (ed.). 163 glamor, studio photos of 106 stars of the 1940s: Rita Hayworth, Ava Gardner, Marlon Brando, Clark Gable, many more. 176pp. 8⅜ x 11¼. 23546-7 Pa. $12.95

BENCHLEY LOST AND FOUND, Robert Benchley. Finest humor from early 30s, about pet peeves, child psychologists, post office and others. Mostly unavailable elsewhere. 73 illustrations by Peter Arno and others. 183pp. 5⅜ x 8½. 22410-4 Pa. $6.95

YEKL and THE IMPORTED BRIDEGROOM AND OTHER STORIES OF YIDDISH NEW YORK, Abraham Cahan. Film Hester Street based on Yekl (1896). Novel, other stories among first about Jewish immigrants on N.Y.'s East Side. 240pp. 5⅜ x 8½. 22427-9 Pa. $6.95

SELECTED POEMS, Walt Whitman. Generous sampling from *Leaves of Grass*. Twenty-four poems include "I Hear America Singing," "Song of the Open Road," "I Sing the Body Electric," "When Lilacs Last in the Dooryard Bloom'd," "O Captain! My Captain!"—all reprinted from an authoritative edition. Lists of titles and first lines. 128pp. 5³⁄₁₆ x 8¼. 26878-0 Pa. $1.00

THE BEST TALES OF HOFFMANN, E. T. A. Hoffmann. 10 of Hoffmann's most important stories: "Nutcracker and the King of Mice," "The Golden Flowerpot," etc. 458pp. 5⅜ x 8½. 21793-0 Pa. $9.95

FROM FETISH TO GOD IN ANCIENT EGYPT, E. A. Wallis Budge. Rich detailed survey of Egyptian conception of "God" and gods, magic, cult of animals, Osiris, more. Also, superb English translations of hymns and legends. 240 illustrations. 545pp. 5⅜ x 8½. 25803-3 Pa. $11.95

FRENCH STORIES/CONTES FRANÇAIS: A Dual-Language Book, Wallace Fowlie. Ten stories by French masters, Voltaire to Camus: "Micromegas" by Voltaire; "The Atheist's Mass" by Balzac; "Minuet" by de Maupassant; "The Guest" by Camus, six more. Excellent English translations on facing pages. Also French-English vocabulary list, exercises, more. 352pp. 5⅜ x 8½. 26443-2 Pa. $8.95

CHICAGO AT THE TURN OF THE CENTURY IN PHOTOGRAPHS: 122 Historic Views from the Collections of the Chicago Historical Society, Larry A. Viskochil. Rare large-format prints offer detailed views of City Hall, State Street, the Loop, Hull House, Union Station, many other landmarks, circa 1904-1913. Introduction. Captions. Maps. 144pp. 9⅜ x 12¼. 24656-6 Pa. $12.95

OLD BROOKLYN IN EARLY PHOTOGRAPHS, 1865-1929, William Lee Younger. Luna Park, Gravesend race track, construction of Grand Army Plaza, moving of Hotel Brighton, etc. 157 previously unpublished photographs. 165pp. 8⅞ x 11¾. 23587-4 Pa. $13.95

THE MYTHS OF THE NORTH AMERICAN INDIANS, Lewis Spence. Rich anthology of the myths and legends of the Algonquins, Iroquois, Pawnees and Sioux, prefaced by an extensive historical and ethnological commentary. 36 illustrations. 480pp. 5⅜ x 8½. 25967-6 Pa. $8.95

AN ENCYCLOPEDIA OF BATTLES: Accounts of Over 1,560 Battles from 1479 B.C. to the Present, David Eggenberger. Essential details of every major battle in recorded history from the first battle of Megiddo in 1479 B.C. to Grenada in 1984. List of Battle Maps. New Appendix covering the years 1967-1984. Index. 99 illustrations. 544pp. 6½ x 9¼. 24913-1 Pa. $14.95

SAILING ALONE AROUND THE WORLD, Captain Joshua Slocum. First man to sail around the world, alone, in small boat. One of great feats of seamanship told in delightful manner. 67 illustrations. 294pp. 5⅜ x 8½. 20326-3 Pa. $5.95

ANARCHISM AND OTHER ESSAYS, Emma Goldman. Powerful, penetrating, prophetic essays on direct action, role of minorities, prison reform, puritan hypocrisy, violence, etc. 271pp. 5⅜ x 8½. 22484-8 Pa. $6.95

MYTHS OF THE HINDUS AND BUDDHISTS, Ananda K. Coomaraswamy and Sister Nivedita. Great stories of the epics; deeds of Krishna, Shiva, taken from puranas, Vedas, folk tales; etc. 32 illustrations. 400pp. 5⅜ x 8½. 21759-0 Pa. $10.95

BEYOND PSYCHOLOGY, Otto Rank. Fear of death, desire of immortality, nature of sexuality, social organization, creativity, according to Rankian system. 291pp. 5⅜ x 8½. 20485-5 Pa. $8.95

A THEOLOGICO-POLITICAL TREATISE, Benedict Spinoza. Also contains unfinished Political Treatise. Great classic on religious liberty, theory of government on common consent. R. Elwes translation. Total of 421pp. 5⅜ x 8½. 20249-6 Pa. $9.95

PIANO TUNING, J. Cree Fischer. Clearest, best book for beginner, amateur. Simple repairs, raising dropped notes, tuning by easy method of flattened fifths. No previous skills needed. 4 illustrations. 201pp. 5⅜ x 8½.   23267-0 Pa. $6.95

A SOURCE BOOK IN THEATRICAL HISTORY, A. M. Nagler. Contemporary observers on acting, directing, make-up, costuming, stage props, machinery, scene design, from Ancient Greece to Chekhov. 611pp. 5⅜ x 8½.   20515-0 Pa. $12.95

THE COMPLETE NONSENSE OF EDWARD LEAR, Edward Lear. All nonsense limericks, zany alphabets, Owl and Pussycat, songs, nonsense botany, etc., illustrated by Lear. Total of 320pp. 5⅜ x 8½. (USO)   20167-8 Pa. $6.95

VICTORIAN PARLOUR POETRY: An Annotated Anthology, Michael R. Turner. 117 gems by Longfellow, Tennyson, Browning, many lesser-known poets. "The Village Blacksmith," "Curfew Must Not Ring Tonight," "Only a Baby Small," dozens more, often difficult to find elsewhere. Index of poets, titles, first lines. xxiii + 325pp. 5⅜ x 8¼.   27044-0 Pa. $8.95

DUBLINERS, James Joyce. Fifteen stories offer vivid, tightly focused observations of the lives of Dublin's poorer classes. At least one, "The Dead," is considered a masterpiece. Reprinted complete and unabridged from standard edition. 160pp. 5³⁄₁₆ x 8¼.   26870-5 Pa. $1.00

THE HAUNTED MONASTERY and THE CHINESE MAZE MURDERS, Robert van Gulik. Two full novels by van Gulik, set in 7th-century China, continue adventures of Judge Dee and his companions. An evil Taoist monastery, seemingly supernatural events; overgrown topiary maze hides strange crimes. 27 illustrations. 328pp. 5⅜ x 8½.   23502-5 Pa. $8.95

THE BOOK OF THE SACRED MAGIC OF ABRAMELIN THE MAGE, translated by S. MacGregor Mathers. Medieval manuscript of ceremonial magic. Basic document in Aleister Crowley, Golden Dawn groups. 268pp. 5⅜ x 8½.

23211-5 Pa. $8.95

NEW RUSSIAN-ENGLISH AND ENGLISH-RUSSIAN DICTIONARY, M. A. O'Brien. This is a remarkably handy Russian dictionary, containing a surprising amount of information, including over 70,000 entries. 366pp. 4½ x 6⅛.

20208-9 Pa. $9.95

HISTORIC HOMES OF THE AMERICAN PRESIDENTS, Second, Revised Edition, Irvin Haas. A traveler's guide to American Presidential homes, most open to the public, depicting and describing homes occupied by every American President from George Washington to George Bush. With visiting hours, admission charges, travel routes. 175 photographs. Index. 160pp. 8¼ x 11.   26751-2 Pa. $11.95

NEW YORK IN THE FORTIES, Andreas Feininger. 162 brilliant photographs by the well-known photographer, formerly with *Life* magazine. Commuters, shoppers, Times Square at night, much else from city at its peak. Captions by John von Hartz. 181pp. 9¼ x 10¾.   23585-8 Pa. $12.95

INDIAN SIGN LANGUAGE, William Tomkins. Over 525 signs developed by Sioux and other tribes. Written instructions and diagrams. Also 290 pictographs. 111pp. 6⅛ x 9¼.   22029-X Pa. $3.95

ANATOMY: A Complete Guide for Artists, Joseph Sheppard. A master of figure drawing shows artists how to render human anatomy convincingly. Over 460 illustrations. 224pp. 8⅜ x 11¼. 27279-6 Pa. $10.95

MEDIEVAL CALLIGRAPHY: Its History and Technique, Marc Drogin. Spirited history, comprehensive instruction manual covers 13 styles (ca. 4th century thru 15th). Excellent photographs; directions for duplicating medieval techniques with modern tools. 224pp. 8⅜ x 11¼. 26142-5 Pa. $11.95

DRIED FLOWERS: How to Prepare Them, Sarah Whitlock and Martha Rankin. Complete instructions on how to use silica gel, meal and borax, perlite aggregate, sand and borax, glycerine and water to create attractive permanent flower arrangements. 12 illustrations. 32pp. 5⅜ x 8½. 21802-3 Pa. $1.00

EASY-TO-MAKE BIRD FEEDERS FOR WOODWORKERS, Scott D. Campbell. Detailed, simple-to-use guide for designing, constructing, caring for and using feeders. Text, illustrations for 12 classic and contemporary designs. 96pp. 5⅜ x 8½. 25847-5 Pa. $2.95

SCOTTISH WONDER TALES FROM MYTH AND LEGEND, Donald A. Mackenzie. 16 lively tales tell of giants rumbling down mountainsides, of a magic wand that turns stone pillars into warriors, of gods and goddesses, evil hags, powerful forces and more. 240pp. 5⅜ x 8½. 29677-6 Pa. $6.95

THE HISTORY OF UNDERCLOTHES, C. Willett Cunnington and Phyllis Cunnington. Fascinating, well-documented survey covering six centuries of English undergarments, enhanced with over 100 illustrations: 12th-century laced-up bodice, footed long drawers (1795), 19th-century bustles, 19th-century corsets for men, Victorian "bust improvers," much more. 272pp. 5⅜ x 8¼. 27124-2 Pa. $9.95

ARTS AND CRAFTS FURNITURE: The Complete Brooks Catalog of 1912, Brooks Manufacturing Co. Photos and detailed descriptions of more than 150 now very collectible furniture designs from the Arts and Crafts movement depict davenports, settees, buffets, desks, tables, chairs, bedsteads, dressers and more, all built of solid, quarter-sawed oak. Invaluable for students and enthusiasts of antiques, Americana and the decorative arts. 80pp. 6½ x 9¼. 27471-3 Pa. $7.95

HOW WE INVENTED THE AIRPLANE: An Illustrated History, Orville Wright. Fascinating firsthand account covers early experiments, construction of planes and motors, first flights, much more. Introduction and commentary by Fred C. Kelly. 76 photographs. 96pp. 8¼ x 11. 25662-6 Pa. $8.95

THE ARTS OF THE SAILOR: Knotting, Splicing and Ropework, Hervey Garrett Smith. Indispensable shipboard reference covers tools, basic knots and useful hitches; handsewing and canvas work, more. Over 100 illustrations. Delightful reading for sea lovers. 256pp. 5⅜ x 8½. 26440-8 Pa. $7.95

FRANK LLOYD WRIGHT'S FALLINGWATER: The House and Its History, Second, Revised Edition, Donald Hoffmann. A total revision–both in text and illustrations–of the standard document on Fallingwater, the boldest, most personal architectural statement of Wright's mature years, updated with valuable new material from the recently opened Frank Lloyd Wright Archives. "Fascinating"–*The New York Times.* 116 illustrations. 128pp. 9¼ x 10¾. 27430-6 Pa. $11.95

AUTOBIOGRAPHY: The Story of My Experiments with Truth, Mohandas K. Gandhi. Boyhood, legal studies, purification, the growth of the Satyagraha (nonviolent protest) movement. Critical, inspiring work of the man responsible for the freedom of India. 480pp. 5⅜ x 8½. (USO)   24593-4 Pa. $8.95

CELTIC MYTHS AND LEGENDS, T. W. Rolleston. Masterful retelling of Irish and Welsh stories and tales. Cuchulain, King Arthur, Deirdre, the Grail, many more. First paperback edition. 58 full-page illustrations. 512pp. 5⅜ x 8½.   26507-2 Pa. $9.95

THE PRINCIPLES OF PSYCHOLOGY, William James. Famous long course complete, unabridged. Stream of thought, time perception, memory, experimental methods; great work decades ahead of its time. 94 figures. 1,391pp. 5⅜ x 8½. 2-vol. set.
Vol. I: 20381-6 Pa. $12.95
Vol. II: 20382-4 Pa. $12.95

THE WORLD AS WILL AND REPRESENTATION, Arthur Schopenhauer. Definitive English translation of Schopenhauer's life work, correcting more than 1,000 errors, omissions in earlier translations. Translated by E. F. J. Payne. Total of 1,269pp. 5⅜ x 8½. 2-vol. set.   Vol. 1: 21761-2 Pa. $11.95
Vol. 2: 21762-0 Pa. $11.95

MAGIC AND MYSTERY IN TIBET, Madame Alexandra David-Neel. Experiences among lamas, magicians, sages, sorcerers, Bonpa wizards. A true psychic discovery. 32 illustrations. 321pp. 5⅜ x 8½. (USO)   22682-4 Pa. $8.95

THE EGYPTIAN BOOK OF THE DEAD, E. A. Wallis Budge. Complete reproduction of Ani's papyrus, finest ever found. Full hieroglyphic text, interlinear transliteration, word-for-word translation, smooth translation. 533pp. 6½ x 9¼.
21866-X Pa. $10.95

MATHEMATICS FOR THE NONMATHEMATICIAN, Morris Kline. Detailed, college-level treatment of mathematics in cultural and historical context, with numerous exercises. Recommended Reading Lists. Tables. Numerous figures. 641pp. 5⅜ x 8½.
24823-2 Pa. $11.95

THEORY OF WING SECTIONS: Including a Summary of Airfoil Data, Ira H. Abbott and A. E. von Doenhoff. Concise compilation of subsonic aerodynamic characteristics of NACA wing sections, plus description of theory. 350pp. of tables. 693pp. 5⅜ x 8½.   60586-8 Pa. $14.95

THE RIME OF THE ANCIENT MARINER, Gustave Doré, S. T. Coleridge. Doré's finest work; 34 plates capture moods, subtleties of poem. Flawless full-size reproductions printed on facing pages with authoritative text of poem. "Beautiful. Simply beautiful."–*Publisher's Weekly.* 77pp. 9¼ x 12.   22305-1 Pa. $6.95

NORTH AMERICAN INDIAN DESIGNS FOR ARTISTS AND CRAFTSPEOPLE, Eva Wilson. Over 360 authentic copyright-free designs adapted from Navajo blankets, Hopi pottery, Sioux buffalo hides, more. Geometrics, symbolic figures, plant and animal motifs, etc. 128pp. 8⅜ x 11. (EUK)   25341-4 Pa. $8.95

SCULPTURE: Principles and Practice, Louis Slobodkin. Step-by-step approach to clay, plaster, metals, stone; classical and modern. 253 drawings, photos. 255pp. 8⅛ x 11.
22960-2 Pa. $10.95

PHOTOGRAPHIC SKETCHBOOK OF THE CIVIL WAR, Alexander Gardner. 100 photos taken on field during the Civil War. Famous shots of Manassas Harper's Ferry, Lincoln, Richmond, slave pens, etc. 244pp. 10⅝ x 8¼. 22731-6 Pa. $9.95

FIVE ACRES AND INDEPENDENCE, Maurice G. Kains. Great back-to-the-land classic explains basics of self-sufficient farming. The one book to get. 95 illustrations. 397pp. 5⅜ x 8½. 20974-1 Pa. $7.95

SONGS OF EASTERN BIRDS, Dr. Donald J. Borror. Songs and calls of 60 species most common to eastern U.S.: warblers, woodpeckers, flycatchers, thrushes, larks, many more in high-quality recording. Cassette and manual 99912-2 $8.95

A MODERN HERBAL, Margaret Grieve. Much the fullest, most exact, most useful compilation of herbal material. Gigantic alphabetical encyclopedia, from aconite to zedoary, gives botanical information, medical properties, folklore, economic uses, much else. Indispensable to serious reader. 161 illustrations. 888pp. 6½ x 9¼. 2-vol. set. (USO) Vol. I: 22798-7 Pa. $9.95
Vol. II: 22799-5 Pa. $9.95

HIDDEN TREASURE MAZE BOOK, Dave Phillips. Solve 34 challenging mazes accompanied by heroic tales of adventure. Evil dragons, people-eating plants, blood-thirsty giants, many more dangerous adversaries lurk at every twist and turn. 34 mazes, stories, solutions. 48pp. 8¼ x 11. 24566-7 Pa. $2.95

LETTERS OF W. A. MOZART, Wolfgang A. Mozart. Remarkable letters show bawdy wit, humor, imagination, musical insights, contemporary musical world; includes some letters from Leopold Mozart. 276pp. 5⅜ x 8½. 22859-2 Pa. $7.95

BASIC PRINCIPLES OF CLASSICAL BALLET, Agrippina Vaganova. Great Russian theoretician, teacher explains methods for teaching classical ballet. 118 illustrations. 175pp. 5⅜ x 8½. 22036-2 Pa. $5.95

THE JUMPING FROG, Mark Twain. Revenge edition. The original story of The Celebrated Jumping Frog of Calaveras County, a hapless French translation, and Twain's hilarious "retranslation" from the French. 12 illustrations. 66pp. 5⅜ x 8½.
22686-7 Pa. $3.95

BEST REMEMBERED POEMS, Martin Gardner (ed.). The 126 poems in this superb collection of 19th- and 20th-century British and American verse range from Shelley's "To a Skylark" to the impassioned "Renascence" of Edna St. Vincent Millay and to Edward Lear's whimsical "The Owl and the Pussycat." 224pp. 5⅜ x 8½.
27165-X Pa. $4.95

COMPLETE SONNETS, William Shakespeare. Over 150 exquisite poems deal with love, friendship, the tyranny of time, beauty's evanescence, death and other themes in language of remarkable power, precision and beauty. Glossary of archaic terms. 80pp. 5$\frac{3}{16}$ x 8¼. 26686-9 Pa. $1.00

BODIES IN A BOOKSHOP, R. T. Campbell. Challenging mystery of blackmail and murder with ingenious plot and superbly drawn characters. In the best tradition of British suspense fiction. 192pp. 5⅜ x 8½. 24720-1 Pa. $6.95

THE INFLUENCE OF SEA POWER UPON HISTORY, 1660–1783, A. T. Mahan. Influential classic of naval history and tactics still used as text in war colleges. First paperback edition. 4 maps. 24 battle plans. 640pp. 5⅜ x 8½.   25509-3 Pa. $12.95

THE STORY OF THE TITANIC AS TOLD BY ITS SURVIVORS, Jack Winocour (ed.). What it was really like. Panic, despair, shocking inefficiency, and a little heroism. More thrilling than any fictional account. 26 illustrations. 320pp. 5⅜ x 8½.
20610-6 Pa. $8.95

FAIRY AND FOLK TALES OF THE IRISH PEASANTRY, William Butler Yeats (ed.). Treasury of 64 tales from the twilight world of Celtic myth and legend: "The Soul Cages," "The Kildare Pooka," "King O'Toole and his Goose," many more. Introduction and Notes by W. B. Yeats. 352pp. 5⅜ x 8½.   26941-8 Pa. $8.95

BUDDHIST MAHAYANA TEXTS, E. B. Cowell and Others (eds.). Superb, accurate translations of basic documents in Mahayana Buddhism, highly important in history of religions. The Buddha-karita of Asvaghosha, Larger Sukhavativyuha, more. 448pp. 5⅜ x 8½.   25552-2 Pa. $9.95

ONE TWO THREE . . . INFINITY: Facts and Speculations of Science, George Gamow. Great physicist's fascinating, readable overview of contemporary science: number theory, relativity, fourth dimension, entropy, genes, atomic structure, much more. 128 illustrations. Index. 352pp. 5⅜ x 8½.   25664-2 Pa. $8.95

ENGINEERING IN HISTORY, Richard Shelton Kirby, et al. Broad, nontechnical survey of history's major technological advances: birth of Greek science, industrial revolution, electricity and applied science, 20th-century automation, much more. 181 illustrations. ". . . excellent . . ."–*Isis*. Bibliography. vii + 530pp. 5⅜ x 8¼.
26412-2 Pa. $14.95

DALÍ ON MODERN ART: The Cuckolds of Antiquated Modern Art, Salvador Dalí. Influential painter skewers modern art and its practitioners. Outrageous evaluations of Picasso, Cézanne, Turner, more. 15 renderings of paintings discussed. 44 calligraphic decorations by Dalí. 96pp. 5⅜ x 8½. (USO)   29220-7 Pa. $4.95

ANTIQUE PLAYING CARDS: A Pictorial History, Henry René D'Allemagne. Over 900 elaborate, decorative images from rare playing cards (14th–20th centuries): Bacchus, death, dancing dogs, hunting scenes, royal coats of arms, players cheating, much more. 96pp. 9¼ x 12¼.   29265-7 Pa. $11.95

MAKING FURNITURE MASTERPIECES: 30 Projects with Measured Drawings, Franklin H. Gottshall. Step-by-step instructions, illustrations for constructing handsome, useful pieces, among them a Sheraton desk, Chippendale chair, Spanish desk, Queen Anne table and a William and Mary dressing mirror. 224pp. 8⅛ x 11¼.
29338-6 Pa. $13.95

THE FOSSIL BOOK: A Record of Prehistoric Life, Patricia V. Rich et al. Profusely illustrated definitive guide covers everything from single-celled organisms and dinosaurs to birds and mammals and the interplay between climate and man. Over 1,500 illustrations. 760pp. 7½ x 10⅛.   29371-8 Pa. $29.95